D1301768

Holding Up the Sky Together

Exploring the National Narrative about People with Intellectual Disabilities

Ron Bishop

WITH SADIE PENNINGTON AND MORGAN WEISS

Hamilton Books

Lanham • Boulder • New York • Toronto • Plymouth, UK

Copyright © 2018 by Hamilton Books
4501 Forbes Boulevard, Suite 200, Lanham, Maryland 20706
Hamilton Books Acquisitions Department (301) 459-3366

Unit A, Whitacre Mews, 26-34 Stannary Street,
London SE11 4AB, United Kingdom

All rights reserved
Printed in the United States of America
British Library Cataloguing in Publication Information Available

Library of Congress Control Number: 2017953709
ISBN: 978-0-7618-7002-9 (pbk : alk. paper)—ISBN: 978-0-7618-7003-6 (electronic)

∞™ The paper used in this publication meets the minimum requirements of American
National Standard for Information Sciences Permanence of Paper for Printed Library
Materials, ANSI/NISO Z39.48-1992.

Contents

Acknowledgments

I am particularly grateful to the individuals who shared their stories of living society's narrative about folks with intellectual disabilities. I hope that reading them will embolden others to follow suit.

My heartfelt thanks to Morgan and Sadie, who continued on with this project after the classes in which we met had concluded. Morgan, in fact, took two additional independent studies in order to complete the story that appears later in the book. Their stories are poignant and brave, and underscore that even the most enlightened and compassionate individuals have moments of confusion and darkness.

Out of the blue this past summer, I approached Sarah Saxton, our department's crack research administrator, for help in finding a grant that would defray the cost of publishing *Holding Up the Sky Together*. Sarah quickly and expertly found sources and patiently answered every last one of my rookie questions about Drexel's grant apparatus.

Similar patience was exhibited by the fine folks at Hamilton Books – Holly Buchanan, Emma Richard, and Nicolette Amstutz – as we moved the project forward. This is my second collaboration with Rowman and Littlefield; both have been enjoyable, productive, and trouble-free.

My wife Sheila did not read the manuscript that became *Holding Up the Sky Together* until right before it went to press. This is because she at times holds up most of it on her own, keeping Neil and I in line, sustaining the family with her vast intelligence, talent, and compassion. She is the love of my life. And Neil, I hope that you know how much I love you, despite some of the bumps and skirmishes we have had along the way. Sometimes your mom and I need a break from you, but our love for you is boundless.

Introduction

Our son Neil is 15 as of this writing. It is fair to say that his three favorite places on earth are (in no particular order): a swimming pool, where he can engage in Olympic-caliber slap-splashing; a set of stairs—*any* set of stairs, any size, any height, carpeted or not, anywhere, including those in various buildings at Drexel University, where I'm on the faculty, and at one time in neighbors' homes visited on Halloween; and the escalator at a local bookstore at the Christiana Mall here in Delaware.

Finishing a close fourth is Neil, parked in his wheelchair/stroller, opening and closing—and slamming with varying degrees of intensity and resulting volume—the large refrigerated cases at Target or at our local supermarket. In fifth place are three tree houses—and their multiple sets of steps—at Longwood Gardens, a beautiful botanical garden built on 1,100 acres of land owned by the DuPont family in Kennett Square, Pennsylvania. His activity at all of these venues is accompanied by repeated shouts or huffs of joy—think Phil Dunphy of the ABC television show *Modern Family* when he revels in his status as an alumnus of the fictional university whose team nickname is the Bulldogs (or Bullfrogs, as his wife Claire (played by Julie Bowen) calls them to his ongoing chagrin.

The bookstore's staff from the start of Neil's fascination with their escalator have been extremely kind and accommodating. My wife Sheila and I know many of them by name. We greet them as though they were co-workers, even friends, though a few of them aren't completely sold on the idea of allowing a teenaged boy with special needs to commandeer their escalator for 90 minutes at a time. "Hey guys," says Sean, a bespectacled millennial who resembles Matthew Broderick. "How's it going?" asks Tony, a New Orleans Saints fan whose stellar Afro rivals the one sported back in the 1970s by former Major Leaguer Oscar Gamble. Some days it's almost like a scene from the classic television show *Cheers*, when Norm Petersen trundled into the fictional Boston bar to enthusiastic shouts of "Norm!" Other kids have been castigated for their rambunctious escalator behavior, but Neil rolls merrily on, up and down, laughing and observing. Once, when one of the escalators was shut down for repairs, a genuine look of sadness crossed the face of Tom, who like many of his colleagues has come to know what these visits meant to Neil and has graciously given him space. We improvised, of course; the malfunctioning escalator became a set of stairs. We cruised up and stepped down.

Neil's plan of attack has changed somewhat as he's gotten older, but the weekend and school holiday afternoons spent on the escalator still feature several recurring segments: gripping the moving hand rail, which conveys the impression that he thinks he is assisting the escalator as it moves, riding up and then down multiple times, and watching the escalator from various vantage points and through black metal railings on the store's second floor. Kneeling down about 10 feet from the escalator—but not in anyone's way, which sometimes requires a hotly contested position shift—to focus on people's feet is a new addition to his escalator agenda. We've even picked up a few friends, including a young woman in a motorized wheelchair who calls Neil her "wheelchair pal" and asks if there's anything she can do or get for him.

But while the store's employees have been kind—so much so that Sheila and I sent a letter thanking them to bookstore's corporate offices—it's the range of reactions to Neil from the store's patrons that coalesced into the leaping off point for our journey. I haven't yet followed through on plans to keep accurate counts or to develop discrete categories for classification, but with apologies to the very talented people who created the hit movie *Inside Out,* their looks typically reflect:

Disgust, as if the person is thinking—but could never muster the guts to say—"how could these people bring him here?" Some sneer visibly at Neil. Some change direction to avoid any contact with him—not that he seems to care. Some act as though they might catch his challenges. Others grumble when he cuts—with no malicious intent—in front of them to get on the escalator, or when he screams when we move to enable someone to pick a Lean Cuisine or a frozen pizza out of the refrigerated case. For the record, we try to restrict our fridge door closing to sections in which odd or unpopular foods are stored.

Indifference is the look we most frequently experience, as if Neil isn't even there. Maybe *intentional indifference* is more accurate; these folks see him, they just don't *see* him. To be fair, it may be that they're wrapped up in what's taking place in their own lives—needing a book for school, trying to find just the right holiday gift, or quieting a grouchy child.

Curiosity, as though they've come upon an animal seen only in the wild or are gawking at a museum exhibit. Kids most often display this look, although to be fair, it probably originates in a lack of exposure to folks like Neil. It's actually a mix of wonder and...

Fear. Neil doesn't notice it—thankfully—but Sheila and I have been brought to tears more than once by kids, usually young ones, who cringe when they see him, as though they've seen a monster, and either head in the other direction or duck behind a parent.

Happiness. It's heartwarming when folks express gratitude to Neil for keeping the escalator moving. "Are you helping us get to the top?" they'll ask. "Thanks a lot buddy," we hear now and then. Others just smile at him—some out of a sense of obligation, others to check off "was nice to a disabled person" on their list of behaviors that ensure entry into heaven, and still others just because they recognize that he's a very compelling individual. A couple of weeks before Christmas last year, a middle-aged couple who had observed Neil for about an hour from a table in the café adjoining the bookstore stopped us between descent and ascent and handed us a $25 gift card. They told us he was a beautiful young man—this is quite true of course—and asked that we use the card to by him a present.

Finally, in limited quantities, we see *emulation*. Neil has inspired a small but dedicated legion of imitators, kids who watch the escalator, cup and imaginarily propel the handrails, and now and then follow us on our forays. During a bookstore visit this past October, two young girls, probably 12 or 13, hitched about a 10-minute ride one step behind us. It's a stretched application of Robert Cialdini's groundbreaking research on how humans tend to "bask in the reflected glory" of excellent sports teams and accomplished individuals, but these kids seem to bask in Neil's coolness. Others meanwhile dip into the escalator shenanigans songbook, sitting on the steps, running up and down, and attempting the time-honored "go down the up" and it's just as exciting cousin, "go up the down." Sheila and I cringe with fear—and a little embarrassment—when a kid gets in trouble with a parent or a staff member for wanting to hang out and ride.

So for those of you scoring at home, I'd guess the breakdown of looks is about 40 percent indifference, 20 percent curiosity, 20 percent disgust, 10 percent fear, and 5 percent happiness and emulation. But I'd also guess that for all of these folks—the nasty, the encouraging, even the kind—Neil's presence at the foot of the bookstore escalator or in front of the refrigerated cases at a local big-box store is anomalous. We've learned during our travels that families that include children with challenges like Neil's are often reluctant to go out in public. And when they do, they carefully monitor their child's behavior so as to not arouse the ire of others. Even though we've had many adventures with Neil—four long airplane rides (including a six-hour jaunt to San Diego marked by loud, persistent crying—and then radiant smiles at passengers ready to ring his neck as we got off the plane), repeated trips to New York City and Washington, D.C., an annual excursion to Phila- delphia to see the renowned Christmas light show at a local department store—we also monitor his behavior and theirs, although we also try to enable him to experience these places and people as he wants to. This means pretending he's causing the beeps during the checkout at the local grocery store or scraping chairs on the tile floor at the Please Touch Museum in Philadelphia even if other families cover their ears now and then. For even as our tolerance of and kindness toward individuals with intellectual disabilities has increased, thanks to the work of organizations like Special Olympics, encountering an individual and his or her family whose lives revolve around the daily challenges that come with a shitty hand is atypical, or is experi- enced and narrated as such, particularly by folks in the media. We don't, despite school outreach programs, PSAs, *Sesame Street*, and, a little further back, *Life Goes On*, see these folks as a regular part of life. In fact, by laboring so hard to encourage or compel tolerance, these well-intentioned efforts, we believe, worsen the marginalization or create a completely differ- ent version of it that brings to mind recent debates about whether we live in a post-racial and post-feminist society (We don't). Even when there is progress, making such a leap provides rhetorical cover or at least a distrac- tion while intolerance regroups and those who fight the intolerance are hung out to dry. And for some, it becomes less about showing love and compas- sion than about being able to pat oneself on the back when an interaction with a person like Neil is over.

When Sheila and I review Neil's encounters, we try to be fair and empa- thetic. Maybe, we say, it was the person's first meeting with someone like Neil. Maybe the person was having a bad day—he or she was fresh from a fight with a loved one or a battle over a parking space (the Christiana Mall is always teeming with customers, even on weekday afternoons)—or they wanted to be nice but have been raised not to be or simply didn't know how. We've scaled new heights in assigning benefit of the doubt (a TED talk—one that true to form would offer no real solutions—is in the offing). True, we do our share of grousing and bemoaning the declining levels of kindness and patience in the world, but we leave our dismay with admissions that we at times lack both qualities. It took me quite a while to realize that the escalator was our version of catch, and that I should stop resenting him for not being able to pop on the mitts and head to the backyard. For the record, we enjoy Neil's variations on catch; they include "step ball" and "deck ball"—both revolve around letting a ball bounce down the steps; the goal is to coax the ball into hitting all of the steps as it falls.

We veer off and talk about what these folks probably don't know: that these places, along with local playground swings and the summer camp program at the Mary Campbell Center, a Wilmington, Delaware residential facility for folks with disabilities, provide the stages for pretty much the extent of the activities in which we can engage outside the home without Neil getting extremely angry. We can't, for example, just go to the Costco located adjacent to the Mall without first hitting the escalator for an hour, otherwise Neil will cry, scream, and thrash. We then can't leave the Costco without 15 minutes of fridge closing/slamming. They probably don't know that we space out the visits to the bookstore so as not to wear out our welcome and shudder whenever other kids are disciplined for fooling around on the escalator, lest the staff end Neil's playing privileges. Neil would be crushed—not to mention supremely pissed off—if we arrived one day to find a sign that reads, "You must be here to shop in order to use the escalator." We're fairly certain that the staff at the nearby Nordstrom, home to the Mall's only other escalators, would not be receptive to regular visits from Neil.

They don't know that we're always on the lookout for pockets of patience that don't materialize very often—and that our at times exhausting surveillance is stacked on top of the knowledge that despite advances in the treatment of Cystic Fibrosis, a genetic disease that relentlessly damages the lungs of its sufferers, we will likely outlive Neil (that fact is the centerpiece of the angry retort we break out only when folks are being particularly intolerant or mean, as in "Oh yeah (asshole is implied), you'll probably outlive him."

But it's *why* they don't know, or are curious but reluctant to engage, or just flat out lack empathy, that compelled us to write this book. Fueling the misimpressions and misanthropy we believe are portrayals of individuals with intellectual disabilities in the mass media, sporadic though they are. We should always be skeptical of those in my line of work who argue that the onslaught of information we take in from an ever-widening array of sources can magically change our behavior—the so-called "hypodermic needle" theory of media effects. But these messages do help us craft our realities and develop and share our own narratives about folks with intellectual disabilities, as James Carey would argue. We'll explore this later in *Holding Up the Sky Together*, but you'd be excused for concluding that folks like Neil, when discussed in a newspaper article, a blog post, or in a television show, are either the hopeless victims of unchecked avarice or brave, spunky competitors who sink a basket after sitting on the bench. We see either unspeakable tragedy visited upon them or celebrated triumphs, often over adversity, in which they revel but which mean more to us. Rarely, I contend, do we see individuals with intellectual disabilities portrayed as, well, individuals - celebrated for who they are, not for their ability to adapt to our attempts to normalize, as much as we feel we can, their behavior. We either cajole them to change or marginalize them. We don't change—they do, or at least we impose those changes on them; they must if we are to include them in the "mainstream" world. Often unbeknownst to them, we compel them to fit in according to *our* expectations, or compel ourselves to believe they're fitting in, even as we claim to be providing them the fullest possible lives.

And for folks like Neil, who sits somewhere between suggestible and unreachable, there are even fewer examples, fewer folks like him represented meaningfully in the national dialogue about intellectual disabilities. Thus, each chapter of *Holding Up the Sky Together* includes stories or vignettes drawn from our lives that will serve as a leaping off point for a deeper discussion of the social history of what we someday hope will no longer be called mental retardation and of examples of the dominant narrative of intellectual disabilities offered up by the mainstream media. We will unpack and dissect the myth to which we subscribe of life for and with a person who has intellectual disabilities. Thus, the book is part memoir, part analysis, part well-intentioned prescription for a society that has made some progress in treating folks like Neil with more kindness, but that still has difficulty recognizing them as individuals.

As I've already hinted, we include ourselves in the latter category. An example: I talk a lot about Neil and Sheila in my classes. In addition to keeping my heart from collapsing, they are the source of most of my relevant and compelling discussion examples. But sometimes I, well, edit the extent of Neil's challenges; I pump up his resume. I ask my students not to call me in the evenings, primarily because Sheila and I will be feeding Neil and administering his breathing treatments—and our post-game recovery, which involves copious amounts of television, a Saturday night movie, and more than a little wine. If they do call, I say, I'll put Neil on and "he can deal with you," as if he can talk. He can't.

One assertion we hear from a few people a month as they encounter us moving through our days we believe neatly sums up the main strand of our narrative about folks with intellectual disabilities. They've seen us cruising the escalator, or wrestling with him to get him into his stroller, or trying to stay calm as he thrashes again to let us know we're not doing what he wants to do, and feel compelled to say (drumroll please!): "He's so lucky to have you."

What a dumb-ass thing to say, we think. How glib—how telethon, how *After-School Special*, how cloying final segment of the local news. As if folks like Neil don't matter until they're saved by well-meaning well-heeled white knights like Sheila and me. And don't forget the related, but still ignorant "you're doing such a great job—thank you" as one woman told us while we stood at the base of the escalator a week before Christmas last year. Thank you for what—for keeping him out of your hair while you shopped? It's a little like when the dedicated iconoclastic teacher swoops in to save underperforming, impoverished and/or repressed students in movies like *Dead Poets Society* or *Freedom Writers*. Those teachers nearly always move on or are pushed out of the classroom after the forces of bureaucratic mediocrity regroup. That's what we're used to from the media on this issue—that these kids have no shot of thriving unless this brand of benevolent help comes their way.

These folks can't possibly know what we go through, unless they too have a family member who faces similarly significant challenges. And we certainly don't mean to dismiss your daily challenges. We're not here to scold or to criticize; our apologies in advance if it our discussion hits you this way. Even our own empathy goes missing on days when Neil is at his most raucous. And we certainly can't know what they go through with their families. But imagine if a couple that made less money than we do or didn't have the Clintonesque "village" of friends, family members, teachers, paraprofessionals, and special education students from a local university to give us a break now and then so we could do our work and take time to relax, or that lacked the knowledge to safely administer his meds, or couldn't muster the temerity to confront officious bureaucrats and spineless teachers who want to turn Neil into a living experiment designed to boost their test scores and justify their narrow-minded pedagogical methods, were charged with caring for Neil.

He would be screwed.

But what I think they mean is that he's really more trouble than he's worth, and that if it weren't for our kindness, he'd have no shot whatsoever. Like he owes us. Like he's less of a person than we are.

Though we can't dictate your reaction to what's to come, please know again that we write not out of a need for sympathy, to castigate you, or to dispense advice in all-American self-help fashion. We've written this only to inform, to perhaps provoke discussion, and most certainly to challenge our society's narratives about folks with challenges like Neil's that day after day frustrate the hell out of us.

We also want to get his story out there before he dies. Though the life expectancy for people with CF has increased significantly as treatments and drugs have improved, and the disease has only done minor damage to Neil's lungs, we face the possibility, referenced in our comeback, that we will outlive him.

While Sheila is the source of most of my decent ideas - and for sure of the titles for my articles and books - the vast majority of the thoughts and ideas in these pages are mine, except later on where my talented contributors weigh in. Some will surprise Sheila, even though I have been for the most part open about how this ride has psychologically and emotionally affected me. So it may turn out that this is the strangest love letter of all time.

Chapter One

A Day in the Life

During the school year and when he attends summer school, Neil gets up at about 5:30 a.m. When he attends camp in mid-August at The Mary Campbell Center—which we can now officially add to the list of favorite places on earth mentioned in the introduction—he gets up at 7 a.m. It's a pretty heavy lift for all concerned—literally when he fights us as we dress him—but it's necessary that we allot enough time to feed him, complete his breathing treatment and chest percussion (either by hand—the "artisanal" method, as Sheila has taken to calling it—or by wrapping him in a vibrating vest that when inflated with air makes him look as though he's sitting in a lifeboat), run a bolus feeding, and leave a little time to change his diaper should the need arise before the school bus comes at 7 a.m. or when we leave for camp a little after 8 a.m.

Though we'd much rather not still be doing it, we frequently get to practice our diaper changing skills. On school days, this means sitting on the padded floor with legs apart as Neil slowly wakes up. But even half asleep, he will usually try to a) roll away from you—we use our legs like bowling alley bumpers to nudge him back to a laying flat position; b) sit up, something his first team of physical therapists concluded he would never be able to do; c) push against your thigh as though he was testing your ability to do a split; or d) kick you in the face, knees, or shoulder. The latter two actions are usually repeated; it's like trying to grab a bucking horse around the waist. Sheila, whose arms are shorter than mine, has to endure the added thrill of Neil reaching out to grab her shirt or, with more gusto, her hair. When he's not trying to grab it, he's looking up at it like a fan in the strands tracks a foul ball. With my flamingo-like arms, I can still elude him, though my defense is helped by the fact there's not much of a target left on my head.

1

Lately Neil likes to grab the armholes of his shirts as we try to slide them over his head. Sometimes giving up works; it's amazing how calmly and quickly he'll push his hand through a sleeve. About four years ago, we added sleeveless t-shirts to his wardrobe after he pulled out his g-tube several times. Out of sight, out of mind—that was the theory anyway. He seems to know that we're skittish at best about the tiny protruding button; when he's tired or wants to redirect us to another activity, he'll tug on it through both shirts. So to have the desired effect, the t-shirt must be tucked in; the tucking has the added benefit of containing the poop that would up until recently otherwise push out from his diaper during particularly prodigious number twos. A new brand of diaper—larger and designed for folks with incontinence issues— have solved the escape problem. We keep them on a shelf in his closet, a closet that no longer has doors because Neil would open and close them all night. Next to them are wipes and plastic—not paper—bags from the local grocery store used to dispose of his dirty diapers in the garbage can at the side of the house.

Up until about a year ago, I carried him down the stairs to his Rifton chair, where his feeding and breathing treatment takes place. Now, to save our backs, and with a piece of advice from his eighth grade teacher, we position his feet in front of him after getting him into a sitting position and offer our hands. He now frequently grabs them and slowly stands up. We then haltingly head toward the top of the stairs. On his less cooperative days, I'll gently (much of the time) drag him on his hands and knees to the stairs. He'll then usually grab the railing and head down. More on his obsession with stairs later in the book.

I prefer that he sleeps through his treatments until right before the bus arrives, I'd like to tell you that it's because I want to make sure he's well rested. That's part of it, I guess. He's not exactly the world's most accomplished sleeper. He rarely stays on the twin mattress we've placed on the floor in a corner of his room. We usually find him in the morning tucked into a sleeping position on the interlocking multicolored mats that for his safety and comfort—but mainly for his safety—cover the floor. We tell people that he's often up "partying"—which means keeping tabs on the air moved through the floor vent or tugging on and snapping cobalt blue baseball-themed curtains (known as "curts"). He snaps them with precision and ferocity; it sounds like he's aiming at someone's rear end in a locker room. Or he'll kick the custom-made maple gate that prevents him from leaving his room. Or peer up through the now opened curtains and hope to spy an airplane or two. Or he'll rearrange the books in his bookcase—his "library," we call it in honor of Sheila's brother, a talented librarian to whom we refer as "Uncle Fuzzy" because of his exceptionally hirsute body. Or he'll just chatter until finally, mercifully, he falls asleep.

We've done the best we can with his room. Ideally, Neil would stay in his bed for eight hours, but we knew right away that wasn't going to happen. Yet true to our personality types, Sheila continues to hope that someday he'll sleep a full night in a bed, which we every so often come close to buying; I believe the mats will always be his main space, with a few bed stays per month on the docket. I understand her concern and love (and envy) her hope. Seeing little waffle impressions on his face was cute, but the mats, despite our best efforts get quite dirty. They hold the remnants of number ones and twos, dog hair that's wafted in (Beebo's not allowed in his room to prevent an even bigger buildup), and of us walking around the room to play with Neil and care for him. Mopping helps, as do the twice-monthly deep cleanings done by the folks from the local company who help us clean the house, but it's never enough. His face looks pretty irritated most mornings—almost like acne. Perhaps it is acne, with a mat chaser.

Mainly though, I just like the quiet in the morning. I too often nod off, sometimes while I'm doing his percussion. When I stir, I'll find myself with my head down or nibbling on my sleeve. Sheila and I have different but equally valid approaches to his morning ablutions. She talks with him about the day, shows him pictures on her iPhone (one of his favorite pastimes), and is generally quite chipper, as she is almost always. On those days when *The Tavis Smiley Show* or the rebroadcast of the news from the local PBS affiliate doesn't put him back to sleep, I'll take a page out of Sheila's book and talk with him—although as reflects our differing approaches to life, my focus is the next 30 minutes. I have of late expanded the menu of topics: we'll talk about swimming, or bowling, or the friends he'll see on the bus. About a month ago, the bus driver and aide let us know that Neil was helping to push a friend who thanks to an injury was using a wheelchair to get around. Full disclosure: I've been freaked out about being late after I dreamed when I was 6 that I was late for school and then forgot to put on my pants. I've been 90 percent successful ever since at being 15 minutes early for everything. Feedings and breathing treatments, like so many of the events in Neil's life, require a level of choreography that would exhaust Derek Hough, who Sheila and I agree is the best of the *Dancin' With the Stars'* instructor/choreographers. For example, for the last two or three months, Neil, in order to move through the morning routine without screaming or thrashing, has required us to put his school backpack—as well as the "backup" backpack filled with supplies for day trips to the mall or the park—on the leather chair located catty corner to the Rifton chair in our living room.

Once everything is in place, and after a few head bobs and weaves, he consumes a container of yogurt and one of applesauce, on which is sprinkled six the contents of six digestive enzyme capsules and two crushed tablets of a recently approved CF medicine that retails for more than $200,000 a year. The yogurt can't be too thick or contain fruit. Either attribute is an engraved invitation to Neil to gently and deftly move the fruit out onto his lower lip, or to a coughing fit. Dish towels must always be kept nearby. After Beebo is allowed his proscribed five licks of each container, on go Neil's "no-nos"—cushioned, colorfully decorated (the current pair sports a school theme) arm restraints that prevent him from deflecting the neb cups or pulling at his feeding tube. The no-nos must be wrapped tightly, otherwise Neil will work them down and off his arm. I check his hands repeatedly to make sure I haven't hindered his circulation. I gently attach the connector on the one end of the extension to the button that sits on his belly. I wind the tubing that carries the food from the pump through the frame of the chair—again to ensure Neil doesn't pull on it—then attach it to the other end of the extension. Tightly—otherwise it might come loose if Neil thrashes. The extension is then tucked under Neil's shirt.

Nebulizer treatments are next. I turn on the nebulizer, pick up the first of the cups, which contains an Albuterol/Pulmocort/Atorvent mix, hook it to the tubing, sit back, and position the business end of the cup in front of his face. I aim for his philtrum. Next up is his Pulmozyme and then, every other month, Tobrimyacin (TOBI), an inhaled antibiotic. If his CF symptoms worsen, we aren't able to skip a "TOBI Month." Neil's breathing treatments have always been a tumultuous ride—this is why I so fervently wish for him to fall asleep on school mornings. If he's awake, the tumult almost always ramps up during "artisanal" treatments—or "bangings" as I call them. For a long time, episodes of *Barney* or *Rachael Ray's 30-Minute Meals* along with some play-by-play commentary would calm him. But we've now changed the accompaniment several times. Lately, we talk about what we'll put in his properly located backpack: the communication book with which we communicate with his teacher and an insulated bag that once carried a container of water or fruit juice (his teacher now ensures that he drink at least a few ounces of water during the day). We'll surmise that both Sheila and our dog, Beebo, need their own backpacks. We'll discuss the backpack tastes of his classmates and celebrities we see on TV. If we cover our backpack bases, our attention will turn to a rousing game of "which downstairs ceiling fan will come to a complete stop first" (if I don't include a head start when designing the play, the larger one in our kitchen with three blades—as opposed to the Florida room fan, which has four—always wins. "Clanking"—and announcing the clanks—while I make my lunch for days up at Drexel or unloading or reloading the dishwasher keep him laughing. All of these activities keep me from worrying that he'll pull out his g-tube. In fall and winter, it's on to locating our coats and placing them on top of the backpacks on my chair. Right before the bus arrives, we'll toss in a load of laundry and cajole him to perform the "washing machine dance," which we'll ask him to "give half a chance" as he undulates like the agitator. I clean his face, brush his teeth (most days), comb his hair, pop on his coat and mine, and grab his backpack.

I gently pull him out of his chair. He usually plops down on his knees, even as I'm listing the friends he's about to see, and who call out his name as he climbs on to the bus. I drag him—gently—out to the front door. We could probably pick up some extra income hiring him out as a freelance political protestor. Neil finally relents; he stands up, rights himself, and slowly makes his way down our sidewalk and driveway and toward the bus. If Neil doesn't veer off to open the car doors and after several short stops to register his displeasure, he and I are met by his extremely kind bus driver, Bonnie ("Miss B"), and Connie ("Miss C"), she of the very colorful wardrobe and the firm but gentle reminders about what he needs at school.

On off days and weekends, we let Neil sleep in, hoping for a little compensation for his late nights with Jagger and Richards. We change his diaper at about 9 a.m. and then let him play in his room until about 10:30 a.m. with some toys from the famed "toy tub" we keep on the shelf in his closet. We try to rotate the toys taken out of the "tub" so he doesn't get tired of them and so he gets the joy of "rediscovering" older toys. At one time, it was possible to change his diaper while he stood and peered over the gate that replaced the door to his room. It wasn't quite as precise as when he was lying down, but this is now a moot point since he outgrew his pull-up diapers and uses larger diapers held in place by four tabs. We grab his clothes from dressers in an adjacent guest bedroom. If we kept them in his room, he would open and close the drawers to the point that they would break—as we learned when he had dressers in his room a few years back. School shirts, undershirts, and socks are in the top drawer; long pants and shorts (in season) are in the middle drawer; short-sleeved shirts not sanctioned for school wear are in the bottom drawer. About five years ago, we bought a "days of the week" clothes organizer that resembles a closet sweater caddy. We do a pretty good job of stocking it with his clothes for the week, particularly when we're able to do most or all (a rare occurrence) of our laundry. He is rarely happy when I head back downstairs to catch up on laundry or some work or to just read the newspaper. But his screams eventually dissipate, and I can soon hear the musical strains from his keyboard and/or happy huffs as he spins toy car wheels and helicopter blades.

We had been insisting that Neil wear "traveling shoes"—a pair of slip-on loafers—for walking down the stairs in the morning. But like so many of our rules ("We have our standard!" is a frequent refrain), it was undone by a combination of his dogged resistance and his slowly improving physical capacity. He can now make it down the stairs in his stocking feet, one hand on the railing, one hand in mine or Sheila's. He often livens up these excursions by bouncing down on his rear end—or, if left to come down himself, by going down a few steps and then back up a few until Sheila or I recapture his hand. Ironically, one of our few remaining rules requires Neil to wear shoes whenever he's on the steps.

Neil's bus arrives here from school at about 3 p.m. When it's warm, and even when it isn't, he'll try to persuade you to take him for another ride, this time in the car. At times he can be persuaded to scale back to a game of "open and close the car door," or my particular favorite, "quickly and furtively honk the horn so he laughs." He also now and then enjoys a sit-down on the wooden blue bench on our porch. Once inside, we let Neil choose whether to head out to the back deck for some "Deck Ball" (bouncing various balls down the steps) and some time on the swings and in his little play scape cabin; b) stop at the stairs for a rousing game of "Step Ball"; or c) spend some time in the Florida room building structures with his cardboard bricks or watching miniature doggies and penguins go up two toy escalators. About two years ago, Neil added to his post-school repertoire watching Sheila or me or one of the very kind and patient undergraduate students from the University of Delaware's early childhood education program walk up and down the stairs...one at a time...repeatedly. Sheila and I usually instruct him to "get started" by going up and down for a time before we fall in. When he's ready for the changeover, he'll plop down into a "W" sit at the top or bottom of the stairs and signal that he wants (a repeated slap on his chest) you to take over (a tap of the thigh) the upping and downing of it all. We try to mix in lengthy segments of "Step Ball" and "Up and Down Boy"—more earnestly as we've gotten older.

Activity in the Florida room has been sporadic of late; Neil usually heads right for the stairs. But when he does venture back there, the soundtrack is the *A Child's Celebration of Song* CD. It's almost always ready to go in the ancient Casio player that sits on the bookcase against the back wall. He might turn a toy car on its roof to spin it or repeatedly play a hip-hop version of "Twinkle Twinkle Little Star" on a tricked out toy keyboard (we have two—the other is in his bedroom, minus the microphone and its cord). Or he might indicate that he wants you turn our ceiling fan on and off. Or he might ask that you "do stickers" with him; this usually means peeling them off the backing and handing them to him to put on a piece of paper or cardboard inserts saved from boxes of yogurt purchased at Costco. He's also quite good at ensuring with his pointer finger that a sticker is completely stuck. Of particular interest to him is the material typically left over after all the stickers are gone. He usually wants you to peel that off before—and often instead of—the stickers are removed, and affix it to the cardboard.

If the weather is warm—and my spirit is willing (not a sure thing after a long drive back from Drexel)—we'll take a short drive or head to the park. We're lucky to have a county park in our development, about ½ mile from the house. Another one is located about a mile away, but it doesn't have a handicapped accessible swing. This became required equipment after I almost could not extricate Neil from a toddler's swing as three or four not so concerned parents looked on. The new swing came courtesy of our local county councilperson—lefty friends take note: she's a Republican—after we wrote to her about Neil not being able to swing like the other kids. He was too small and too unsteady for the "big kid" swings. Neil typically starts out on the swing and then moves on to the nearby playscape, where he goes up and down its stairs—and then cajoles you into doing it.

New to Team Neil are registered nurses with experience caring for kids with special needs. They visit on most weekday afternoons to administer Neil's evening breathing treatment, percussion, and bolus. Even though Sheila and I are for the most part warm and friendly folks, we like our privacy— we'll return to that idea later. Having a new person on the scene takes considerable getting used to. Compounding our discomfort is the feeling we share that we've somehow failed by having to add a player to our roster—it's an admission that we can't handle Neil on our own. We don't do well with asking others for help. Then again, Sheila didn't miss a single day of work in 2005 as she battled what turned out to be a rare form of cancer, and I asked for my laptop to catch up with students the morning after I had surgery in 2011 to stem the damage done to my hand and arm by a flesh-eating bacteria. We keep our heads down and forge ahead, battle, struggle. Dare I say it—we "get 'er done!"

It took only a couple of weeks for us to begin to enjoy having the UD students around. Most have taken to Neil right away; one, a young woman from Pennsylvania, came darned close to equaling the level of engagement— not to mention calm—achieved by one of Neil's former paraprofessionals (we call her "The Neil Whisperer"). Only two or three have been less than interested in engaging with Neil. Sheila can do a dead-on impression of the young woman with the put-upon sigh who spent a significant amount of her time here texting her friends. But for the most part, we see them as surrogate daughters. But they come and go; they're here twice a week and then only for a couple of hours. And they only play with him—walk the steps (with more variations—slides, kicks, spins, ascending and descending on tiptoes—than Sheila and I have come up with), do stickers, hit the swing in the backyard, toss the ball. We want very much to keep them in Neil's life, but they have the audacity to grow up, embark on careers, get married—or not, have kids— or not. Some have made return visits, but they typically graduate and go on with their lives. We'll get an occasional email. Ironically, both Sheila and I are devoted members of the "parents should work themselves out of a job" club. We wish them the best.

Now, we've offloaded some of his care to a total stranger who as of this writing hasn't shown that she has the strength to handle him. Further, she has yet to master Neil's rhythms—this is a fancy way to say that he wants to engage in only certain activities after school and that even well-intentioned variations are not tolerated. He can't be cajoled traditionally into changing course, although we have had some success with explaining what we're about to do and promising him that we'll do what he wants once we completed our appointed rounds. You can sneak in an unprogrammed activity now and then, but Sheila and I learned after about a thousand screaming fits—not all of them Neil's—that at times you have to let him dictate the itinerary. I can get away with Tavis Smiley and NJTV News in the morning, but he insists during his afternoon ablutions that a constant stream of escalator, stair workout, and dogs sliding on their bellies down the stairs videos be played on the iPad as he sits in the Rifton chair. Others in our inner circle engage him in the same way; Sheila's sister mixes in pronouncements about what she believes Neil wants to do or he's thinking. "Look—he wants to color!" she says. No, not really. "He wants to pet the puppy!" Nope. When we visit them at their home, it's right to their stairs—and then to their other set of stairs.

Our main worry is that he won't be able to do only the things he wants—not to mention his tendencies to pull hair and pinch arms—if we decide when he's older to move him to a group home or to the Mary Campbell Center. Maybe because I usually drop him off at MCC and see how the residents act and how compassionately they are treated by staff, I don't worry quite as much, but in any event we want him to be safe and happy. Nor have the nurses' presence mitigated the tension that comes with others taking care of Neil while we're here working. As Josh Lyman told Charlie Hill early in the run of *The West Wing*, that feeling "never goes away." It's a din, a hum. When the UD folks are here, we often have to intervene—to change a diaper, for example, or to move Neil away from something that might hurt him. On top of that, I at least feel like I'm lazy for not being able to work and keep him occupied. After a recently resolved run of self-pity explained later, we worry that we're "outsourcing" (Sheila's word) our son's care—and even though I see him going to live in a residential facility sooner than Sheila does, Dawn's presence suggests that we actually are getting closer to that milestone.

But back to the daily schedule: other weekend entertainment possibilities include the wonderful but underfunded Delaware Children's Museum. Located on Wilmington's slowly rebounding waterfront (the water furnished by the Christina River), the DCM features a host of really cool interactive exhibits—and a mammoth set of winding stairs right inside the main entrance. A three-step set awaits Neil in the back, next to the aquarium and the interactive garden with the plastic veggies. Again, there's a short, but slowly growing "greatest hits" list: the steps, the steering wheels on the scaled down train and speedboat, the reflex reaction machine, and the wooden blocks kept in a set of cubbies near the area where kids can imitate construction workers by building with what looks like giant plastic Tinkertoys.

If we've recently pulled the Longwood Gardens treehouses or the bookstore escalator out of our quiver, we might head off to the "Can-Do" playground located about five miles away in Wilmington's Alapocas State Park (like our park, it features swings for disabled kids) or to a local family-owned grocery store in tony Greenville whose staff kindly indulges Neil's at times erratic shopping cart driving and his burning need to open and close their fridges. The guilt Sheila feels as Neil slams has meant that we end up buying some pretty odd frozen goods on those trips.

We try to return home by 5:30 at the latest; I've become a lot less insistent (I think) about this deadline. It's back into the Rifton chair for another breathing treatment and bolus. He is more willing these days to head right into the living room without a detour to the steps. With a little coaxing—and complaining and a quick stop at my leather chair—Neil will sidle over and shimmy into the Rifton. In fact, on numerous occasions in recent months, he's climbed without any prompting from us into the Rifton. It is essential, however, that he be strapped in (that sounds punitive—it's only one strap) to the chair; otherwise, his wanderlust will reemerge. He'll drop out of the chair onto his knees and head off.

In contrast to the brave and thorough parents of kids with intellectual and physical disabilities we see often in the media, our life with Neil, as rich and fulfilling as it is, often revolves around getting through the next ten minutes. And making peace with the fact that we tend to our lives' other quadrants by taking a shortcut or two—or not giving him the undivided attention he so vigorously seeks. Example: both Sheila and I have assured Neil's CF nutritionist that he has progressed to eating thick soups in addition to his usual menu of yogurt and applesauce. This is at best partially true; a few times more than a year ago, he did indeed eat pureed versions of Sheila's phenomenal chicken noodle soup and slummed it with some Campbell's, but that's it. Trying new things with Neil has to be properly timed. He has to be in a good mood if there's to be a shot in hell of accomplishing the new thing. And the care he requires, frankly, has dampened our drive to innovate. We just want to get through the next ten minutes.

He won't tolerate the mask that most CF patients wear to maximize the effectiveness of the nebulized medicine—so, with the approval of our respiratory therapist (who no longer is vomited on when she swabs the inside of his cheek for a culture), we just point the neb cup at his lip and trust the "blow by" to do the job. We always sterilize his neb cups by "putting them in the cooker (microwave), booker" for 10 minutes, but we don't always wash them first. We long ago gave up using the "artisanal" method of percussion during the evening sessions and for extra sessions prescribed by Neil's CF doctor when bacteria appear on a throat culture or when he contracts a cold. It was then that Neil was at his pinching, flailing, and swinging worst. Sheila bought me compression sleeves to wear on my forearms, but Neil grabbed them and ripped them off to get at my skin. More than once, I regret to say, I've in anger thrown the small blue rubber compression cup against the

Florida Room wall. If he hasn't fallen asleep during our pre-school sessions, I often wear the Hawkeye Pierce-style bathrobe purchased for me by Sheila or my New York Mets jacket (also purchased for me by Sheila) to fend him off.

By the weekend (pre-nurses), I was doing anything I could to delay the start of the bolus escalator video festival—moving clothes from the washer to the dryer, folding dried clothes, running outside to get the mail, sneaking in a check of my email on the way back into the living room, cleaning off dusty ceiling fan blades, gathering and bagging the piles of newspaper strips fashioned by Neil—but only with Sheila's help. We joke that there have to be teachers out there, even in our test-obsessed time, who still introduce their charges to papier mache. Or we could put the bags of strips up on eBay in the hope a struggling artist might buy them.

Eventually though, I settle in. A surgeon put in Neil's g-tube in 2008. Without it, he would never take in a sufficient number of calories. CF sufferers must consume 1/3 more calories than you or me. Neil has struggled from birth to gain weight, thanks in part to poor muscle tone in his mouth. Because of severe gastrointestinal reflux, he refused for a long stretch to eat anything at all. At one point, we were using an eyedropper (actually, one of us used the eyedropper while the other held his head) to get the formula into him. We were lucky if he'd take in a few ounces in addition to the applesauce he's eaten since he was two weeks old to ensure that he received the digestive enzyme mentioned earlier. We augment the tube feedings these days with a pinch of salt, a splash of Vitamin D, some protein powder, and a few ounces of tap water (Neil drinks maybe five or six ounces of fluid all day).

When the bolus is done—and if we've managed to get through it without having the connection between the bag that holds the formula and the feeding extension come dislodged and spill the contents—we disconnect him and gently flush the extension with some warm water from a syringe. A counterclockwise turn detaches the extension from the button. We pull off the old split gauze pad there to collect discharge, clean around the button site with an alcohol wipe, and arrange a new pad around the button, securing with it tape.

Neil walks, knee-walks, or is dragged by one of us to the steps. With encouragement, funny noises, and a little singing, he scales the steps and heads into his room. After a diaper change, we select the tub toys du jour, close the gate, pop on the iPod that sits in our guest bathroom down the hall, select a playlist (usually Nat King Cole or "Mellow Mix," which leads off with "New Soul" by Israeli singer Yael Naim—as of this writing still Neil's favorite song), tell him we love him and head downstairs for a few hours of wine, conversation, and staring at the television. During his sabbatical, Neil plays a little, "curtains" a little (he tugs them and snaps them with a flick of the wrist—a matador without a bull), lays on the floor, parties a little with himself, and almost always poops. Neil is quite regular—early morning and early evening, without fail.

We revel in the peace, though it is punctuated by screams from upstairs if the front door is opened. He's the world's loudest upstairs neighbor. Our friendly but neurotic dog ensures that this happens at least once, when I take him for his walk—after he's taken care of his business and chased a squirrel or two in our spacious back yard. Neil also weighs in on taking out the trash or hopping into the car to run a late errand. During the week, we try to head back up to get Neil by 9 or 9:30. We give ourselves more chill time on weekends; we've been successful of late at scheduling Saturday night movies, or reruns of *The West Wing*. Loved *Dr. Strange* and *Trolls*, but I had to walk out on *Batman v. Superman*—it's cool to see that superheroes have flaws, but they should have titled the film *Total Crank v. Martyr*. On top of that, I was vibrating and nauseous about 30 minutes in. We're nearly always greeted by a pungent number two when we reach the top of the stairs— although the new diapers, in addition to containing his work product, kill more of the smell. The trick once you have Neil on his back to change him is distracting him from the collegiate-level wrestling that accompanies the diaper change, as referenced earlier. Lately, we've been talking about how efficient the floor vent—"Mister Vent"—is in delivering cool or warm air into the room. Every time our heating system kicks on, Neil happily watches the air cause the curtains to flutter. If he's awake during the morning change, talking about his buddies on the bus, or "Miss B" and "Miss C." Evening colloquies revolve around how many airplanes he's spotted from his window, a task to which we assign when we bring him up. YouTube videos of planes taking off and landing don't cut it; he likes the real thing. During sessions of "deck ball," he stops and looks skyward whenever he detects a plane. "Nice spotting, Mister N!" is our usual reply. We put his toys back on the closet shelf; he rarely plays with them these days. He is begrudgingly slid to the steps. He rises to a standing position just as we are try to find the second step. Neil usually complies with our requests to traverse *all* the steps, though now and then he'll slip his hands from yours, grab the railing, and reverse direction. Subsequent course adjustments are met with screams. At the bottom of the stairs, Neil will typically grab the last style in the banister and/or drop to his knees, ready to play ball and resume the "up and down" game that we started earlier in the day...or on the weekend. More sliding moves him to the living room, and even more to his Rifton, though if Sheila or Beebo are on the couch, a brief discussion of what they're up to may move the drop out of his mind. If his symptoms are flaring up, one more non-artisanal breathing treatment is administered; if it's a "TOBI month," we'll blow that by. After some applesauce and yogurt and a quick wash of the face, it's back out of the chair—although to be honest, we often milk a few more minutes of stillness out of the ritual before "popping" him out of the chair.

Extensions typically happen while Sheila and discuss the heartily delivered talking points by the guests on *Real Time with Bill Maher*.

And then the end of the day chase begins. Neil may head out to the Florida Room for some more "tunes" and some mild tormenting of the dog, but just as often, he'll decide to a) tear up some more newspaper; b) pull everything off of the large square leather-covered ottoman positioned in front of our end table to prevent; c) throwing objects at the lamp on the end table to make it jiggle and/or the pull chains "clank" against the stem. If Sheila has left the couch, he sometimes will climb slowly onto it and sit next to Beebo, but that's a rare turn of events. The iPad is often brought back (Sheila has so far expertly kept hidden from Neil the new larger iPad I bought her for her birthday). Without the containment provided by the Rifton, Neil is better able to bite or pinch your arm—or pull Sheila's hair—as the escalator or stair workout or dogs being afraid of stairs presentation is underway on the iPad. One more trip outside for Beebo and medication all around for us, and then it's a drag back to the stairs. Beebo heads up first and pokes his head through the banister styles in wait. Sheila gets him in his crate and heads to Neil's room as I cajole him up the stairs. By this time, we're usually singing or recounting the day's events. "Let's talk about all the fun Neil had today," Sheila will say cheerily from the edge of his bed. After more political protest, I slide him on his knees into room, then drag him gently toward the bed by his arms, and use my shoulder for leverage while on my hands and knees to shove him into bed. Not following these steps—to the letter—causes Neil to scream. If the light is mistakenly left on in the hallway bathroom, he screams. If Sheila forgets to turn out the hallway light, he screams. If I'm up first and Sheila's ascent is delayed by something and/or Beebo wanders the hallway pining for her and/or cases the trash and the toilet in the middle bathroom, Neil screams.

We soak in the slowly growing calm as Neil drifts off—or fakes drifting off to placate us only to relocate to the floor, sometimes within seconds of our departure. We sing to him from the sanctioned bedtime songbook; we are eternally grateful for the musical talents of Elvis Presley *(Can't Help Falling in Love)*, Paul Williams and Kermit the Frog *(The Rainbow Connection)*, Nat King Cole *(L-O-V-E, Answer Me My Love, It's Only a Paper Moon)*, Billy Joel *(Vienna, You're My Home)*, and Louis Armstrong *(What a Wonderful World)*. It should be an iPod channel, in case something happens to us; otherwise, whomever tries to coax Neil to sleep in our stead will be in for a rough ride. Variations—Dylan, the Beatles even—are rarely tolerated. The length of the playlist depends on how tired we are and how chipper he still is. We usually perform five or six numbers, and end with the closing theme from *The Lawrence Welk Show*. Cue the bubble machines, Guy and Ralna, and the Lennon Sisters: "Good night, sleep tight, and pleasant dreams to you/ Here's a wish and a prayer that all of your dreams come true/And now 'til we meet again/Adios, au revoir, auf wiedereshen." We kiss him, hope he doesn't roll out of bed and onto the mats before we leave the room, secure his gate, turn on the standing oscillating fan ("fanny") in Sheila's craft room across the hall, and practically sprint to our room and close the door behind us. The gravity of Neil's challenges—and our challenges in taking care of him— often hits as we're getting ready for bed. He's come so far, we say—from not being able to lift his head as an infant to walking on his own in 2010, after his physical and occupational therapists told us kindly but plainly that he never would sit up on his own, much less walk. We decompress from having to redirect the relentlessness Neil (and the dog) dish out. What happens after he graduates from high school? A school district transition program will offer support until he's 21—but will he get to 21? One of us reminds the other that the CF hasn't yet done all that much damage, but how many more meds can the doctors throw at him? What's in the research pipeline? Or we'll consider the biggies: He'll never get married, never have kids—although he now and then throws innocently flirtatious smiles at young women. We'll have to take care of him in some fashion for the rest of his life—a life we hope lasts just a second longer after the start of true suffering. How much longer can we battle him and his near total lack of empathy? And then he'll get a huge kick out of something—an escalator video, watching people walk up the stairs, or a toy. He outstretches his arms, swings them back, thrusts out his chest, and makes an "O" shape with his mouth. He looks like an Irish dancer trying to master a safe call. Just beautiful—or maybe the world's most enthusiastic practitioner of naval semaphores. It's like living as though *The Office's* Dwight Schrute was shouting "adapt!" at us as he did at Michael Scott in the episode titled "Baby Shower"—or for you older folks out there, like living in a driver's ed training film. But it works and works itself out.

I'm usually asleep within five minutes. The lovely Sheila checks out a book or a series or two on her iPad, and then drifts off. By that point, the dialogue from down the hall usually has dissipated—although even now, the Rolling Stones now and then stop by to party, as we tell friends.

Chapter Two

The Saddest I've Ever Been

Sheila and I went through three unsuccessful attempts at in vitro fertilization before shifting gears to head down the road to adoption. Our doctor had all the warmth of a Moscow winter. To paraphrase Carly Simon, we really didn't give ourselves time for the pain caused by those tries, though we to this day recall with fondness "Z1" and "Z2," and project what our lives would be like if Neil had them as siblings. Actually, I boxed up the sadness and stashed it on a mental shelf somewhere. Sheila was crushed. But then, I usually cry only when something on TV or in a movie serves as a catalyst.

Adoption in Delaware is the province of the glad-handing zealot. Couples are not allowed to adopt in our state without enlisting the aid of an agency. And boy to do they give aid. We attended the mandatory classes, where we heard one of our classmates, she of the Anderson Cooper infatuation, definitively demand that her eventual child be "spunky." Other attendees had similarly unrealistic wishlists. We heard from a birth mom who in our view had way too cozy (as in proximity and frequency of visits) a relationship with the couple who adopted her child. We endured lectures, read overly chipper materials, and collected enough paper from the organization to keep a recycling facility busy for a week. Officials at the agency let us know in no uncertain terms that the young woman whose baby would soon enter our lives was "making an adoption plan," not putting her baby up for adoption. At least we didn't have to say "adoption - yay!" and then clap, as Cam and Mitch of *Modern Family* felt compelled to do around their then infant daughter Lily in the Season 2 episode titled "Two Monkeys and a Panda."

We were gymnastics-caliber flexible when it came to informing the agency what characteristics we'd embrace in order to adopt a child - African-American, Asian-American, Latino/a, transracial, international, conservative, liberal. It didn't matter. We were a little less flexible when it came to the child's health challenges; we let the agency know that given our even then frantic lives, we worried that we couldn't give a special needs child adequate care. More than adequate love for sure, but not adequate care. But as Sheila often notes, and her husband, the atheist, is willing to acknowledge, "man plans and God laughs."

I lack knowledge of how this transpires in other states, but adoption in Delaware calls for more than a little prevaricating of the "wink-wink/nudge-nudge/something has to be on the form" variety. Sheila created a lovely two-page guide to us, then placed it in a clear plastic sheet cover. We thanked the birth mother "for making this difficult and generous decision" and said we knew "a lot of thought went into your adoption plan (*adoption- yay!*)." Then came the dating service portion of the show - or the pregame lineup an-nouncements, if you prefer. We talked about how we met, gave snapshots of our personality, which appeared directly across from one of my favorite snapshots of the two of us: Sheila's head is behind mine; she's lightly strok-ing my hair, blue eyes the center of the universe as my nose and chin vie for "most bulbous" honors. Descriptions of the families and our jobs followed, and then a brief account of our world travels. "When the baby is a little older," we wrote, "we hope to continue exploring the world and to teach the baby as much as we can." Soon he or she would be sitting behind the drums with me, or hanging out in the garden with Sheila before heading off to knit another masterpiece. And finally, a deftly executed bookend to our initial attempt at ingratiation: "we want to know again how thankful we are for the brave decision you've made." The flip side of our profile was a montage of small photos of us in different family combinations, and, to cement our rep as travelers, in Ireland and in San Francisco. With significant financial help from Sheila's employer, we wrote the checks to pay what seemed like an endless list of fees. Between our purchases and a festive baby shower thrown for Sheila by her friends, sisters, and mom, we were equipped and ready to go.

And we waited.

I was at Drexel when Sheila, in tears, called to let me know our first prospective birth mother had decided to go another way, citing the fact that the adoptive mother who had won the sweepstakes was a fan of the novelist Danielle Steel. I barely made it home. Yet as I pulled into the driveway that night, there Sheila was to tell me that we had again been picked. We hugged and cried.

Soon it was on to a series of mandatory meetings with Neil's birth mom held at neutral locations closer to her home than to ours, and within a reason-able distance of the hospital in which Neil would be born. To protect her privacy - and Neil's - I won't go into much detail about her, but I can say this: I ticked off in my head during our meetings many of the cliches in the national adoption narrative: how her life would be different if her family wasn't poor and in addition, more accepting of her and her pregnancy; how we came off, though not intentionally, as the "white knights" saving her baby from the family's poverty; how we might possibly reprise the white knight role by adopting her too (cue the ay-i-yi-i sound effect from *Bugs Bunny* cartoons); how a baby wouldn't fare well with a teenager who already had run afoul of law enforcement (and would again more than once after Neil was born) and who received no prenatal care until about halfway through her pregnancy - and took Ritalin until about the same time. Yet at the same time we found ourselves sympathetic to her situation - in between the press conferences for how wonderful life was here (which it almost always is).

It was unseasonably warm that winter in central Pennsylvania. We took up temporary residence in a hotel not too far from the hospital. We journeyed to Wal-Mart for some last minute items. And then we got the call.

The birth mom's labor was long and painful. Curled up on the bed in the spacious delivery room, she looked like a frightened child, which she was. All of the nurses we encountered, save one, wanted nothing more than to see us all leave. I don't know if that was because Neil's birth family, one side of it anyway, was Hispanic, or that they preferred sending babies home with their biological parents, or if we got the big well-appointed room by mistake, but their disdain was palpable. And it was a motley crue: Sheila, me, the birth mom, a couple of her teachers, her quite eccentric family, and our very, very overwhelmed adoption caseworker. She left the business not too long after our festivities. Sheila and I were not supposed to be around when Neil made the scene, but because the birth mom's mom insisted that the day be about her - an insistence that permeated our every meeting with her - there we were. More than once, she darted out of the delivery room - it really was almost a suite - screaming out some variation of "I can't take it anymore." Earlier in the afternoon, one of the aforementioned teachers, upon being introduced to Sheila and I, pulled her hand from Sheila's as if it were covered with dog shit. We apparently were the city slickers who had come to their turf to purloin their prized student's baby.

Neil emerged pretty late that evening, with the one understanding nurse and me desperately trying to keep the birth mom from catapulting off the bed as Sheila and the birth mom's OB waited, ready to be the first to welcome him. At one point, I had threaded my arms between the birth mom's torso and arms. I looked as though I was pulling her from a burning car. Forceps were required to ease Neil into the world. But he made it, even if his head did look he was headed to the velodrome, helmet already on, for a race, and that his mom punctuated his birth by rushing into an adjoining bathroom to cry, shriek (and vomit). He was bundled and swaddled, received blow-bys, and spent some time in a warmer - not for the last time on our lives, he became a "baby burrito." In the hallway outside the suite. we met the birth mom's birth father, a wiry man with a thick mustache who worked at one of the area's chicken farms, and her brother, who was maybe 12, and said little. Sheila's sisters soon arrived to lend moral support for which we were extremely grateful. Both clad in leather jackets, we to this day refer to them - with a shout-out to Will Smith and Tommy Lee Jones - as the *Women in Black*. We gazed at Neil in the warmer, told him we loved him, made sure our shaken social worker - who left the business not too long thereafter - was in one piece, and headed back to the hotel for alcohol and soup taken from a small cauldron burbling away in the lobby.

The law in Pennsylvania required that we remain in the state until we had received official clearance to head home. That meant hanging out for about a week at the home of one of the "Women in Black," her husband, our niece and nephew, and their families' lovable small boulder-sized dog with a penchant for eating... almost anything, with a special fondness for couch pillows. We swaddled Neil tightly; he at times looked like his face was poking out from a beehive. Close friends stopped by; Neil was passed around, hugged, and kissed; all of this was memorialized in photos actually printed on actual paper. He ended up sleeping with us - on Sheila's chest to be precise. When it was time to feed him, my niece would join me in their kitchen to concoct a fresh batch of Neil's formula, or what she came to call "baby bottle stew." Back in their guest room, it quickly became clear that Neil couldn't generate the sucking power to draw out the formula; his eyes widened and his cheeks collapsed as he desperately tried to eat. We widened the holes in the nipples. We would learn later that Neil had hypotonia, or poor muscle tone, in his mouth - in fact, throughout his body. He sucked with flummoxed ferocity at the bottles - we widened the holes. And then he'd throw up again. We used to use an eye-dropper to feed him. He'd turn away from and push away, spoonfuls of food. It could have been that he was just tired of applesauce - the only food whose texture didn't cause vomiting - but not until we sought the help of two talented feeding therapists at a local university did we achieve/cajole him into eating. Today, at 15, he's 4-3 and about 85 pounds. He's pushing the genetic rock up uphill, but we fervently hoped that he'd climb on to the weight graphs. He's chugged along at his own pace, with a few dips. And now, he wants to eat - he's learned a sign for hunger, hops right up when we mention "snacktime," cranes his neck to look at empties, and opens his mouth like a baby bird. But he still has never eaten solid food. Once we received the "all clear" from state officials - and the Rams, my favorite NFL team since the late 1960s lost Super Bowl XXXVI on a last-second field goal by the New England Patriots' Adam Vinatieri - Sheila, Neil, not quite two weeks old, and I headed home to Delaware.

I was shopping at one of two local Acmes a couple of weeks later when Sheila called to tell me that a genetic test made available to new parents by the state of Pennsylvania revealed that Neil had cystic fibrosis. Since we had ticked all those boxes on the "what health challenges would be willing to accept" form, we had eagerly taken the state up on its offer. I was standing at the end of an aisle, wondering how many people actually buy their hand mixers and digital alarm clocks at supermarkets when she called. My next stop was the deli for some boiled ham and turkey breast. When Sheila broke the news, my mouth formed words, but the rest of my body seized up. I stood there.

She asked quietly: "do you want to give him back?"

We had that option.

"No!" I blurted out emphatically, with not a clue of what that meant. I heard the relief in Sheila's voice, though I'm sure she felt the same way. It would be a couple of months before we even started to chip away at learning the full extent of Neil's challenges. The pediatrician recommended to us by friends admitted on our first visit that he hadn't treated a CF patient in more than 30 years; he suggested we contact a doctor affiliated with A.I. DuPont Hospital for Children. A caring person and a dedicated professional who also adopted (*yay!*) her child, she remains his pediatrician to this day. Soon, the dedicated staff at the still nascent Cystic Fibrosis Clinic at A.I. DuPont would join the effort to keep Neil healthy. They too are still key residents of Neil's village.

Next came a severe case of gastrointestinal reflux that caused Neil to throw up a half-dozen times a day or more until he was about four. Medicines were sporadically effective. We became really adept at anticipating when he'd vomit. Neil would curve his tongue into the shape of a "U" when the fun was about to begin. I don't think family members believed us when we'd tell them about Neil's prodigiousness, but hearing us shout "Curved tongue! Curved tongue!" and seeing him in action rammed the point home. We became adroit vomit catchers, "spitty rags" at the ready no matter where we were. We led the league a few years running in returning home for a clean-up and a change of clothes. Neil threw up in some pretty classy joints, but didn't discriminate. Sheila and I can still see the ashen and horrified faces of the elderly couple at a local chain restaurant who witnessed from a nearby booth one of Neil's full-on bouts of regurgitation. It got to the point either one of could catch and somehow contain his puke from the driver's seat. Call it "barf catching while driving." He made Linda Blair's character in *The Exorcist* look like she had a mild case of indigestion.

I don't remember the nature of the errand that brought me back to that shopping center. It might have been that I was there to buy something at the big box store or at the Acme, or to pick up take out at one of the two restaurants in the row of establishments on the complex's west side. And I don't remember why Neil was with me. Maybe we had just come from riding through the car wash at the Shell station about two miles from our house, or maybe we were headed home from one of his at that point very frequent appointments (for OT/PT, the GERD, as well as the CF) at A.I. DuPont Hospital.

In any event, there he was, happily ensconced in the car seat attached to the right rear passenger seat of my Subaru. Head cocked slightly, he stared out the window, enrapt in a sense of wonder that I have to resuscitate in myself these days. Something caught his attention; he soon began the Irish dancer safe call/naval semaphore practitioner dance. His movements are accompanied by jubilant hoots that both announce the object of his excitement and encourage you to take a look. After completing our mission—let's go with the big box store—I half-placed, half-shoved Neil back into the car seat, a maneuver that resembled a combination of circus acrobatics and sumo wrestling. He often ended up sitting in one of my catcher's mitt-sized hands or grabbing my hair as I blindly aimed his butt at the chair. Today, thanks to his improved coordination and more strength—and bigger cars—he can now climb up and swing his legs around in order to position and lower his butt himself.

With a put upon sigh, I settled into the driver's seat, put on my seat belt, and realized I'd forgotten something: copy paper maybe, or a curtain rod. I first thought that if I moved the car a little closer to the store and cracked open the window, I could dash back in, grab and pay for the forgotten item. It would only take a minute or two—and Neil was still happy, still entertained; he was probably thinking of an amusement park that featured only ceiling fan- and door-themed attractions. Or he could have been that he was transfixed by watching folks come in and out of the automatic doors.

No, I quickly concluded, I wouldn't be one of those careless parents who take unnecessary risks with their kids and ends up having their lives dissected in an overblown local news segment. He wouldn't be left to swelter in a closed car or left to fend for himself after the school bus dropped him off. I wouldn't be like my parents, who were content to let me ride the train into Manhattan when I was barely a teenager. I wouldn't be like our friends who waited until their daughter was 12 and had been asked to leave three schools before seeking the help of a therapist, who promptly diagnosed her as having Asperger's syndrome. Not me—I wouldn't have waited so long to deal with her aggressiveness, her need to control every social situation, and lack of empathy.

Nope, I'd take Neil home, to his amazing mom and the stack of magazines he loved loudly flipping through, and then head back out to obtain the item, whatever it was. Besides, I thought, what if someone was there in the parking lot, set to embark on a plan to kidnap Neil? Even the unprepared dimwits who appear (and insist on talking too much) for a ritual class-driven drubbing on *Judge Judy* would easily surmise that he could neither walk nor talk—that he was, in the chilling terminology tossed around by his school district, "trainably mentally retarded." That he won't go to college, drive a car, dress without help, read a book, or fall in love. Our fictional assailant would conclude it wasn't worth it—that Neil wasn't worth it. Not worth the trouble. There would be no ransom, no urgent, breathless, overhyped coverage of the abduction on CNN, for seizing this damaged kid. I mean, how much could they get for him?

As the scenario ended and my mind slowed, I turned off the engine and began to cry. I'm not sure if my internal rant included the word "damaged" or "broken." But that rant, and all the ones since, internal and external, made me an asshole then, and make me an asshole now. I've never cried with as much self-directed fury as I did that day and do now, when I drop the martyr act, hack through the dense brush of my selfishness, and ponder the unfairness visited on my son, unfairness about which (I've persuaded myself to believe) he thankfully he has no idea. But even with reflection and long conversations between me and Sheila, what usually comes out in public—especially if we're not close to the person we're talking to—is "he's been dealt a shitty hand."

I've had more success lately at tapping my unconditional love for Neil and at looking at our lives as more—so much more—than an exercise in serial regrouping. And even though it's been charitable to me when I don't deserve it, my internal rant could be seen as pretty typical, as just so much steam that had to be blown off. But I can't sit here and tell you that periodically I don't think about how uncomplicated our lives would become if Neil was moved to a residential facility or if we had a full-time nurse on the team. They could worry about him pulling out his g-tube button; they could field the frantic calls and emails from the school nurse every time Neil is just tired and rests his head on the desk; they could tend to the fierce cough that to this day jolts me out of my seat; they could anoint his crotch with anti-fungal cream to stem the yeast infections he gets when he's taking antibiotics for the bacteria that periodically crop up in his lungs. It's a constant looming threat. That din again. Add to that the unrelenting guilt you feel for wanting to get your own work done, for wanting more than 45 minutes a week—less if it makes him cry—to play the drums. At least I've talked myself out of announcing to Neil during his first diaper changes on weekend mornings that "I get until 11!" before I bring him downstairs to feed him and administer his breathing treatments. The rejection in his eyes and his crying as I left tore through me—then it didn't, but did again, so I stopped. Not permanently - I still have an "11" day now and then, but it's better.

Chapter Three

"Making" Disabilities

It is probably true that society is becoming more tolerant and accepting of folks like Neil. Their achievements are publicly celebrated, as when Robert Lewis, the manager of the boy's basketball team at Franklin Road Academy in Tennessee, in February 2016 sank his one and only three-point attempt of the season with five seconds remaining to seal the team's Senior Night victory (Brown, 2016). Morgan will revisit Robert's wonderful accomplishment—and how it was described by journalists—later in the book. Kids with Down syndrome now appear in ads for Target (Heasley, 2015) and for other companies. The newest muppet on *Sesame Street* is Julie, who has autism. Special Olympics, a wonderful organization in which Neil has participated for a decade or more, receives glowing media coverage and the continued endorsement of scores of celebrities—rightfully so, given the positive impact it has on so many lives. But our experiences leave us asking: has the story of the lives touched by intellectual disabilities—the one we tell each other, the one we populate with characters and layer with themes drawn from the media—really changed all that much over the years? How much closer are we toward telling this story in a "disability rights" perspective, where a disability is treated as something created by society rather than as a physical attribute that "resides" (Haller, 2010, p. 40) in an individual, where we direct our energy toward revealing and repairing the social structures that sustain a narrow, at times still intolerant, view of disability, where we acknowledge and celebrate the disabled individual—and where we finally stop thinking of the "disabled individual as the problem" (p. 40)?

We spend a lot of time in my field exploring how communication contributes to the "construction and maintenance of an ordered, meaningful cultural world that can serve as a control and container for human action" (Carey, 1988, pp. 18-19), how our experiences are replaced by "a projection of the ideals created by the community" (p. 19). We have to be taught that our lives must be improved, as any self-respecting self-help guru will tell you. Think of the rituals you perform: Do you tailgate before football games? Sing the National Anthem once inside the stadium? Do "the wave" or engage in a team-specific chant? The goal isn't to change minds or challenge a world-view, it's to affirm the "underlying order of things" (p. 19). We expect and embrace the drama—we become immersed in a "world of contending forces as an observer at play" (p. 21). We don't worry about the effect of a message or whether we learn something, or whether anything in the story is true. The play is indeed the thing—that is, so long as it doesn't threaten the cohesion we strive to maintain. We want communication to bind us together, not challenge what we hold dear—our ideas, our values. A ritual is not per-formed to illuminate or instruct; it is performed to *affirm*.

Narrative is an important tool of affirmation. Think about the stories you repeatedly tell your friends, or that a family member tells about you. Maybe it's one you wish they'd stop telling. I wish, for example, that my mom would stop telling the story about how I, then 2, was caught relieving myself behind a tombstone during a visit to a family gravesite in western Pennsylva-nia that had gone on too long and which tested my intestinal track's patience. And then there's the story of she and my dad met: she was for a few years a Rockette; he maintained the "Mighty Wurlitzer" theatre organ at Radio City Music Hall, where the Rockettes for the last 85 years have done their high-kicking thing. Mom had been asked to imitate playing the organ (a cost-cutting move by execs, if memory serves), but insisted on actually playing and having the right music—which my dad gladly fetched for her. The rest, as they say, is history. If you spent even ten minutes with my family in any capacity—friend, neighbor, letter carrier, intrepid jogger—you'd hear the story. Since my dad died a few years back, the story has become for me less corny and a lot more heartwarming.

And then there's the story about how the lovely Sheila and I met. Actual-ly, we had sort of known each other—known of each other—for some time. Her sister married my college roommate. When I moved with my first wife to Philadelphia, he and I reconnected, and we also became friends with his wife's twin sister (not Sheila). As my first marriage was ending in 1994, my roommate invited me, now living in a one-room apartment, to his annual Christmas party—for which Sheila had kindly agreed to prepare the food (which was delicious). Never a gadfly, I spent most of my time near the kitchen. Sheila noticed my Mets jacket and told me that she loved all sports, but her favorite was baseball. Enthralled, I kissed her goodbye that night—and in so doing knocked her over. She told her mom on the phone later that I had kissed her. After going outside for a cigarette to ponder these develop-ments, Mom took the phone back and suggested that Sheila invite me to their New Year's Eve get together. We've been together ever since.

I get why scholars still look askance at narrative. Certain very narrow-minded pockets of the GOP notwithstanding, we value scientific exploration, respect those who do the exploring, and breathlessly wait for the latest technological advance, oblivious to the fact we're witnessing planned obsolescence in action. Moreover, we tend to believe that a person's psychological life is more worthy of study than culture, mainly because the latter is so messy, a fact celebrated by the postmodernists out there. And finally, we reject activities that don't produce something. But even if narrative as a form of communication is just part of "the ambience of human existence (p. 24)," and seems at times just ordinary, there is, I believe a certain kind of magic in our stories. "They can make us contemplate the particular miracles of social life that have become for us just there, plain and unproblematic for the eye to see," Carey wrote (p. 24). Sure, they become stale as they are told and retold (and retold); some are told to deceive; some reek of sexism and racism—and not a single one of them is accurate. But they do, Carey believed, provide a compelling opportunity to explore how we human beings construct and then inhabit our own realities.

As we'll see, the "stock of symbols" (p. 28) from which we construct and maintain our worlds is often limited, rife with stereotypes and out of date information. But Carey contends we each map the areas of our lives a little differently, even if the goal is the same: to make sense of what's going on in each area by managing the at times staggering amount of information that comes our way. "Different maps bring the same environment alive in different ways, they produce quite different realities," Carey explained (p. 28). Mapping is a social activity that "occurs primarily on blackboards, in dances, and in recited poems" (p. 28)—and through the creation and telling of stories.

Walter Fisher's (1987) work on the centrality of narrative to human experience bears Carey out. Fisher contends narrative "is the basic and essential genre for the characterization of human action" (p. 58). We don't have to debate each other or constantly be working on compelling arguments in order to fine-tune our experiential maps. "By creating stories out of the raw material of our lives," explains Klapproth (2004), "we manage not only to establish coherence for ourselves, but also to create meaningful discursive structures that can be communicated and shared" (p. 3). Narrative is a tool of organization; stories help us "make sense of the people, places, events, and actions of our lives" (Foss, 2009, p. 307). They enable us to determine "what a particular experience is about and how the various elements of our experience are connected" (p. 307). We favor coherence and fidelity in our stories over accuracy; they have to hold together and "ring true" if we are to make our way through the day.

Producers of media content know this. Journalists, for example, craft narratives to explain events to readers; they try to find "in the unfamiliar...that which is familiar, a story type made available by culture," as Eason (1981) notes. Their stories "are already largely written before the journalists take fingers to typewriters or pen to paper" (Hall, quoted in Fiske, 1987, p. 293). Journalists fit "unruly" (p. 302) facts into one of an existing menu of narratives and then, as more information becomes available, borrow from their "mental catalogue" (Berkowitz, 1997, p. 363) of familiar story themes in crafting stories that will attract readers or viewers. John Fiske might argue that it is at this point a "state of equilibrium" (p. 293) is restored. Meanings suggested by narratives, along with their "compelling" vocabulary (Condit, 1990. p. 6), soon drive the public's understanding of an event or issue. Jack Lule believes this repository of story types is "deep but nonetheless limited" (p. 15). They depend on "a mental catalogue of news story themes, including how the 'plot' will actually unravel and who the key actors are likely to be" (Berkowitz, 1997, p. 363). Their editors and readers expect they will explain events in familiar ways. In fact, Carolyn Kitch (2002) claims that a successful news story is one in which "events seem to tell themselves" (p. 296). For example, when members of a union vote to strike, what elements do we always see in news stories about their decision? Folks walking a picket line, folks trying to get to work by attempting to move through the picket line, spokespeople for both sides providing their perspectives, and some indication of how those affected by the strike are inconvenienced. That's usually it. Walter Benjamin (1982) argued that a narrative "preserves and concentrates its strength and is capable of releasing it even after a long time" (1982, p. 90). In fact, a truly skilled storyteller is able to persuade listeners that only one interpretation of a story is possible (Bruner, 1991, p. 9). Only by exploring the "linguistic and cultural resources" from which coverage of individuals with intellectual disabilities is built can we accurately assess how we've been persuaded that their lives are "something that can be told about" (Manoff, 1987, p. 226) and that the media's take on these experiences is valid.

Together, we fashion and revise a "common recollection" (Nerone & Wartella, 1989, p. 85) that enables us to recall events without having experienced them (Kitch, 1999, p. 123). Along the way, the journalist enables us to sustain and celebrate shared beliefs and values. We have to look hard at times to find them; Herbert Gans (1979) contended that they are "rarely explicit and must be found between the lines—in what actors and activities are reported or ignored and in how they are described" (p. 40). Only the "activities" of a narrow range of "actors" are reported on with any real regularity. Nevertheless, from extensive news coverage typically emerges "a confirming, reinforcing version" of society (Fiske & Hartley, 1978, pp. 85-86). And if through these collaborations we "banish contradictions and make the world explicable and therefore habitable" (Storey, 1996, p. 57), we will have created a myth—a "sacred, societal story that draws on archetypal figures and forms to offer exemplary models for human life" (Lule, 2001, p. 15). Myths give us "a stock of stories that hold out the possibility of confronting and suspending the conflicts and contradictions of everyday life," as Campbell (1991) explains (p. 137). Readers invoke myths—even though they are "at once true and unreal" (Barthes, 1957, p. 239)—to try and understand the world around them. By that point, Roland Barthes argued, events and information have coalesced into "Common Sense, Right Reason, the Norm, General Opinion" (p. 165).

But what if our narratives and myths are no longer able to help us figure out, describe, and explain life to each other? What if, as Carey noted, our reality "breaks down" when a new generation with an opposing or even radical view of the world, hits the scene? "Finally, we must, often with fear and regret, toss away our authoritative representations of reality and begin to build the world anew," (p. 30) he asserted. As anti-war protestors, environmental activists, feminists, Muslims, and African-Americans, and the Occupy movement have learned, we don't do this willingly. We'll push back and make opposing and divergent views seem odd for as long as we can—and banish those who hold them to what Dan Hallin (1987) calls the "Sphere of Deviance." Reporters build and fortify rhetorical boundaries between the public and individuals who have the temerity to challenge the conventional wisdom on a topic—who attempt to let the air out of our myths. Every so often, a dissenter or a hot-button issue will make it into the "Sphere of Legitimate Controversy," where actual discussion ostensibly begins. The key word in that last sentence is *ostensibly*. Though they should be lauded for calling national attention to the Civil Rights movement, for example, it took a while for reporters to decide that the nation should be made aware of the African American struggle for equality. Complicating the transference is the tendency of reporters to bend over backward to maintain the appearance of objectivity—even if that means distorting the dissenter's view. This is the leaping off point for the false equivalencies seen in recent coverage of settled issues like our role in causing global warming. Dissenters can only dream of admittance to Hallin's "sphere of consensus," the rhetorical space where hallowed institutions and cherished values and ideas are kept and protected. Think Mom, democracy, the flag, the loyalty of a fine dog (the last two put on our list by the creators of the classic television series M*A*S*H in the episode "The General Flipped at Dawn"). Journalists fiercely guard this space, deflecting attempts by dissenters to provoke dialogue or even to weigh in. Once a myth is entrenched, we tend not to treat competing information "thoughtfully," to paraphrase *Project Runway* guru Tim Gunn.

These arguments pop to mind every time I drive through local neighborhoods and see parents waiting in their cars 10 feet away from their children as they, in turn, wait for their school busses. So-called "free range parents" have incurred national wrath for letting their kids walk alone to school. For an aging former hippie wannabe, that's a revolting development. I walked to school every day by myself (there and back, up hill both ways)—and I was never abducted, or even threatened. But to push for keeping parents out of their kids' back pockets is to sound uninformed, even neglectful. We've so fully embraced the "stranger danger"/*To Catch a Predator* line of fear mongering offered up primarily by companies that benefit handsomely from keep us scared that it would take a public information effort of Herculean proportions to convince even a small fraction of the U.S. population that walking alone to school, or playing outside without supervision, is not tantamount to child abuse. Of course, repeated accounts of how "my mom opened the door on Saturday morning at 9 and didn't expect us back until dinner" have also risen to the level of myth. As part of my research for a book on pick-up games published a few years back, I heard this myth reverently told time and time again. I was struck by how fondly the folks who submitted their stories remembered their freedom—but equally struck by how emphatically most of them rejected the idea of allowing their children to enjoy the same freedom.

Morgan, Sadie, and I embarked on this project fully at peace with the idea that the best we'll be able to present is a broader and more nuanced version of the intellectual disabilities narrative, but one still "governed by convention and narrative necessity," as Bruner (1991, p. 4) instructed. Still, coming to know how we come to know something is a worthwhile endeavor. Carey (1992) likened it to "attending a mass, a situation in which nothing new is learned but in which a particular view of the world is portrayed and confirmed (p. 20)." Thus, our goal is to unpack and explore "the interpretations of meaning and value" contained in recent news media coverage of intellectual disabilities and how those meanings and value find their way into "the rest of life" (Christians & Carey, 1981, p. 347). Stated differently, what is the "cultural work" (Thomson, 2001) performed by journalists in compiling these stories? What do they tell their readers and viewers about how we make sense of intellectual disabilities and the people whose lives are touched by them?

As we construct our realities, we "make disabilities," claims scholar Paul Higgins (1992, p. 19) through our choice of words, of media content, and in the narratives about disabled people that we create and tell. More precisely, "we do not see the world, rather we are taught by representations of the world about us to conceive of it in a culturally acceptable manner" (Gilman, 1982; quoted in Thomson, 2001, p, 336). While we've of late been more kind to and tolerant of individuals with intellectual disabilities, the national conversation about their lives still proceeds from the idea that they are different. As acclaimed author Barbara Ehrenreich (2009) explains, a disability replaces the person who lives with it. It becomes a performance, with each part following a script with required emotions. You are not supposed to refer to those who deal with cancer as "victims" or even "patients"—violates the convention, the protocol (p. 25). They battle, they fight—and, it is hoped, survive the disease. "It is the 'survivors' who merit constant honor and acclaim," (p. 27) she writes. We might memorialize those who have lost the fight, but the true stars of the play are the survivors. Some even view cancer as a gift, an experience they would want to have if life's clock was reset (p. 28). It offers us a shot at redemption (p. 28). But does the redemption distract us from viewing these folks as individuals?

Higgins claims that we still "present disability as primarily an internal condition that estranges disabled people" (p. 19) from the rest of us. We still "other" them, though perhaps with less discriminatory force than in the past. Our narrow-mindedness may actually stem from how conflicted we are about disabled people, argues Rosemarie Garland Thomson (2001). "[W]e are at once obsessed with and intensely conflicted about the disabled body. We fear, deify, disavow, avoid, abstract, revere, conceal, and reconstruct disability—perhaps because it is one of the most universal, fundamental of human experiences," she writes (p. 337). You'd think we'd be more enlightened or tolerant, she contends, since advancing age will disable all of us to some degree. But our intolerance persists largely unabated, Thomson believes. We go on making "the familiar seem strange, the human seem inhuman, the perverse seem exceptional" (p. 337).

Nevertheless, we should consider the possibility that what we pinpoint as we "other" someone is not a quality inherent in the person. *We* in effect create the quality, and go on to establish a category and the criteria for including someone in that category. It become that person's role, their social identity; we use it to structure our interactions with them—mainly so that we can encounter them without thinking, as Erving Goffman (1963) argued more than a half-century ago. We may no longer banish disabled people by segregating them in institutions, exploiting them in freak shows, and by enacting "ugly" laws as we did until the 19th century, but the information and images on which we build our knowledge of the disabled enables us to encounter them from a safe distance—and usually without having to actually interact with them (Thomson, 2001, p. 338). Thus this activity "has less to do with what they are physiologically than who we are culturally," claims sociologist Robert Bogdan (1988, p. 146). In his compelling history of the freak show, Bogdan contends that a disabled person's appearance is actually less powerful than the story we have constructed in our minds about them from the cultural material furnished by "those in charge of telling us" who these individuals are and "what they are like" (p. 279). Thus, we see intellectually disabled people through a lens focused by doctors, officials, journalists—even laudable organizations like Special Olympics.

A "stigma," suggested Goffman, has to be presented and promoted if it's to stick around. And it's not like we're lazy about maintaining them. Reducing full-fledged human beings to a single aspect of their identity takes work; as mentioned earlier, we vigilantly correct those who would offer a competing, more tolerant view. Rachel Adams (2001) might argue that othering is "the performance of a stylized presentation" (p. 6) where the disabled person's identity is created and entrenched by our sheer repetition of these behaviors. While Adams, like Bogdan, is best known for exploring the history of freak shows, her arguments are particularly applicable to our journey.

Thus, the othering of Neil that we witness—and that we at times do ourselves—does not stem from a quality inherent in him. It is, to use Bogdan's words, "something we created: a perspective, a set of practices, a social construction" (p. 92). And it doesn't matter if those practices or that construction are more positive or tolerant than it had been in the past—our behaviors are about us, not him. We've assigned him a role that he must now play for the rest of his life. Bogdan also contends that in a way, *we're* the performers. The organizers of freak shows created a demeaning deception that appealed to our curiosity, but also to our status. They persuaded us to perform for them and for each other. Even when a depiction of disability is positive—suggesting, for example, that we should be impressed by a disabled person's physical accomplishments or recognize the depth of the challenges they face—it is for *our* benefit. As Thomson (2001) writes, "disability exists for the viewer to recognize and contemplate, not to express the effect it has on the person with a with a disability" (p. 346). What we "recognize," or have reinforced for us by experiencing the disabled person's body, are the significance of and the status conferred by the physical qualities we value so highly—for example, beauty, health, fitness, intelligence (p. 348).

Adams argues that freak shows were not so much about the physical characteristics of those on display as they were the "spectacle of the extraordinary body swathed in theatrical props" (p. 6). Bogdan urges us to focus on how an "othered" group is packaged for public consumption. So it becomes important, Adams tells us, to be mindful of what's happening in society when a label is affixed to someone and the "set of practices" (p. 6) both she and Bogdan discuss is developed and performed. Encouraging a particular way of thinking and representing a group of people soon becomes a tradition that is sustained by our repeated performance of behaviors. It would be nice if we could stop ourselves along the way for a little reflection. We must at least entertain the idea, proposed by Susan Sontag (1977) in *Illness in America*, that we should step away from the metaphors that guide our thinking about illness—or about disabilities—and start to be honest about what we think having a family member with an intellectual disability suggests or says about that person, their family, and about us. We began our analysis of these texts under the assumption that none of them—not even the positive ones—would be, to use Thomson's words, "in the service of actual disabled people" (p. 340). We hoped, however, that we would find some that eclipsed using the intellectually disabled person "for the purposes of constructing, instructing, or assuring some aspect of an ostensibly non-disabled viewer" (p. 340).

We used to believe, Sontag asserted, that a person suffering from cancer was insufficiently passionate, repressed, and inhibited. Discussion of the disease was discouraged—and still is in some families. Shame came with the diagnosis. That came after a period in the 19th century where we felt it appropriate to express emotions using the disease as the mechanism. Then we went back to corralling our passions—and came to think that self-repression caused the disease. Cancer came to be seen as "a failure of expressiveness" (p. 48). Having a disease caused by too much passion brought with it some glamour. Cancer patients were treated as failures. Today we characterize those with cancer and their families as engaged in an ongoing battle to ward off a relentless invader. Patients who lack the strength or inclination to fight—to follow the cultural script—are marginalized. Conversely, those who contracted tuberculosis were by the 1820s seen as being consumed by passion; Sontag asserted that we eventually came to think that looking sickly as a result of TB was romantic, an indication that a person came from good stock, was creative, and was spiritually refined. In fact, the TB sufferer became a model for what aristocracy should look like. TB was the first illness that we saw as affecting the individual (p. 30). We came to believe that TB sufferers were more compelling—and that being perfectly healthy was boring (p. 32). Being sick made us more interesting.

So we spend way too much time, Sontag argued, pondering and creating stories about what we *think* happens in the lives of folks dealing with these challenges, as opposed to trying to recognize what actually happens—how these challenges are actually experienced. Built into our stories are judgments about these folks, even about their character. Further, serious illness offers us a shot at redemption—or at least a chance to tick off the entries on our bucket lists. It is essential, Sontag cautioned, that we exercise skepticism when someone comes along who posits an emotional cause for a disease, or an emotional aspect to its cure. Maintaining a positive attitude, or being feisty, or insisting that one play an active role in one's care—all of these are fine, but they absolutely don't contribute to a cure. They reflect how little we know about a disease (p. 55). These actions may make us feel that we've achieved a small measure of control in a trying situation, but Sontag believed that what ultimately happens is that we place the blame for getting the disease—and the onus for a cure—on the individual (p. 57).

Our performance begins with the simple act of looking. We learn as kids that a person's disability "is a potent form of embodied difference that warrants looking, even prohibited looking" (Thomson, p. 346). But it goes a little further than that: looking usually turns into staring. A stare, unlike a passing glance, confirms that a relationship between the starer and the disabled person has been established. "The starer," writes Thompson, "becomes the subject of the act of staring while the stare becomes the object acted upon" (p. 346). Not always: Neil has no idea that the folks in the mall or at one of our local parks are staring at him. Or he does but can't vocalize his reactions. We know they're staring, of course, but his role in the relationships described by Thomson is purer, more volitional; he sees them as helping him—or failing to help him—get what he wants. And he smiles at them and sometimes blows a few kisses. But in most cases, the person staring has deemed the disabled person different and, sadly, the disabled person has acknowledged and perhaps internalized that difference (pp. 346-347). This produces the disabled person's identity and is how we end up perceiving the disability as "aberrant" (p. 347). Those who look at Neil on the Barnes and Noble escalator or the steps of the Franklin Institute are able to remain essentially anonymous while he is in effect on display, even if he doesn't realize it and likely doesn't experience their stigmatization. He certainly has no idea, though we do, that he's part of a "ritual enactment of exclusion" (p. 347) performed so that the rest of us can feel better about ourselves.

Yet not all of the stories and photos are negative, even if they are rooted in misconceptions and outright fear of folks with intellectual disabilities. Media texts describe disabled people living rich, happy, fulfilled lives. But that "message of success" becomes a bar that disabled folks must clear. "If we fail, it is our problem, our weakness," asserts author Irving Zola (1991, p. 161). Way too often, Mitchell (1989) argues, we read and see stories of what she called "supercrips" and "helpless victims" (pp. 18-19). Coverage also suggests that we have little actual sustained contact with disabled people. Our interactions are one-offs which journalists often imbue with "cheap sentimentality" on the way to their heartstring-tugging portrayals of "handicapped heroes" (Krossel, 1988, pp. 46-47) who inspire us with their courage. Biklen (1987) believes there's a sort of continuum at work in coverage, with disabled people "[t]ypically cast in terms of tragedy and its attendant emotion, pity, or of struggle and accomplishment" (p. 81).

Perhaps more destructive is the fact that the texts and photos let us off the hook—they make it acceptable to stare, to repeatedly tell our incomplete narratives without challenge or correction. We usually don't take time to get to know a disabled person, so ensconced are we in our narratives, so intense are our stares. We also are left unable to figure out when our fealty is redirected to sell products and services, Thomson (2001) suggests. Thomson's (2001) taxonomy of visual rhetorics evident in photographs of disabled people found in popular culture are a helpful guide. She posits four: the *wondrous*, the *sentimental*, the *exotic*, and the *realistic*. As part of the *wondrous* rhetoric, the viewer looks in awe at the disabled person and is inspired by feats that the viewer is unable to do. We cheer on the "courageous 'overcomer (p. 352),'" Thomson writes. But we are not humbled or inspired to act—or to treat the disabled person as anything other than "distantly strange" (p. 352). Instead, the wondrous rhetoric deploys "the extraordinariness of the disabled body in order to secure the ordinariness of the viewer" (p. 341).

Pictures imbued with this rhetoric enable us to keep the disabled at arm's length and fails to obligate us to treat them as does not suggest we treat them as equal.

The *sentimental* rhetoric typically positions the disabled person as helpless, as a victim who needs our protection—needs us to come to their rescue. Think Jerry Lewis Telethon; we're instructed to pity the disabled—and, as Thomson points out, to express our pity in the form of monetary donations. We're made almost to feel like the person's parents and that we're obligated to help them overcome their disability, which is transformed from "internal and narratable into something external and narratable" (p. 341). We don't learn much about the reality of struggling with a disability; instead, we're treated to a more enticing and easy to digest spectacle. Thomson argues that in these images disabled people are "domesticated" (p. 356). Children are often depicted in photos that suggest this rhetoric—they both "contain the threat of the disability" and give us the authority to act to help. We're given the stage and encouraged to be the hero. Sympathy gives way to unbridled hope for a cure—that the disabled person will be "fixed." Buoyed by faith in progress, we'll improve their lives. But if we fail in our effort to improve the disabled person's body, it becomes "intolerable" (p. 355) and is banished—permanently, Thomson suggests. But we still bask in the pats on the back that come from our "conspicuous contribution," as Longmore (1997, quoted in Thomson, p. 356) calls it. Former *Tonight Show* host Jay Leno characterized it this way: "In America, we like everyone to know about the good work we're doing anonymously" (May, 2008).

The *exotic* rhetoric asks us to think of the disabled person as "alien, often sensationalized, eroticized, or entertaining" (p. 341). Our curiosity is piqued; we objectify the disabled person. It's almost as if we're on a self-guided tour of another country. We think of ourselves, Thomson argues, as "diverted, enlightened, or titillated" by an "encounter with the figure of the remote, alien body brought before them" (p. 342)—and kept at a safe distance. Finally, the *realistic* rhetoric of disability appears to indicate that a disabled person is more like us than we realize or previously acknowledged. Images play down the "visual mark of disability" (Thomson, p. 344) but they aren't accurate, nor do they reference how life is rendered complex by a disability. Images trading in this rhetoric suggest that the disabled person and the viewer are on equal footing, but in actuality an ulterior motive drives the image's creator: provoking concern in the viewer about a repressive or destructive governmental policy or action or a pressing social issue. But even as these images ask us to identify with disabled people, they reassert their status as "other," Thomson contends. They tell us that the disabled person is someone "the viewer does not want to be" (p. 346). Disabled people, she writes, "variously been objects of awe, scorn, terror, delight, inspiration, pity, laughter, and fascination—but we have always been stared at" (p. 348).

Chapter Four

The Legend of "Scooter Boy"

We begin our journey through texts depicting intellectual disabilities with Rosemary Kennedy, eldest child of the celebrated Kennedy family. With the recent release of several books, including *Fully Alive* by Timothy Shriver (2014), longtime chair of Special Olympics, son of the organization's indefatigable founder Eunice Kennedy Shriver, Rosemary Kennedy's life has again moved up a few slots on the public's agenda. After finishing Shriver's book, I located a pdf copy of a 1962 *Saturday Evening Post* article written by his mother about Rosemary's life. Before we go further, a statement for the record: Sheila and I, like millions of families around the world, are grateful to the Shriver family for the joy and the sense of inclusiveness that permeate every Special Olympics event. Neil participates every year in several Special Olympics events; more than a dozen medals hang from his feeding tube pole and from doorknobs in our house or are tucked away in memory boxes. The Shrivers and the Kennedys deserve the praise they have received for their tireless advocacy on behalf of intellectually disabled people.

And yet, given the scope of his challenges, we are unsure if for Neil these events mean anything more than another venue in which to engage in favored activities after placating the adults in the room—or on the court, or the field. A few years ago, we attended a Special Olympics medal ceremony at a nearby community center. We swelled with pride as his name was announced and he walked up with a caring school paraprofessional, now a good friend of ours, to receive his medal from a county police officer. He had spent much of the afternoon walking—he had just started flying solo—around the gym or throwing balls into baskets. He had to be cajoled and/or wasn't interested in taking part in much else. But that's Neil: we've taught him to do what we'd like him to do for 15 minutes or so—carefully stacking his brightly colored cardboard bricks, for example—before he is permitted, to quote Fleetwood

Mac, to "go his own way" and throw the bricks across the Florida Room or at its windows. You know what? "Permitted" sounds like we have a pedagogical purpose. We're just thankful that he's come this far; we've recognized that he is a unique individual with a compelling personality all his own—and feel it's just fine now and then to let him rip.

We jubilantly celebrate Neil's gains, as when he earned the moniker "Scooter Boy" for propelling himself around the house on a Little Tikes scooter, learned to rock on a large blue plastic dog we named "Azul" to honor his Puerto Rican heritage, when he first walked on his own, or when he proved he no longer had to sit strapped into his wheelchair while riding the bus to school. We cried and hugged as he made his way for the first time up the steps at the front of the bus and took his seat next to a classmate. An aide then secured him to the seat with a chest harness (which he no longer needs). A few days later, more tears and hugs: with only a gentle prompt, he turned slightly and waved to the bus as it pulled away, punctuating the departure with a soft "buh-buh." Soon, he was "schootching" (knee-walking) at an Olympic level from the floor into his first Rifton chair to be fed and treated. And if we had known whom to email at the White House, he would have most certainly been considered for the Congressional Medal of Freedom for announcing "O-ba-ma!" from his chair as the 2008 election returns rolled in. A neurosurgeon who treated Neil when he was an infant for the larger than usual space in his corpus callosum told us that we could throw all the therapies we could arrange at him; he might not hit all of the milestones, but if he did, it would be in his own good time.

A second statement for the record: while the many books by and about the Kennedys that reference Rosemary are compelling, we proceed fully aware that not a single one of the accounts of Rosemary's life discussed in those books "can be believed with any certainty (O'Brien, 2004, p. 226)," as historians Barbara Gibson and Ted Schwartz (1995) contend. Fearful of ostracization and controlled by the desire to compete, the Kennedys lied to varying degrees about Rosemary's disability her entire life. So with all due respect to the Shrivers and to the Kennedys, the language in Eunice Shriver's *Post* article is so jarring, so intolerant. In the subhead (likely written by a *Post* staffer), Rosemary is referred to as the "Kennedy family's own misfortune" (p. 71), her disability called a "widely misunderstood affliction" (p. 71). Rosemary was born at a time when the practitioners of eugenics, who sought to protect white middle class folks from "the supposed threat posed by individuals seen as genetically inferior" (Castles, 2004, p. 352), were at the height of their influence. Her low IQ score and a dearth of schools in which the family could enroll Rosemary left Eunice Kennedy Shriver "terribly frustrated and *heartbroken*" (Shriver, 2014, p. 39; Shriver's italics). It's oddly reassuring to read that Tim Shriver considered the possibility that his mother was embarrassed that Rosemary might not be as smart or accomplished as her other children (p. 39). The fear that Rosemary would be rejected, that she would never be loved or valued for who she was, also troubled Shriver. O'Brien (2004) contends Eunice and the other Kennedy children were trying "to make up for the deficits" (p. 232) perceived by their parents in experiencing Rosemary's disability. It is likely too that they made their own goals even more challenging in order to alleviate their parents' disappointment—their "torment" (p. 231, 232) at having a child who was less than perfect, who couldn't compete with her siblings.

Sheila and I have experienced all of those feelings—all but the last few—but I don't think we've ever thought of our efforts as an attempt to "fix" him (Shriver, 2014, p. 21) - keep him quiet for more than 10 minutes a time, dissuade him from grabbing and pinching us, but not "fix" him. It's been a haul, and Sheila's optimism burns brighter than mine, but we've always thought of Neil's life as intrinsically having value. Like Rosemary Kennedy, Neil doesn't "have to *do* anything to prove" (Shriver, 2014, p. 22; Shriver's italics) that he matters. But this is where once again the other items on the packed menu of Neil's health challenges come into play, at least for me. I'm thrilled that he can now identify numbers and letters and that he can indicate, with a little modeling by us, what he wants by pressing the colorful icons on his communication device. I still tear up when I remember the first time we saw him, then about 11, get up himself and start walking. His IEP meetings, where we sit at three carefully positioned rectangular tables which makes me feel as though we're part of a Congressional hearing, are now more positive than negative, a far, far cry from fifth grade when we had to threaten a lawsuit that if successful would have forced the district to place Neil in a private school if they refused to reunite him with his kind and compassionate fourth grade teacher. Neil now joins us for the IEP meetings, his attention improving every time out, though he eventually wants to get back to his friends. It feels to me like we're talking over and past him much of the time. I wonder if he has any idea of what's being discussed, about why it's necessary in the first place. Goal by goal, benchmark by benchmark, we plot out Neil's next year. We wonder if "sufficient progress to meet annual goal" means that they've tired of waiting for him to comply or have dialed back their expectations.

Yet when his very positive, very friendly speech therapist contacted us recently about upgrading the device, I wondered if it would really accelerate his learning—and if it would be worth continuing the insurance fight that had already begun. I'm happy to report that it will and and it is. I'm saddened every year when the state sends out the results of its annual test—and Neil is once again rated "below average." The plan of care from the nursing agency lists his medicines, "functional limits," "activities permitted," and "mental status" in small capital letters that serve only to reacquaint us with his fragility. His block-building now lasts 20 minutes instead of 5, but he still ends up throwing them at the windows and ceiling fan in our Florida Room and the ceiling fan. He can place and with his first finger elegantly press down stickers on paper and pieces of cardboard salvaged from cartons of yogurt bought at Costco, but he eventually decides to tear up his work (hence the cardboard). It was a lovely surprise though, when he knee-walked his latest sticker creation into Sheila, who was working in the office. It's hard to know if he was feeling pride in what he had helped to make, or if it was because he loves his mom - who's very lovable. But it is now on the list of experiences that we've taken imaginary photos, a la Pam and Jim when they married on *The Office*. Meanwhile, the math and vocabulary workbooks purchased by the lovely and optimistic Sheila gather dust in the bookcase and he maybe lasts 10 seconds with a crayon in his hand.

Conventional medical wisdom when Rosemary Kennedy was growing up dictated that intellectually disabled children be institutionalized to stem the damage to the family caused by the focus on a disabled child required of parents. Or as O'Brien (2004) explains using the terminology of the time, "the degree of stigma attached to feeblemindedness during the 1920s and 1930s was extraordinarily high" (p. 228). Despite the fact that having an intellectually disabled child was seen by the medical community as "charac-teristic of an underlying weakness in the biological constitution of the par-ents," (pp. 229-230), the Kennedys instead decided to keep Rosemary with them at home—at least at first. "For a long time my family believed that all of us working together could provide my sister with a happy life in our midst," Eunice Kennedy Shriver recalled (p. 71). Rose Kennedy demanded that Rosemary be included in family activities. She played tennis and touch football, attended dances (Shriver, 2014, p. 40). She was part of the family crew during races in Hyannis Port. "[S]he usually could do what she was told," Shriver recalled. "She was especially helpful with the jib and she loved being in the winning boat" (p. 71). Rosemary loved kids, and according to Shriver often asked Rose if she could take the younger ones from the sur-rounding area out on the boat.

Her siblings' inclination to include Rosemary waned, although Tim Shriver asserts their interactions "forever imprinted them, just as she herself was forever imprinted by their lives and adventures" (p. 40). Found within that imprint, however, was her siblings' struggle to both "explain" and "inte-grate and hide" Rosemary to and from their friends. If Rosemary had been sent away, Shriver believes, "they would have never have known the mean-ing of difference in quite the same way" (p. 40). Yet that's exactly what the Kennedys eventually did: they turned Rosemary's life into a tragic travel-ogue, and for largely selfish reasons, asserts author Kate Clifford Larson.

Rose Kennedy had essentially Taylorized the lives of her children; she stoked their competitive fires, obsessively monitored their weight, and trans-formed family dinners into extended history lessons (pp. 35-37). Post-mortems were conducted if a Kennedy child didn't win or succeed at something. When Rosemary's disabilities manifested themselves, the Kennedys found the development "overwhelming," Larson explains (p. 40). They could not understand why "they are all not alike," Rose said of her children (p. 41). As they experienced "the pity and fear and shame and loneliness" (Shriver, 2014, p. 38) with which Tim Shriver believes all families with intellectually disabled children must deal, Rose and Joe Kennedy first and foremost had to "make sense" (p. 38) of Rosemary. While some accounts—like the *Post* article by Shriver's mother in 1962—paint a picture of Rose and Joe bravely soldiering on in the name of family loyalty, Larson asserts that it was a captivating fear of being pushed from the social and political heights to which they had ascended that motivated them to act. In the public version of this narrative, they steadfastly believed Rosemary would realize her potential; Rose would somehow "transform disability into achievement" (Larson, p. 44) by insisting that she be treated "just like the other children" (p. 51) at the elementary schools she attended during the 1920s. Their drive—and tendency to blame Rosemary when she was unable to meet their standards—was only intensified by the fact that Rosemary's disability was not severe; she did not appear to be disabled (O'Brien, 2004, p. 231). So Rose and Joe Kennedy zealously labored to "mold Rosemary into the likeness of themselves and her siblings" (p. 58)—which would not have afforded her siblings the chance to comprehend "the meaning of difference," as Tim Shriver believes. By the end of the decade, the Kennedys were educating Rosemary at home.

Rosemary's at-home instruction lasted a year. Scared they might be ostracized and mindful, Larson claims, of the influence of eugenics on their friends, the Kennedys sent her to an experimental boarding school for the "feebleminded" in Pennsylvania run by Helena Devereux, a former student, though according to Shriver not a disciple, of the eugenicist Henry Goddard. Devereux was a pioneer of individualized education for children with intellectual disabilities; her goal was to move "each child closer instead of farther away from a sense of belonging to the larger humanity to which each child longed to be a part" (Larson, p. 61). Rosemary adapted socially, but struggled academically. That struggle made her anxious and damaged her self-esteem. Back for a second year, teachers observed that her lack of confidence shortened her attention span and caused her to make a less than adequate effort to finish her schoolwork (p. 65). Gripped with worry that Rosemary might run away, be kidnapped, or explore her sexuality, the Kennedys brought Rosemary home, where she spent a good deal of time "helping with housework and caring for her younger siblings" (Shriver, 2014, p. 41). The Kennedys all were fully involved in what Rose called a "conspiracy of kindness" (p. 42); they hid Rosemary's disability from everyone—including Rosemary. Tim Shriver suggests that it was equal parts fear of being ostracized and concern for Rosemary's well-being that compelled them to conspire. The family believed wholeheartedly that being honest with Rosemary would bring about "the disaster of disasters" (p. 42), Shriver asserted.

The Kennedys two years later dispatched Rosemary to a school in Rhode Island and then, when she didn't make satisfactory academic progress there, to work with a tutor at a private school outside Boston. At the tutor's suggestion, they subjected Rosemary to experimental hormone injections. They consulted with Walter Dearborn, a pioneer in educating children with learning disabilities (Larson, pp. 82-83). Rosemary was not asked back for a third year at the private school; its director said Rosemary was "the most difficult child to teach so that she may retain knowledge that I have ever encountered" (p. 88). Soon it was on to another school, this one in New York. A new tutor, Amanda Rohde, was hired to make Rosemary "face reality" (Shriver, p. 43) and, essentially, stop acting out. Rohde believed she had "taken advantage of her weakness" and "used it as a weapon to have her way too much" (Larson, p. 90). She became "unpleasant" (p. 91) when asked to concentrate on her work. Dearborn believed that "tense social situations" (p. 91) caused Rosemary to stumble intellectually and become frustrated when "concerned" (p. 90) onlookers took notice. The school later refused to re-enroll Rosemary. Once again, the Kennedys had purposely understated the breadth and severity of Rosemary's disability in the misguided belief that she could be "fixed"—"cured," her "backwardness," as Joe Kennedy put it (Larson, p. 71), conquered. They labored to sustain the illusion that Rosemary's disabilities "were something easily overcome" (p. 69).

These accounts direct our attention to a shift, taking place as the Kennedys were putting into effect their plan to hide Rosemary's struggles, in how intellectually disabled people were—and still are—viewed by society. When the eugenics movement receded, it became the goal of newly formed advocacy groups like the National Association for Retarded Children (NARC) to sustain "normal" white middle class families, to teach them how to become part of their communities, and, claims scholar Katherine Castles (2004), "how to deal with those children who would never be normal or (by postwar definitions) well adjusted" (p. 352). It was as important for NARC to help the family as it was to help the intellectually disabled child. Castles claims that for some doctors, this help took the form of "invoking perceived threats to the family to justify fearful and punitive attitudes toward" (p. 353) intellectually disabled children.

Meanwhile, Americans were joining community organizations of all stripes at a rapid pace, Castles notes. The number of non-profit organizations whose missions centered around illnesses and disabilities mushroomed at the same time. For most of them, raising awareness and money was uncomplicated; their causes, as Castles notes (p. 355), were socially acceptable. Yet many of the parents who joined NARC struggled with the decision to disclose and discuss their experiences; those that decided to engage with the stigma left over from the eugenics movement "had to constantly argue that their families were normal and respectable," Castles explains (p. 355). At first, NARC reminded people that intellectual disabilities were experienced by families of all economic strata; Castles contends deepening radicalization, characterized by mistrust of established mental health professionals, narrowed the group's focus. This vehemence insulated them from "some of the stigma attached to mental retardation as a problem of deviant lower classes," Castles writes, "but also helped them shape an alternative definition of mental retardation as a social problem faced by ordinary Americans—which, for the most part, meant middle class and white" (p. 355). To counter the isolation felt by these families, and to coax some sympathy from the public, they in essence infantilized intellectually disabled children, building messaging on the idea that the children were helpless. This approach, Castles claims, reflected their own interests "far better than the interests" of individuals with intellectual disabilities (p. 360).

Soon, medical professionals moved from infantilizing to demonizing, Castles argues. In a shockingly high number of cases, doctors persuaded parents that their families had to be "rescued" (p 360) from their intellectually disabled children. Many parents had shifted their attention from the "concrete demands" (p. 361) that come with caring for an intellectually disabled child to seeing the child as a threat to the family. Siblings would be neglected; they also would be ostracized by peers. The adage "create a need then fill it" is apropos here; the anguish nurtured in middle-class parents by doctors and amplified by the community turned into demand for more institutions, into which more of these families placed their intellectually disabled children in the decade after the end of World War II (p. 362). Organizations like NARC in the ensuing years partially reversed the rhetorical course charted by doctors by arguing that it was community narrow-mindedness that had fomented the anguish. Still, the texts we've analyzed, including those referenced later in this chapter and the next, reveal that society has some distance to travel before it embraces the idea that families with intellectually disabled kids can actually be happy, be whole—be themselves—as Castles (p. 365) suggests, without parents constantly trying to show society that they're working to cure their kids or laboring to ensure that their kids act as normal, whatever that means, as possible in public.

Or as we might say these days, to stop making it all about them (the parents and other family members). Empathy is without question the first casualty of living with a child with intellectual disabilities, but accounts suggest that Rose and Joe Kennedy were more concerned with how Rosemary's behavior might impact their political aspirations and status within society than they were about her health and welfare. The best the Kennedys could do, Tim Shriver asserts, was to on occasion achieve an "exclusive intimacy" around Rosemary, "a place where caring for her yielded to being happy with her" (p. 44). Yet I believe the family's fear that Rosemary was a growing "distraction" (p. 45) was a preliminary indication that they too wanted to be "rescued," as Castles suggests—whether or not that fear was heightened by the experts who seemed to enter Rosemary's life through a revolving door.

What confirmed this for me—and only for me—were the accounts of how Rosemary flourished in London when Joe Kennedy was appointed Ambassador to Great Britain in 1938. Rose deployed her children as an ongoing photo opportunity, primarily, Larson claims, to burnish her bona fides as a mother (p. 99) and to bask in the publicity that until then had been lavished only on Joe. Rosemary stayed behind for a time in New York, in part so that plans could be made to ease her transition. Yet even as her family, in true *Rudolph the Red-Nosed Reindeer* fashion, continued to keep Rosemary's disability a secret, she, well, had a ball—or a presentation to Britain's king and queen, to be precise. "She felt dazzling and adored rather than slow and lonely," Shriver wrote (p. 45). British reporters fawned over her, even though she nearly fell in front of the king and queen (Larson, p. 110). She danced and conversed—and no one was the wiser. The glitz and glamour continued at a coming out party a few months later (p. 111). And despite the relentless passive-aggressive criticism coming from her parents, Rosemary felt comfortable at a Montessori school in London (p. 120). When the Kennedy children returned to the United States less than two weeks after France and England declared war on Germany, Rosemary stayed in England. No longer stressed by the family's social schedule and under the supervision of teachers who believed in individualized instruction, reinforcement, and the discouragement of brand of competition that damages confidence, Rosemary was happy, even though her temper flared now and then (p. 123). Unsupervised, she looked after younger students; she read to them and made their lunches (p. 127). Joe Kennedy, with customary kindness, acknowledged that she was "no bother or strain at all" (p. 125). He thought Rosemary should stay at the school "indefinitely" (p. 126). But she still had not mastered writing—at least not to Joe's satisfaction. Worried that the family would be embarrassed if her letters were leaked, he had them sent to the U.S. as official diplomatic correspondence (p. 126).

The swath cut by the Nazis through Europe led the Kennedys to fly Rosemary back to the United States, where almost immediately she felt disconnected from her competitive siblings, left out of the intense dinner conversations led by Joe about world events. Without the kind but firm support of her teachers back in London, she struggled. Gone, Larson points out, was "the structured life that had given Rosemary a sense of purpose and self-determination" (p. 135). She was, in short, left out. Soon, she began to lash out and became physically violent; she suffered convulsions. The Kennedys also feared what might happen if Rosemary began to express her sexuality. Her time in a summer camp in Massachusetts (Larson, pp. 144-147) was disastrous—largely because Rose failed to inform the directors of the full scope of Rosemary's needs. They also erroneously claimed that Rosemary was a counselor at the camp. She was soon "whisked off" (p. 148) to a convent school in Philadelphia, where her she continued to lash out, and then to another in Washington, even as Rose began to research possibly committing Rosemary to a psychiatric institution. Tim Shriver speculates the school, "compared with her situation in England...must have felt like a prison" (2014, p. 47) to Rosemary, now in her early 20s. She suffered more tantrums and frequently wandered from the school's grounds.

Perhaps as early as the spring of 1941, Joe and Rose Kennedy put into motion plans to have Rosemary lobotomized. Joe had come to regard her behavior as "a menacing disgrace to the Kennedys' political, financial, and social aspirations" (Larson, p. 158). As a result, he rushed to have the procedure performed on Rosemary, despite its rejection by the American Medical Association, exaggerations by practitioners about the procedure's effectiveness, and the fact that patients typically ended up permanently disabled. Rose acquiesced, perhaps having tired of the push "to make Rosemary able to function in society appropriately and independently" (p. 160). What Joe and Rose wanted was a "more docile, less moody" (p. 169) Rosemary; what they got was a daughter who could no longer walk or talk and who was barely able to speak.

Rosemary was then essentially hidden away for the rest of her life. Rose didn't visit her for more than 20 years. Joe believed seeing Rosemary would "shatter" (p. 175) Rose. Joe visited her a few times as she recovered until 1949 at a psychiatric facility near New York City that provided for the well-to-do "a discreet rehabilitative environment" (p. 178), then never saw her again (p. 189). Eunice Shriver claimed she had no idea where Rosemary was for almost 10 years (p. 178) and may have been compelled by her grief to leave Stanford. The youngest Kennedy girl, Jean, was told Rosemary had "moved to the Midwest and had become a teacher—or maybe a teacher's assistant" (p. 176). Ted Kennedy was apparently scared the same fate might befall him if he didn't behave. Rosemary eventually was moved to the Saint Coletta School for Exceptional Children in Wisconsin.

I have a hard time believing, as Tim Shriver asserts, that the family was so caught up "in such a flurry of activity" that they "never questioned one sister's absence until much later" (p. 49). Reaching what they believed was a satisfactory resolution was in Joe Kennedy's words, "a major factor in the ability of all the Kennedys to go about their life's work and to try and do it as well as they can" (Larson, 2015, p. 192). But it also gave them the opportunity to amend the "code of secrecy" (Shriver, p. 49) they had for so long observed and seize control of Rosemary's narrative. Rose, for example, asserted that she had "felt grief and pain hardly lessened by the years" (p. 49), yet also lied about when she had learned Rosemary had been lobotomized (Larson, p. 191).

Rosemary seemed happy, comfortable, and unburdened by family expectations, Larson contends, while in the care of the nuns—who knew also to shield her from any contact with the press. Meanwhile, family subterfuge continued; John F. Kennedy made a "secret side trip" (p. 194) during his re-election campaign in 1958 to see his sister. Nevertheless, he changed his mind about supporting legislation that would fund rehabilitation and education programs for intellectually disabled people (Larson, pp. 194, 197). Eunice Kennedy dove headlong into promoting research (p. 196), and pushed her father to devote more money to the cause via the Kennedy Foundation.

The true nature of Rosemary's challenges eventually was revealed. *Time* reported during Kennedy's campaign for President that she had suffered as a child from spinal meningitis and that she lived in a Wisconsin nursing home (Larson, p. 198). The *New York Times* did not reference the illness. "I used to think it was something to hide," Joe said in the *Time* article, though not specifically in reference to Rosemary's intellectual disability, "but then I learned almost everyone I know has a relative or good friend who has the problem" (p. 198). A footnote to the article, however, mentioned the millions spent by the Kennedy Foundation on homes and hospitals for the intellectually disabled (p. 198). Perhaps unburdened, Joe then asserted to a reporter, "I don't know what it is that makes eight children shine like a dollar and another one dull. I guess it's the hand of God. But we just do the best we can and help wherever we can" (pp. 198-99). It was NARC that in 1960 that disclosed Rosemary's disability—though not the lobotomy. Eunice Shriver, meanwhile, persuaded JFK to launch several governmental bodies whose mission it was to protect and advance the interests of individuals with intellectual disabilities.

But Shriver did not mention the lobotomy in the 1962 *Post* article, either. Instead, she referenced the advice of doctors to put Rosemary in an institution, "where competition was far less and where our numerous activities would not endanger her health." Shriver said it saddened her "to think this change might not have been necessary if we knew then what we knew today" (p. 72). At St. COletta, she had achieved an "agreeable" life where she did not have to worry about "keeping up" (p. 72). A "liberated" Rose Kennedy (Larson, p. 206) traveled around the country, giving speeches to raise awareness about intellectual disabilities. The narrative was now set in stone: after watching as Rosemary's "limitations slowly emerged" and persistently trying to find a "medical cure," the Kennedys came to grips with the scope of her disabilities. Upon the family's return from England, she "showed disturbing signs of going backward;" the Kennedys could only "accept the unanimous verdict" (p. 206). So it was off to St. Coletta, where she could escape "the pressures and complexities of the world" (p. 206). Rose didn't visit her until the early 1960s—motivated perhaps by the positive public reaction to the *Post* article (Larson, p. 208). The visit did not go well; Rosemary "recoiled" from Rose. Rose didn't contact St. Coletta again until 1969 (p. 208). When Joe Kennedy died the same year, Rose became more involved in keeping track of Rosemary's care, but soon shared the responsibilities with Eunice Shriver. Meanwhile, all Rosemary wanted, the sisters said, was "love and attention" (p. 212). Larson intimates that Rose's renewed interest might have been precipitated by work on her new memoir. She told her ghostwriter that Rosemary's mind "is gone completely" (p. 214), but stopped short of revealing that her disability was likely caused at birth, when a nurse held Rosemary in the birth canal while waiting for the doctor to arrive and deliver her (pp. 3-4). "[I]t would be discouraging for other people to think then she suddenly retrogressed" (p. 214).

Rose's lack of compassion continued; she believed she "shortchanged" (p. 215) Rosemary's siblings by devoting so much attention to her; she struggled to understand "why God took three sons who were equipped and wanted to work for the government and for humanity, and left my daughter who is incapacitated" (p. 215). She demanded more of the nuns at St. Coletta, and would pay for only one to accompany Rosemary on her first trip to the family compound in more than three decades (pp. 217-218). When Rosemary was informed about the visit, Larson reported, she said "Bronxville"—the last home she knew before her tour of institutions began—and "European"— which meant London and the school in which she thrived (p. 217). At one point during the visit, Rose said softly, "Oh, Rosie, what did we do to you?" while trying to persuade her to swim. Yet the secrecy continued; Rose tried to dispose of Rosemary's diaries while writing her memoir. A Kennedy family secretary then claimed the John F. Kennedy Library didn't want them (pp. 220-221). Finally, upon publication of her memoir, a moment of clarity: ""I do believe that Rosemary's gift to me is equal to the gifts of my other children" (p. 229). By that point, the public, thanks to her family's efforts, had learned that people with intellectual disabilities were not prone to going "berserk," (1962, p. 72) as the director of a work training center was quoted by Eunice Shriver as saying, that they were stable and productive, and that the "weary fatalism" (p. 72) that compelled institutionalization was lifting. Still, I don't think that despite our progress society now regards intellectually disabled people as more than "little flames," as the psychologist Maria Egg wrote (and was excerpted by Shriver in the *Post*).

I was touched by Shriver's assessment that Rosemary "belonged at the center of the Kennedy family story" (p. 225), that her experiences had "trans-formed them all" (p. 225). But somehow these sentiments fall under the heading of "too little, too late" or as just so much brochure copy, part of the family's continuing mission—which just to be clear, we applaud and are thankful for. One of his chapters is titled "Pity or Purge," referring to a typical emotional reaction to individuals with intellectual disabilities and the decision about them made by so many families. How would we amend that chapter title to include the today's tenor of treatment and discussion? By perhaps adding the word "parade?" Do we, as a condition of increased tolerance, always have to be entertained? Can't we just accept people for who they are?

Reading these accounts, I found myself bouncing among several thoughts, some of which were less than charitable, ignorant of context, and evidence of my own lack of empathy. Rosemary Kennedy was able to walk, talk, read, bathe, dress, and eat! Even allowing for the time, the limited medical knowledge, the quacks who took advantage of beleaguered parents—what a bunch of self-involved and self-aggrandizing wimps! You outsourced her, lobotomized her, and then outsourced her again—and *now* you call her "[t]he *most* extraordinary of my mother's siblings" (p. 21; Shriver's italics)? *Now* you find your empathy and claim it was "triggered by countless moments when their sister was alone and the only response that made sense was to sit by her side" (p. 34). You papered over politically motivated decisions by saying Joe and Rose "struggled to help her, to cure her, to protect her in a society that had no place for people like her. They had many moments of joy, happiness, and love. But despite their intentions and in part because of them, she suffered terribly" (Shriver, p. 50)? The thing is, I've advocated for some time having Neil live at the Mary Campbell Center as soon as he's eligible. It's a wonderful place staffed by caring people, but it would still mean not having him with us. Remember when I wrote that empathy is the first casualty in a parent who has a child with intellectual disabilities? For no one is this truer than it is for me. I joke with Sheila that he's perfect for us because we can get angry with him—yell at him, even smack his hand when he pinches our skin for the 200th time—and his pain, his sadness, his rejection will quickly go away, as if we were shaking an Etch-A-Sketch. We do this by lying to ourselves that our flashes of anger have no lasting impact on him.

I don't look directly at him during our early morning sessions in the hope that he'll sleep right through his "artisanal" breathing treatments. I blame him for everything from not having enough time to play the drums to my relative lack of close friends. I do everything I can to avoid scrolling through pictures and escalator videos with him on the iPad while he's sitting in his chair receiving treatments for nearly four hours a day: I fold laundry, do dishes, get the mail—all the while spinning a narrative about these events. "Time to get the mail, Mister Neil!" I'll announce and then head to the front door. I'll flick dishtowels still warm from the dryer and shout "fwap!" This makes him laugh. I guess that's engaging him.

And while I enjoy invoking Neil and Sheila in class discussions—in class projects, class Facebook pages, and in comments on my students' papers—I can just as easily be moved to think of him as a relentless intrusion, an inconvenience, much as my dad did when my brother and I were growing up and dad was running his business. Sheila and I have never believed, much less avowed, that we could "fix" Neil, but I've certainly done my share of temporarily outsourcing him. But I think what differentiates me from the Kennedys, or at least from their public treatment of kids and adults with intellectual disabilities, is that I bristle at the idea endorsed by society that we can't act as if the lives of these folks matter unless it's accompanied by the intervention of celebrities or heroic, zealous volunteers. It's a little like the teachers in movies like *Freedom Writers* and *Dead Poet's Society* who parachute into the lives of downtrodden or oppressed kids, spread some inspiration, and then are forced out by bureaucrats who have had enough time to regroup as the teacher implores students to for the first time think for themselves or see the value—not just instructional—in their own experiences. Parents of special needs kids are either completely inept and neglectful, or plucky and determined, always smiling, muddling through, true heroes, like Dick Hoyt, who pushes his disabled wheelchair-bound son through triathlons all over the United States—and now in FitBit ads. This is why when someone affirms that Neil is lucky to have us, we mostly want to reach out and pull the person's lower lip over his or her head. Call it the "Dick Hoyt" effect. We only see Hoyt in a few interactions with his son - feeding him, helping him maneuver his wheelchair, running behind him in the marathons. We don't see the desperation, the anger, the bile. Who knows? Maybe he is that supportive all the time. But to serve the system, and to affirm our expectations, portrayals focus on the doggedness, the support, the love, the triumphs, the putting the disease in its place.

Raising a kid like Neil is a 15-round heavyweight bout. Joy spars violently with teetering hope against a backdrop of bitter frustration. Or as Billy Joel put it in *Angry Young Man,* "just surviving" is indeed "a noble fight." The gap in Rosemary's narrative suggests that folks who experience intellectual disabilities now are required to be role models; they must compete bravely in Special Olympics, sink a three-point shot that brings the crowd, who likely didn't know all that much about the person, to its feet. They are persuaded to "represent" folks who have similar experiences. They have to put up with fund-raisers and athletic competitions—though to be fair, they do so willingly and with great talent and enthusiasm. Day to day acceptance, tolerance is a little harder to come by—and isn't as promotable. In some cases, Ehrenreich contends, diseases like cancer are experienced as rites of passage, like getting your driver's license, your first kiss, or your first job. The ribbons and the rituals normalize the disease.

But what if you're just pissed off? We certainly are—about Neil's CF, his CP, his developmental delays, inflexible insurance companies, having to schedule ten or more doctor's appointments a month, about making sure he takes a dozen or medicines, about the fact he'll likely never read or write, go on a date, get married, have kids, make us grandparents—you get the idea. Ehrenreich argues that those who rightfully shake their fists at cancer are marginalized by the folks who go down the accepted "survivor" path. "Cheerfulness is required, dissent a kind of treason," she writes. The attitudes of patients "are subtly adjusted, doubters brought gently back into the fold" (p. 31). It should be noted that Rosemary Kennedy had that cheerfulness—or as the daughter of the director of Camp Fernwood where Rosemary was supposed to serve as a "junior counselor" wrote, she was "full of girlish wistfulness and social good cheer" (Marotta, 2010). This requires the kind of packaged access the Kennedys—and most celebrities and politicians—have mastered.

While we are grateful for the professionals, paraprofessionals, teachers, friends and neighbors, colleagues and strangers for their expressions of support and kindness during Neil's time on the planet, the fetishization of a disease or condition actually leaves the healing, the care—and the fear—to the individual and to the family, and lets the people and institutions that often complicate lives like ours off the hook while allowing them to burnish their public "cred," as the kids say. We saw this first-hand when a few years ago we arranged for the installation of a heated therapy pool in our basement— the therapy for us includes the laughter from Neil and he paddles around, splashing all corners of the room. We went back and forth between the pool and a trip to Walt Disney World, but settled on the pool—the highlight for Neil of every trip that includes a hotel stay. Two representatives of the local Make-A-Wish chapter soon descended on the house carrying balloons (also a Neil favorite) and toting gifts. They took pictures for the organization's website and made enthusiastic small talk as Neil took it all in while seated in his Rifton chair. It was like a Publishers Clearing House commercial—minus the big check, TV cameras, and having to subscribe to seven magazines that we would never read. Scripted earnestness delivered in chipper fashion. Like they were doing us a solid, as the kids also say. It's not their fault, of course, but we haven't been in the pool in going on six months. Pools require a lot of upkeep, something we rarely have time for, other than now and then tossing in a couple of Solo cups full of Clorox to "shock" the water. We recently had a repair person out to make sure the pool was in working order—and if we don't begin regularly using it, we'll talk again about having it taken out. Come to think of it, we never checked to see if they used Neil's picture.

Part of our performance, it turns out, is having to publicly soak in and be grateful for all that Neil's experiences supposedly can teach us. "You must learn so much from him," friends, neighbors, and passersby tell us. "He's there to teach you, to teach all of us," say others—kindness, consideration, compassion. Why not add the zither and Esperanto to that list? He's there to be Neil. "She taught us all to appreciate the simplicity of life," Koehler-

Pentacoff said of her friend Rosemary (McNeil, 2015b). Yes, but after her parents had holes drilled in her brain for no other reason than to make her docile. She also taught Koehler-Pentacoff that "love and empathy were key in the success and happiness of everyone's lives" (Nowakowski, 2016). I see—not ambition, aspiration, clearing space to have affairs, the blind pursuit of power—the goals that compelled Joe and Rose Kennedy to permanently damage their daughter? And then she's converted into a shill for Special Olympics—and cast in a role subordinate to her sister Eunice, who had to be prodded into partially admitting Rosemary was an inspiration for the organization's creation? How completely thrilled we would be if Neil could write, even if it came with "typos and lopsided sentence structure" (Gordon, 2015). And how angry was I when Koehler-Pentacoff recounted Rosemary's post-lobotomy "major accomplishment—she was reading billboards" (McNeil, 2015b). She was, the author said, "so proud—queen for the day" (McNeil, 2015b). Koehler-Pentacoff came to admire the "knowing side" (McNeil, 2015b) of Rosemary. Rosemary was probably able to do all of this before the surgery, but we now all get to purge that image from our brains and pat ourselves on the back for recognizing it now. Such is the value to these publications of keeping Rosemary *exotic*, to use Thomson's term.

Before she slipped on our stairs and injured her foot, Tabitha, the second private duty nurse, made a strong connection with Neil. She was calm and patient, varied cleverly how she walked up and down the steps, and was able to endure the endless escalator videos with a supportive smile on her face. Her predecessor, the cranky and petulant Danielle, had experience working with kids who have special needs, but she still expected Neil to act in a typical fashion. She refused to adjust her expectations so that the time they spent together could go smoothly. Sheila and I looked at each other around our computer screens one afternoon and practically in unison said "enough." We then made sure that we had reviewed with Danielle the actions that might cause Neil to get angry. We concluded we had, but to be fair we might have gone over them with more than a little dispatch, as when we shout last-second instructions to our excellent weekend sitter and "We love you!" to Neil as we're practically ripping the door knob off so that we can head out to the gym or to dinner. Yet Danielle would still whine "stop it!" and its ever-popular cousin, "stop it Neil!" when he'd begin pinching her arm or pulling her hair during his tube feedings. She moved the pole that holds his bolus to the sink to wash it out. She'd insist on playing ball on the steps her way, requiring that he land two or three on the steps and then knock them off with another ball, causing them all to land in his lap (that one he likes). She'd complain about having to walk up and down the steps and then give a far too detailed announcement about how many more times she would do it. Successful provocations are just fuel for his fire. Sheila and I made sure the ramped up aggressiveness was not due to illness or to a worsening of his CF symptoms. A throat culture came back clean—we checked that off our rationalization list. It reached the point that we weren't able to get any work done. We ended up performing many of the tasks we had asked Danielle to perform, and even asked her to leave early a couple times—and cited Neil as the cause, claiming he was tired, or had been overstimulated at school. We'd then passively aggressively say that we'd "try again tomorrow" as she wrote up the daily report required by her employer. We joked that we could teach master's classes in constant regrouping.

So I guess even the most loving families that include kids with special needs have their "make it about us" moments. True, we didn't take the abhorrent, disastrous, drastic, tragic, self-serving steps taken by Rose and Joe Kennedy. There are times th0ugh, especially when we're nearing the end of his summer break—or even a particularly raucous weekend—when I'm more than ready to dispatch my amazing son to a residential facility. The pinching, the grabbing of Sheila's hair, the sudden, powerful screams when one of us, for example, removes or puts something in the freezer, the end of day knee-walking to Sheila and then to me and then to Sheila, imploring us to rip the newspaper into thin strips, or to look once more at the iPhone, or to turn "fanny" on and off, or to give in for once and let him throw pens and books at the lamp on the end table, the four hours a day spent watching escalators and ceiling fans (and now folks on trampolines) from across the nation and around the world gets to us. Unlike Sheila, who has the brains to walk away when the pinching and grabbing begins, I sometimes descend into short fatigue-fueled stretches of arrogance and anger. I make a series of silly clicking and popping noises, ostensibly to let off steam, but mainly to announce to myself what a great guy I am for not going off on him. I chew and suck near the shoulder seams of my t-shirts to nullify the anxiety—not to mention the boredom—that comes with feeding Neil and administering his treatments. Evidence of my teething remains on a few shirts, even after several washings. Sitting here right now—and for probably the tenth time in the last 24 hours—I'm thinking about how uncluttered life would be if Neil were happily trolling the stairs at the Mary Campbell Center. I love and admire how optimistic Sheila is about keeping him with us, though I also unfairly seethe in her general direction when she puts her impressive organizational skills to work to carve out time for a bath or a visit with friends. I am jealous—of those skills, and of how much she gets to do that doesn't involve Neil.

So while I'm maybe not an entitled, power-hungry, self-aggrandizing Naziphile jerk like Joe Kennedy, it turns out I'm not a hell of a lot more enlightened than those in our universe who with the best of intolerance-tinged intentions recommended when Neil was a baby that as one put it, we "get one that's right" the next time we adopted.

Chapter Five

Catch the Wind

It felt like I had to petition Congress—after moving and heaven and earth and making peace with my inner Sisyphus—to persuade my father to play catch with me. Picture Kevin Costner's father in *Field of Dreams* saying "You know what son? I'm good" as the sun sets and the cars roll in during the movie's last scene. After all you and I have been through in dissecting the news media's Rosemary Kennedy narrative, you'd be justified in raising an eyebrow—perhaps even two—about the veracity of these statements, but rest assured I've picked through my many disorganized mental files; it was always a fight. True, Dad bought me my first glove—a Dick McAuliffe-autographed Spalding he delivered to me with only minutes to spare before the start of my first Little League game—and he had a fair arm. But Dad just wasn't a fan—of catch or of baseball. The wonderful woman who helped my grandmother raise Dad after my grandfather died in the late 1930s said Dad hated accompanying her to Ebbets Field to cheer on her beloved Dodgers. Remembering her describe Dad's reluctance still makes me shake my head in disbelief.

Fast forward to the late 1960s and then through the 1970s: Dad limited my baseball viewing to one or two games a week—I snuck in an episode of *This Week in Baseball* late on Saturday mornings as he slept—on the trusty Admiral in our living room. Until my great-grandmother bequeathed me her old black and white set, that was it. Dad and I attended a handful of games—a few as part of class trips—but we really didn't bond, other than about how cool it was that we often received the tickets for nothing from a rich relative.

It didn't help my cause that Dad's business was, to be kind, always just a few feet from the brink of collapse. He constantly stanched the financial bleeding caused by his being too lenient with clients who hadn't paid him on time and being too willing to take on jobs before thinking through whether he could complete them and without compromising on the quality of materials. Even when he was present in my life, he wasn't, such was the pull of business matters. I tried to connect with him by working for him during the summers and on weekends (when school was in session)—trading my fealty, I guess, for conversation that went beyond parts orders and which of his employees he didn't like that week. I'm sure I still did my share of shrill "are we there yet" style whining and wheedling to persuade him to play. Eventually though, I gave up.

By now, it's possible that Harry Chapin's *Cats in the Cradle* is playing in your head, or through your earbuds, or you're thinking I should seek professional help. Fair enough. But before we adopted Neil, I vowed that I would do my damnedest to be available whenever and wherever my daughter or son wanted to slip on the mitts and toss the ball around—or partake in an activity more in line with their interests. Hell, I even keep a pair of mitts, a bat, and a baseball in my office at Drexel in case one of my students—or a colleague, a visiting dignitary, or passerby—wants to toss. In my syllabi I let my students know that I'm available for a catch during my office hours. "You always wanted a kid to play catch with," Sheila said at one point during the adoption process, rubbing my shoulders as I sat the bottom of our hallway stairs.

But for quite a while after Neil was born and as the true scope of his physical challenges materialized, I pouted and pissed and moaned about his inability to play catch. I thought a lot about what had been taken away from me. We'd never have that *Field of Dreams* moment. Fortunately for Neil, I got it together when it came to taking him to his three weekly physical therapy sessions, but even then I'd duck out to the hospital's gym to shoot hoops while the plucky and optimistic therapists worked with him. I did so with their blessing, and had stayed for many of their early sessions, but I still rushed out of there and told myself I deserved the break, given all Sheila and I went through with him. His first two therapists confessed that he might never walk, or even sit up. At first, he couldn't even raise his head or get into a side-sitting position. But they persevered—we followed suit at home. Eventually, Neil learned to throw—and, we joke these days, hasn't stopped. He went from holding a ball to rolling it to throwing it in short order. He had no particular target in mind for his early throws, but he soon was able to toss balls in boxes, wastebaskets, clothes baskets—anything with a large opening. His teachers were less thrilled that his arsenal soon included crayons, spoons, cups, blocks—anything you put in front of him—but it was a significant first step.

I got greedy. Before school on warm days, Neil would sit in his wheelchair, his thin legs holstered in AFOs to give them some stability. He was barely able to hold a baseball; I'd place it in his little hand, and his wrist would tilt back, like Charlie Brown's Christmas tree before his friends get to it. I found a tennis ball in my gym bag and switched out the baseball. Neil was at first only interested in throwing at things in the garage—the propane tank, rakes, the workbench, even the retracted garage door. But then it happened. His arm moved slowly forward; the ball left his hand, traveled less than a foot, and plopped on to the driveway. A couple of meager bounces, and it reached me, standing five or so feet away in front of our car. "Way to go, buddy—that was awesome!" I shouted, not caring for once if anyone else heard me. I began to cry as my first-baseman's mitt closed on the ball. He flashed the smile that suggests equal parts mirth and mischief as I handed him the ball to try again. Take that, Kevin Costner. The Mets' World Series wins and the Rams' sole Super Bowl title in that moment were supplanted as my favorite sports memory. I'd be lying if I said I no longer envision Neil and I standing 20 yards apart on a field tossing the ball around, but watching him these days make nearly perfect throws into my mitt from the top of the stairs will do nicely, although I still fantasize about exchanging throws on the diamond.

Neil's teachers and paraprofessionals tell us he enjoys participating in Special Olympics. We have quite a few pictures of him at meets and competitions, and one special video of him receiving an award from officials and a local police officer. Where once he took it all in from his wheelchair, he's now able to walk around—with a little help—and enjoy more of the action. But we suspect his enjoyment comes from the busy day, the young girls with long hair, and the willingness of the folks running the show to bend the day's protocol a bit and let him walk around and throw balls into baskets and at targets. We suspect because Sheila and I, thanks to life's endless interventions, haven't attended many of the Special Olympics events that have included Neil. We *say* it's because of life's interventions—and that's true to a point—but it's also because of our busy at times complicated work schedules, the fact that we want Neil to have his own experiences, our theory that he might not want Mom and Dad hanging around while he goes about his day, that we, or at least I, don't want to see him stumble or struggle—and frankly, because we're so wrapped up in taking care of him that we're happy that someone else has to sit through his master class in persistence.

Neither one of us is big on organized, well, anything. My involvement in organized activities amounts to two, maybe three years of Cub Scouts (I left when I surmised I'd have to learn to swim to make Webelo—not a happy development for someone afraid of the water), three years of Little League, two unsuccessful attempts to make my high school's baseball team, two seasons of rec softball in Philadelphia, and a few seasons with Sheila in a bowling league she joined while working for a previous employer. We've made noises about joining a local support group for folks with kids who have chronic illnesses, and we've circled a local park during a few annual Cystic Fibrosis walks, but we're just not joiners—although with no fanfare whatsoever I did leave the Democratic Party in 2015 to cast my ideological lot with Bernie Sanders, and Sheila expertly dashed off a beautiful pussycat hat and marched here in protest of Trump's election.

Still, we have nothing against Special Olympics. We make annual - almost annual - donations to show appreciation for its mission and support for the athletes, and perhaps to assuage our guilt for not attending events or volunteering. In a past life, I served on a committee of Philadelphia-area white-collar types charged with generating publicity for the Philadelphia chapter's annual May Games. My employer, a regional cable channel, overcame initial reluctance and came through with coverage and financial support, and Sheila got to play ping pong during the group's Celebrity Sports Festival with NFL Hall of Famer Franco Harris and meet former Flyers defenseman Joe Watson (she grew up in Philadelphia and is an avid Flyers fan). The chapter's general manager, who along with his wife attended our wedding, was a friendly, driven, charismatic man who made Dale Carnegie sound like a prickly malcontent. We met a few athletes and I helped our production crews put together the May Games broadcasts and promos, but we haven't gone further than that. While Neil smiles, and can be moved from anger to contentment, when we talk about Special Olympics, his involvement with the organization outside of school is limited to clanking his medals as they hang from our Florida room door.

The organization's goals are positive and admirable: according to the Special Olympics International website (2016), it seeks primarily to "show the world the true nature of people with ID (intellectual disabilities)." Sports provide the public stage on which to "showcase the skills and dignity of our athletes" (2016). Along the way, the organization strives to bring together "people with and without intellectual disabilities" to "see and take part in the transformative power of sports" (2016). These goals would seem to exemplify the principle of normalization first put into practice in the late 1950s by Niels Erik Bank-Mikkelsen, a Danish reformer and advocate for those with intellectual disabilities. At the time, his home country was involved in a debate about whether individuals with intellectual disabilities had a right to "a life as near to a normal one as possible" (Kumar, 2013, p. 669). Bank-Mikkelsen fervently believed that they did. An individual with an intellectual disability, he wrote in 1969, "is first of all a fellow being and so, he must from a point of view of equality, have full rights as a fellow citizen" (quoted in Kumar, p. 669). Resistance to this idea ends in "sentimental pity, in theories of over protection, in group discrimination, or in something worse" (pp. 669-670). Bank-Mikkelsen then operationalized ideas first put forth in 1967 by Swedish scholar Benjt Nirje. Nirje argued that individuals with intellectual disabilities should be given the chance to experience what he called "the normal rhythms of life" (Kumar, pp. 671-675): to experience a typical day, a typical routine that includes living in one place or attending one school, recreational activities, holidays and "family days of personal significance"

(p. 672), a caring co-educational atmosphere and lots of stimuli in adequate and easily accessible settings, the freedom to express themselves, and access to "pocket money for the individual's private use" (p. 674).

Concerned that society had failed to take the concept of normalization "seriously as a tightly-built, intellectually demanding, and empirically well-anchored mega-theory of human service and, to some degree, relationships" (p. 435), scholar Wolf Wolfensberger (2011) began in the 1980s to argue that equal rights and a typical life were not enough for individuals with intellectual disabilities; proponents of normalization had to move toward "the creation, support, and defense of *valued social roles* (Wolfensberger's italics) for people who are at risk of social devaluation" (p. 435). Assignment of a role that society believes has worth is an effective buffer against devaluation, he said. Viewing someone with an intellectual disability as "different" is unkind and narrow-minded; thinking that person lacks a valued social role strikes at the person's very identity, assaults their dignity; it contributes to the perception of the person as deviant. It also determines how we treat the person—the types of settings we permit them to inhabit, the depth of interaction we have with them. Such treatment is uniformly negative, Wolfensberger argued, and makes it likely that the devalued person "will behave in ways that are socially expected of him/her—or at least that are not valued by society" (p. 436). If we perceive the role as having value, however, we are more likely to encourage the person to act positively and to appropriately ramp up our expectations of them. Our respectful treatment results in higher achievement by the person, Wolfensberger contended (p. 436).

So how do we valorize a social role? We begin, Wolfensberger said, by creating the conditions which make it possible for a person to feel they've achieved "competency"—at a task, for example. Neil has become adroit at paper shredding—his love for the activity began in our office at home—pushing a small cart around the school to deliver mail to classrooms, and loading and unloading laundry. Although he was already revered at his middle school (you'll permit me a bit of prideful parental exaggeration), Neil's growing competency at these tasks enhanced his public image, as Wolfensberger might have predicted. It's hard to know if it also changed perceptions of Neil, but his embrace of the shredder, delivery person, and launderer roles came about because of support and encouragement from his teachers and paraprofessionals. But that change in perception has to happen if a devalued person or group hopes to move beyond improved treatment and a nurturing environment to true respect, protection by their peers, being sought out by others as a friend, even becoming someone who is emulated, as Wolfensberger believed could happen (p. 436).

Looking at any Special Olympics flyer or yearbook, you could easily conclude that the organization's athletes have checked most of all of the boxes on Wolfensberger's list. Smiling and determined athletes beam with pride, exult in victory, embrace their fellow athletes, compete with determination. Smiling and enthusiastic volunteers cheer them on, support them, share in their accomplishments. The recently launched Play Unified program, which fields teams made up of folks who have and don't have intellectual disabilities, is designed to demolish "barriers to respect, inclusion, and friendship" (Rabbitt, 2016). A photo of a bespectacled boy from Illinois holds his medal at eye level and admires it. He "remains unpicked when activities" at school that "call for speed or agility." The boy "is reminded daily that he is not as good as his peers." To use Wolfensberger's word, he is devalued. Winning his Special Olympics medal, for the moment anyway, "wipes clean this hurt and gives this self confidence a boost that is priceless" (Turner, 2016).

But is it possible that all of this positivity could be interpreted as meaning that the path laid out by Wolfensberger and his predecessors is a little more arduous for the intellectually disabled person who chooses not to take part in Special Olympics or to do so without the full-throated and enthusiastic commitment seen in the organization's promotional materials? Do you have offer yourself up as a role model in order to successfully complete the path to a valorized social role? For both the parents and the athletes, there clearly is a set of "required emotions" (Ehrenreich, 2009, p. 22) that must be exhibited if not actually experienced. But there also may be a cost—two actually, according to Barbara Ehrenreich: these individuals may suppress their anger and tamp down their fears; and their family and friends may find they like better the person who exudes all that "fake cheer" (p. 41). Again, this is not to say that the folks who take part in Special Olympics are not genuine; it stands to reason, however, that they at least some of the time act as they think officials and the public would expect them to.

Special Olympics events are one of the venues culturally approved for public interaction with people who have intellectual disabilities. An event like May Games "is communal, planned, and, in the end, ritualized," wrote disabilities scholar Paul Longmore (2005, p. 503). Unlike our spontaneous bookstore encounters with other customers, it is not "a casual singular occurrence" (p. 503). It has been deemed one of the "appropriate arenas for dealing with people defined as physically or physiologically anomalous" (p. 503). As heartwarming as the athletes' spirit and drive might be, the organization's events nevertheless remind us—and reinforce, I think—"the power dynamics between nondisabled and disabled people in both the institution and the larger society," as Longmore claimed. We also get to experience the affirmation of society's dominant ideology of disability. Writing in the mid-1970s, Stuart Hall (1975) defined "ideology" as "the mental frameworks—the languages, concepts, categories, imagery of thought, and systems of representation—that different classes and social groups deploy in order to make sense of, define, figure out, and render intelligible the way society works" (p.

15). An ideology becomes dominant "not merely by producing a system of meanings which purport to represent the world but rather, by producing its own system of meanings as the real, natural (i.e. experienced) one" (Grossberg, 1991, p. 145). One perspective exerts significant influence, pushing others to the margins. Those who adhere to a dominant ideology determine how much freedom those with divergent views have to express themselves (Cloud, 1996, p. 304).

Well-known British literary theorist Terry Eagleton (1991) cautioned that an ideology is more than "meaning in the service of power" (Thompson, 1990, p. 7). Dominance by one set of meanings in the cultural narrative about a subject doesn't mean that the audience is unified or cohesive. Dominated groups have "their own rich, resistant cultures" and don't give them up without a fight (Eagleton, 1991, p. 36). They often make use of the same rhetorical devices to sustain their ideology as more powerful groups do. What the audience experiences and internalizes, then, is a mix of the values affirmed by dominant groups and "notions which spring more directly" from its own experience (p. 36). "If there is nothing beyond power," Eagleton writes, "then there is nothing that is being blocked, categorized and regimented"— and dominant social groups would not concern themselves with challenges to their authority. Those with the authority see their ideology in a state of constant negotiation with those held by less powerful groups—this interplay is a key source of their influence, Eagleton explained.

Maybe the most troubling by-product of the experience of disabilities orchestrated by well-meaning groups like Special Olympics is that it ends up shaping casual, spontaneous interactions with individuals who have disabilities—this brings us back once more to Neil and me and the escalator. The ideology embodied by those involved is carried forth by the folks who watch the three of us, whether or not they know it. They have the power "to define normality and abnormality, full membership in the human community and marginalization in or complete exclusion from it" (Garland-Thomson, 2001). Stated with more kindness, if all that a person knows about individuals with intellectual disabilities comes from news stories and publicity about Special Olympics, the odds are slim that they'll be able to engage in a genuine and spontaneous exchange with someone like Neil. While Special Olympics has encouraged a kinder, more inclusive perspective of folks with intellectual disabilities, its officials, not the athletes, are at the ideological controls, as Longmore might have argued. Special Olympics athletes speak eloquently and with passion about their participation and achievements, but they do so within a framework developed by the organization. It's a framework that supports laudable goals, to be sure; the organization stresses on its website that it strives to create "a new world of inclusion and community, where every single person is accepted and welcomed, regardless of ability or disability" (Specialolympics.org, 2016). That world will be "a better, healthier, more joyful place," made so "one athlete, one volunteer, one family member at a time" (Specialolympics.org, 2016). Special Olympics athletes are cele- brated, empowered—not demeaned, as are the disabled individuals who ap- peared in the telethons that were the focus of Longmore's research. Still, the celebration is conditioned on the involvement of nondisabled people—as potential donors, coaches, referees, or as fans. The athletes are not there to serve as props in a donor or volunteer's pursuit of redemption or in the attempt to rediscover their humanity (Longmore, 2005, p. 506). But their quest for inclusion is nevertheless designed at least in part to tug at our emotional heartstrings. What counts as "normal" and as "abnormal" is still confirmed, albeit in a positive, compelling fashion.

A Special Olympics athlete's story is ready-made for a journalist. Ethics professor Deni Elliott (1994) reminds us that the decision to cover a story, like the decision to publicize the subject of what a PR person *hopes* will turn into a story, is an economic one. Sociologist Michael Schudson (2003) argues that much of the news of which we partake these days originates in "planned, intentional events, press releases, press conferences, and scheduled interviews" (p. 6). Journalists are on the lookout for "dramatic, visual, con- cise characteristics" (p. 136); they trade context for convenience, but stories that tick those boxes can be completed quickly and without the need to assemble much in the way of background information.

That would likely trouble Elliott, who argues that media-savvy groups end up attracting more than share of coverage, despite the fact they are "not unique" (1994, p. 74) from groups less skilled at attracting media attention. Journalists compound the discrepancy by often treating the mistreatment of a disabled person as an "episodic" problem. Journalists, she argued, "have a professional responsibility to see the big picture" (p. 74). Highlighting the fact that an organization needs donations and other forms of support "directs attention from the larger question of why people with disabilities should be dependent on private philanthropy" (p. 75) to meet those needs. "It is society and the policy decisions" made by our elected leaders that necessitate crea- tion of events like the Special Olympics World Games, Elliott contends. It's bad enough that society can't care for everyone; "we ought not to extend that embarrassment by allowing exploitation" (p. 75). Sheila and I have had limit- ed exposure to the organization, but still I don't believe that Special Olym- pics exploits its athletes. They are not made to "disappear behind" (Elliott, 1994, p. 76) their disability, as so often happens with charities, particularly those that host telethons. The organization has tried for decades to educate the rest of us that a disability is "nothing more than and nothing less than a characteristic of an individual that may present difficulty with a particular set of tasks" (p. 75). We glimpse what life is like for the athletes when they're not competing, the emotions and experiences that compelled them or their families to involve them in Special Olympics. The organization goes beyond merely having them perform athletic feats "that are hailed as spectacular tricks" (Elliott, 1994, p. 76).

But would Special Olympics pass Wolfensberger's test? Does the organization through its work create a truly valued social role for the athletes? Keith Storey (2004, 2008) of Touro University in California likely would say no. As well-intentioned as Special Olympics officials and volunteers may be, they continue to segregate the athletes—a practice that stands in stark contrast, Storey argues, to the movement over the last 40 years to offering services to those with intellectual disabilities in inclusive—integrated—settings. Despite the recent formation by Special Olympics of its Unified Sports program and its connection to the Best Buddies program headed up by Tim Shriver's brother Anthony, the organization has done little, Storey claims, to foster "a degree of community presence and participation" for its athletes "that is no different from that enjoyed by" (2008, p. 134) nondisabled people. The organization's success and positive public profile are nagging obstacles in the path of integration advocates. Special Olympics officials assert that athletes make an informed choice to participate in its programs. Yet athletes may not have adequate information about integrated recreational programs, or such programs simply may not exist. Thus, "it is easier to 'choose' a segregated program as these are often more readily available," Storey argues (2008, p. 138). For them, Special Olympics literally is the only game in town.

Relationships between athletes and volunteers are brief and rarely turn into long-term friendships (2004, p. 35). By assuming the dominant role, a volunteer coach stunts the equality on which genuine relationships are built. Their charges learn skills that have no real-life application, that "contribute directly to the attainment of greater independence, self-sufficiency, and quality of life" (Brown, Evans, Weed, & Owens, 1987; quoted in Storey, 2004, 2008). Having adults and children compete in the same events and enjoy the same activities causes the public to see the adults as children. "This infantilization," Storey contends, "leads to participants' being denied adult status and dignity" (2008, p. 136). The hordes of "huggers" found at every Special Olympics event dispensing affection to the athletes amplifies the infantilization by suggesting they have to be "helped" (p. 137) by nondisabled people. They also convey the impression that it's acceptable to hug a total stranger. "This can be especially problematic if participants generalize this behavior to other settings and situations," Storey explains (2004, p. 37).

The most troubling of Storey's assertions is that interacting with a Special Olympics athlete does not make a person less prejudiced toward people with intellectual disabilities. In fact, one study suggests we come away from the experience with our stereotypes fully intact—even strengthened. The news media, are no help; past coverage of the organization has reinforced "a negative, self-fulfilling prophecy that evokes sympathy, pity, or stigma" (p. 135). You may recall when former President Obama, appearing on *The Tonight*

Show in 2009, characterized his bowling ability as being "like the Special Olympics or something" (quoted in Storey, 2008, p. 134). Extensive coverage of the President's self-disparaging comment "further enhanced the general public's perception of people with severe disabilities through the lens of Special Olympics" (p. 134). Further, journalists and the public have made only halting progress in adopting less offensive and polarizing terms to describe intellectually disabled people—terms that "lump" (p. 135) them together and which they would not use to describe themselves.

Without question, depending on the media to accurately depict experience can be a fool's errand. But we deserve some of the blame. Famed historian Daniel Boorstin (1982) argued more than a half-century ago that it was our increasingly ravenous appetite for news that caused journalists to seek out what Boorstin famously labeled "pseudo-events"—planned events created solely to generate coverage, set up to be convenient for reporters, and only "ambiguously related to the underlying reality" (pp. 39-40) of a situation. We expected more news than real life could produce, and we expected journalists to find it. Journalists, with the able assistance of folks in the emerging field of public relations who formulated the pseudo-events, obliged. What British journalist Nick Davies calls "churnalism"—receiving a press release and running it without editing or checking the facts contained therein—is now the unfortunate norm. "Spontaneous happenings" have indeed, as Boorstin asserted, been driven "out of circulation" (p. 40). It's to the point where non-pseudo-events are recast as pseudo-events. Think of hastily called press conferences at scenes of great tragedy. Nearly gone are unscripted moments—President Obama singing the classic Al Green song *Let's Stay Together*, for example, Tom Cruise leaping up on Oprah's couch, or a college student shouting "Don't Taze Me, Bro!" at then Presidential candidate John Kerry. French theorist Guy Debord (1995) probably would have gone a step further: we've become quite used to experiencing life as "an immense accumulation of spectacles" (p. 12). According to Debord, "mere representation" (p. 12) has replaced real life. A spectacle, he wrote, is not simply "a collection of images; rather, it is a social relationship between people that is mediated by images" (p. 12). We like copies more than we do originals; we now accept deceptive acts like lip-synching and feign anger at plagiarism. Seeing the world in this way is an assault on reality. It can't compete. We record and celebrate everything—every event, every sentiment, every action, no matter how minor by reality's standards. There is no scale. The Food Network teaches us, for example, that it's not enough to just like food or to cook it competently or joyfully. To participate in that universe, you have to love food—crave it, talk about all the time, act like you're a member of Up with People when you're within 100 yards of it. Hobbyists need not apply.

With so much brash, scripted content to take in, we aren't inclined to go deeper. It's not expected of us. To stay hip and happening, we can't act outside the spectacle; Debord says such activity is "banned" (p. 21). If an organization like Special Olympics showed the depth of the prejudice still felt by folks with disabilities, or the ongoing battle fought on their behalf by disability rights activists, it might "harsh our mellow"—or to put it more eloquently, it might call on us to look closely at the prejudice, or to grapple, even more a few minutes, with our own sense of vulnerability. The media rarely ask to meet our problems head on; instead, messages recast them "into shapes which tame them, which disperse them to the margins of our attention" (Wood, 1975; quoted in Nelson, 1994, p. 4). Put another way: the thought that we might someday be disabled freaks us out, as does contemplating that someone in our family or in our circle of friends lives with one. So we stigmatize, we shun—and celebrate—to get past that feeling. We talk a good game about respecting individuality. What we don't do, even if we do embrace the cause of the disabled, is protest for systemic change that might benefit them, according to sociologist Samantha King. Americans have a deep and abiding faith in their ability to conquer a disease or social issue by throwing money at it either in the form of donations or of items purchased to signify support of a cause. Sheila and I have done our share of both—in my case, it eases my guilt at not having the time to get involved. But in addition, King claims, wearing a ribbon or carrying a PBS tote bag announces to the world our "virtuosity" (p. 38). And since our elected leaders and the news media have persuaded us political dissent is "dangerous and destabilizing" (p. 40), undertaken by individuals who are "naïve, ridiculous, shallow, and juvenile" (p. 40), we're left with consumption as the one uncluttered path to true citizenship. So long as we ditch the anger and the inclination to look behind the curtain and stick to sentimental accounts of how the disabled have touched our lives and enriched our souls, all is well. King has added "ethical serenity, patriotism, and proper deference" (p. 41) to the list of feelings approved for volunteers and fundraisers, where they join Ehrenreich's "fake cheer" (2009, p. 41).

I can't speak for Sheila, but I have days when I endorse Storey's bold recommendation that Special Olympics be disbanded and replaced with something more inclusive. I acknowledge but do not accept the argument by some that the organization is all we have right now, a first step toward something better, that it's been effective in at least opening the door to the lives of individuals with intellectual disabilities. About a year ago, Sheila had an idea for one such program: a non-profit organization that would place for two weeks entitled, jaded, or just plain misinformed teenagers with families that include a child who has intellectual disabilities. They wouldn't have to engage in so many activities per day, or compete with each other to see whose kid makes the most progress. They would just live with the family, observe, play, help out. I might ask them to keep a video diary in which they reflected honestly on the day's events—or just let them decide how they would want to memorialize or synopsize the experience. The as yet unnamed organization would also provide support and counseling—and maybe small grants—to families with intellectually disabled kids that are reluctant to go out in public. We might also reach out to educators—but one step at a time. Or perhaps we could obtain a loan to launch a small hotel chain (or get buy-in from a big chain) that caters to families with kids who have intellectual disabilities. Call or go online and tell the hotel owners what your kid likes to do, and they'll custom build (within reason—perhaps they'd just have materials on hand) and arrange the room for you. She likes banging on drums? You'll find portable soundproofing, a kit (acoustic or electronic), and sticks. He loves stairs? A small portable set will be placed in the room at your request. Escalators? A tour of local up and down hot-spots will be arranged. Call it *Special Stays*. As is typical of us, Sheila's idea is grounded and feasible and mine is out there—but we hope you agree they're both intriguing.

Pretty ironic for a couple of iconoclasts, you say? We're certainly not alone in our reluctance. About three years ago, we asked our helpful former social worker (who has since been replaced by an equally helpful social worker) at A.I. DuPont Hospital if she knew of any support groups for couples who were raising children with chronic illnesses and disabilities. She got back to us right away; we emailed the group's leader for more information. We signed up for their email list—and haven't been to a single meeting. Our aforementioned lack of enthusiasm for organized groups is the main reason for our inaction—not shame or guilt, as Kathleen Jones (2004) explains in her description of how New Jersey-based groups for parents of children with intellectual disabilities came to be. That and we don't want to be defined by Neil's challenges. So that's why we're not out there allowing Neil's face to be used on a Special Olympics flyer or trying to book an appearance on *The Shark*. The rush to help in America is undertaken along with a rush to pigeonhole, and to streamline—to use the same strategies and tactics to meet a need or solve a problem. There's no such thing as custom charity. We've gone from warehousing kids like Neil to parading them around like floats—and then sending them back to their beleaguered, exhausted families. It's a softer form of othering. Our few forays into the nonprofit world are motivated by our concern that we would end up without any kind of help because we don't endorse the approved methods of delivering it. We're on an island—and it's a fine island—but sometimes we have to suck it up and head back to shore for reinforcements. In a 2015 interview on the PBS radio show *Fresh Air*, the great comedian Sarah Silverman told host Terry Gross—I'm paraphrasing here—that you can't win at grief (she had just suffered a great personal loss). You shouldn't aim to win at charity—or condition charity on winning or on cajoling someone into being "brave in the attempt" as the Special Olympics motto instructs.

So we won't attract media attention or condition-laden donations from mega-corporations—big deal. At least we'd be letting them the kids do what they want while we cared for them. So catching the wind will never be a Special Olympics event—so what? We won't have to deal with the ethical complications presented by an organization that models itself after an event whose organizers as a matter of routine evict homeless people, trample free speech, harass dissenters, and fill in as propagandist for oppressive and corrupt host governments (Zirin, 2014). There will no pomp, no coming together as a nation to celebrate exceptionalism and to encounter sports we'll forget ten minutes after the closing ceremonies—until NBC ten minutes later ramps up coverage of the next Olympics.

We may, however, have to pay royalties to the singer Donovan.

Just catching the wind. A simple act. Neil may not love the wind as much as escalators or stairs, but it's close. He savors tiny bursts and long gusts, sticking out his tongue to capture as many molecules as possible, his sandy brown hair fluttering like so many bike streamers. No taste testing, no discrimination. On the way up the steps of his school bus, he pauses, leans back, and takes a last tongueful before his friendly driver allows him to check her iPhone or pull the crank to close the door in order to coax him inside. He tries to keep his friendly hazel eyes open during fiercer squalls, perhaps to prove he's an equal, like a defiant ship's captain staring down a hurricane. If Kate Winslet had stuck out her tongue instead of her arms (or along with them) early in *Titanic*—that's what it looks like. Sitting on a towel on the beach, he adds throwing handfuls of sand into the wind—and at the ankles of passers-by—to the experience. Tongue still out, he bounds down to the water's edge and waits to be pelted by the waves. Their impact is greeted with a hearty laugh—from all three of us. It's comforting—and ironic—that he seems impervious to the uncertainty about his health that Sheila and I experience every millisecond of our lives. He doesn't go there. He refuses delivery—or at least that's how we perceive it. You see it when he charges toward our garage or our bedroom to see if he can eclipse last week's most thunderous door slam, when he fights us coming out of tub and tolerates our rendition of the *Rocky* theme as we put on his robe, when he sort of turns on the fan in the second floor hallway just to get it spin, and as he revels in half-hour long rides on the swing interrupted by our table-shaped dog, Beebo, who now and then wants to hitch a ride. You feel it when he refuses to head to bed and has to be dragged, political protester-style, to the stairs, determined to suck every last drop of marrow out of the day. You see it while we move through a recently opened car wash near the University of Delaware that in addition to the usual massive spinning brushes and blow dryers features as many flashing lights and colorful signs as a fun house. You see it when he walks—toward someone or something he likes. He holds his hands out and bends his elbows, as though he's riding a surfboard or preparing for a 90-meter ski jump. Or he pushes his hands down like he's dancing Fosse or mounting the parallel bars. You see it when he tosses clothes into the washer and/or dryer—and then smacks the adjacent bathroom door with them, usually when someone is inside.

He savors tiny bursts and long gusts, sticking out his tongue to capture each molecule, not discriminating, not testing. Unaffected. Nonjudgmental. On the way up the steps of the school bus, he often pauses, leans back, and gets one more tongueful before taking our friendly bus driver up on her offer to let him close the automatic door. He tries to keep his friendly hazel eyes open, even during fiercer squalls, to get the full effect, to prove he's an equal, like a defiant ship's captain staring down a hurricane—but happily. If Kate Winslet had had the presence of mind to stick her tongue out at Leonardo DiCaprio at the start of *Titanic*, that's what it would look like.

Wouldn't experiencing these activities be at least as powerful and instructive as a 100-meter dash or bowling? Or should these activities be instructive in the first place?

Donovan's song resonates with me for a second reason: Neil's love for us is as elusive as the love Donovan sings about. I wonder if he feels the same deep, boundless love for Sheila and me as we do for him. I know that may come off as petty and self-absorbed. Keeping score in any long-term relationship is a bad idea, but he's so hard to read when it comes to affection. It could be that I'm too lazy to try and understand, even appreciate, how he expresses affection. He more often these days throws warm smiles at us, and kisses us lightly when we lean in. He blurts out "mama," "papa" and a version of "Beebo," punctuating them with more kisses. Yet I still hold out hope that someday his emotional growth will culminate in a heartfelt "I love you." Why aren't his expressions of affection enough for me? I can't shake mental images of he and I walking along the beach, hand in hand, like Bill Bixby and Brandon Cruz in *The Courtship of Eddie's Father*. He owes me for the years of diaper changing, trips to the doctor, the kicks to the groin, the cuts from his pinching. Sheila's right: I too often focus on what it takes to care for him, to just get through the day, rather than on truly experiencing him—the same criticism I've lobbed at Special Olympics volunteers. So I guess it's *my* love that's elusive, expressed with the same conviction as a teenager saying his prayers—fast, flat, monotoned. Before I pick on others, I need to make sure that I've create a valued social role for Neil in my own life and monitor my devotion to it.

As I thought about Neil's involvement in Special Olympics, I remembered my second cousin, Larry, who has Down syndrome. I fleshed out my memories of Larry with a little help from my mom. I was 12 or 13 when I met him. My dad and his crew were installing a pipe organ near Rochester; Larry, his siblings, and my Great Great Aunt Marion and Uncle Harold lived in nearby Scottsville. I don't remember much of what was said or what I felt in the lead-up to the visit. It's a safe bet I felt a little put out, but then again many adolescents, then as now, aren't keen on forced family interaction. I remember only bits and pieces of that section of the family narrative that referenced him: Aunt Marion rejected calls to institutionalize Larry. She was "bound and determined," my mom recalled, "to keep him home." When Aunt Marion's health declined, and Uncle Harold was no longer able to care for both she and Larry, he became a resident at the group home he had visited on and off to learn how to care for himself and to pick up job skills. I recently learned that Aunt Marion was one of the region's early teachers of kids with intellectual disabilities—the headline for her obit inelegantly used the term "retarded pupils" ("Marion H. Stiffler," 1981, p. 9) and followed up with the barely less inelegant "educably retarded" in the story's lead. While teaching in several communities, she also contributed to the creation of Rochester's ARC (Association for Retarded Citizens) chapter.

Like my mom, I remember Larry as a kind, affectionate, demonstrative person. Mom enjoyed his visits when she was a kid to her hometown in western Pennsylvania, but had a hard time reconciling that joy with word from the "adults" that Larry was not permitted to play with kids in his own neighborhood. "I presume they were afraid of him or what he would to do the other kids," she wrote. If my memory is accurate, what he would mostly do is hug them. He loved to hug. He also loved sports-themed magazines, particularly season preview issues. I also loved the season preview issues; I collect them to this day. We spent the day reading them and talking about football. As I tell my students, frame of reference is a powerful thing; context indeed drives communication. We ended the day in his backyard, tossing around the football. I helped him tweak his grip and throwing motion. A few weeks after we returned home, in one of the few truly unselfish acts I have undertaken in my life, I mailed Larry a few of my magazines. In short order, I received a heartfelt thank-you note that I'm sad to report has been lost to the moving gods.

I have no knowledge about the day-to-day operation of Larry's family, but in thinking about him for this book, I am confident based on my memory of that one visit that he was allowed—maybe encouraged—to be himself. I write this fully aware that it could also be wishful thinking. I picture him sitting on the bed in his room, bent at the waist, one leg crossed and perpendicular to the other, poring over his magazines, his head inches from their pages. To borrow a phrase from Ronald Reagan's political strategists—one adapted by Aaron Sorkin for one of the best episodes of his excellent show *The West Wing*—they in my mind at least "let Larry be Larry." Life for he, Aunt Marion, Uncle Harold, and Larry's siblings was more complicated than even a moderately astute newly minted adolescent could grasp, but the love and respect that I perceived they had for him was and is once again inspiring.

Not too long after Neil was born, we took to reciting "Here comes Mister Neil, the baby/toddler/young person with the mass appeal" with great excitement whenever he came into the room. If memory serves, we attempted a Spanish language version to, as we did with the aforementioned "Azul," honor his Latino heritage. We still do it, though not as often. We still frequently call him "Mister Neil," but because of his small stature and slow physical growth, it took us a while to not call him the "baby" with the mass appeal. "Mister Neil" has caught on with many of his close relatives, as well as his pediatrician, his teachers, and the kind folks at the local pharmacy.

Maybe we do it to convince ourselves that he has appeal outside of our little group. Or to tide us over or buttress our defenses for his next spate of cantankerousness and/or aggressiveness. Or to make him more in our eyes—or to build his self-esteem and self-confidence. Whatever the reasons, we think he should have mass appeal. We love him endlessly and wish more folks would get to know him. To paraphrase J.K. Simmons' character in the movie *Juno,* we want to convince the world that "the sun shines out of his ass." But as referenced throughout our journey to this point, what we get from most folks—and even from some family members—is an ersatz or faux admiration that lasts in many cases only until we part company. Folks thank him for his escalator help, or throw a warm smile our way, and it's on to the rest of their day. Part of our task, then, is to set up a scenario that enables them to engage and then go.

Journalists tell us that Special Olympics competitions are among the few spaces in the athletes' lives where they can experience true joy and acceptance. Organization officials and volunteers work tirelessly, it seems, to create and sustain a valued social role for the athletes. But it's still a bubble, even if it is constructed from "acceptance and equality" (Downes, 2015b). The experience of Special Olympians is "virtually self-contained" (B. Kamenetzsky, 2015). While this was meant in the article to be a positive thing, within the bubble, athletes aren't really accepted for who they are—they have to be transformed, worked, packaged, molded—given temporary membership in a class of people from which we get so many of our role models—in order to be accepted. Profoundly disabled kids like Neil aren't that malleable—their stories not sufficiently "incredible" (Lev, 2015) for ESPN producers. Special Olympians are pawns in an ongoing recruitment and fundraising effort; thus, if they are to help the group succeed, we can't engage with them on their own terms. The terms, it turns out, have to sound like they're coming from any other athlete celebrating a win or making peace with a loss—and not causing trouble by piercing the narrative. For example, only the threat of negative publicity—and persistent parents—compelled Special Olympics officials to rescind their earlier decision to bar a young equestrian competitor from marching with her teammates due to her history of epileptic seizures. Turns out even Special Olympics could use "some additional training and understanding regarding this population" (Tomlin, 2015), said an advocacy group official.

The goal is to have them briefly fit in. We don't have any idea about how they actually process what's going on at the Games. We just get boilerplate quotes right out of *Bull Durham*. The athletes are in and out of our lives quickly. Do the athletes *want* to be the "messengers" for the organization? It is too much to expect of them when their home country might not accept them or treat them well. Again, the system that produced that inequality and intolerance and which has barely become kinder over the last hundred or so years wasn't specifically challenged. They're still "the other set of athletes in the room," as one reporter explained (McGinnis, 2014). According to the mother of an athlete, it's important to hold the Games "just to show everybody how special these people are" (Kunthara, 2015). These people? Do they *have* to be special in order to be appreciated? Isn't it possible to like them for who they are? They "deserve to have a presence everywhere," the athlete's mom said. Yes, but this happens only under the terms set by Special Olympics, endorsed by the media, and agreed to by us.

Despite the well-intentioned work and hoopla, despite the scale of the ceremony, the preparations, the celebrities, the competitions themselves, Special Olympics athletes—given this huge stage to show what they can do to the world—are segregated. Revered Special Olympian Dolores Claiborne asserted that thanks to Special Olympics and the bravery, drive, and persistence of its athletes, "the days of being left out are over" (Koffler, 2015). Journalists shaped a Special Olympics narrative that appears to corroborate Claiborne, but it's just not the case. Lawrence Downes (2015a) of the *New York Times* observed that "people with intellectual disabilities are frequently humiliated, abused, and ignored." To be sure, the work of Special Olympics has diminished the frequency described by Downes. But the story of the group told by journalists reads as though "packaged" and "deployed" have simply been added to that list. We are encouraged to perceive athletes who take part in Special Olympics as inspirations, as role models, as brave, joyful, agenda-free competitors who can teach us a thing or two or three about grappling with life's many curveballs. News accounts vividly detail their dedication, their ebullience, their unbridled love for the sports in which they compete. The narrative isn't built for allowing them to be themselves. Nowhere is there evidence of these athletes partaking in the "normal rhythms of life," something for which Benjt Nirje (quoted in Kumar, 2013, pp. 671-675) so strongly advocated. We bear witness to their strength, are moved by their bravery and persistence, tear up at their moments of triumph, maybe pause to reflect on our own shortcomings during the teachable moment they provide.

And then they go home.

Celeste Lacroix and Robert Westerfelhaus (2005) found that the main characters of the Emmy Award-winning television show *Queer Eye for the*

Straight Guy, which aired on the cable network Bravo for five seasons (2003-2007), received similar treatment. The show was hailed for its positive depiction of gay men, for increasing their visibility in the cultural mainstream. The cast members enthusiastically shared their expertise with "style-deficient and culture deprived" ("About Us," 2004) straight men.

And then they went home—more precisely, to the loft set created for the show. The *Queer Eye* cast was given only temporary access to the mainstream. Once their style mission was accomplished, they were exiled to the loft to prevent further "contamination" (p. 12) of mainstream society. This was accomplished by a reworking the rite of passage. To transition from one social role to another, an individual is usually separated from society, struggles to acclimate to the new social role, and then is reintroduced (in that new role) back into society. The trick, at least for the rest of us, is to see the rite through to completion with minimal social disruption—or in the authors' words, "to manage the potential threat these transitions pose to the social order" (p. 13).

In *Queer Eye*, this process was reversed: the experts hopped into an SUV and rushed to help those in need; they "quickly invade[d] their clients' lives and spaces" (p. 13). While there—"a part of and yet apart from society" (p. 14)—they skirted sociocultural rules by touching and flirting with their clients, but safely, the authors claim—and only to help their clients improve their style. The "Fab Five" then returned to the loft where—by themselves—they watched on a large television screen as their clients apply their advice. This application often took the form of clients eliminating "homoerotic contamination" (p. 15) picked up during the consultation by going on a date, for example, or by acting in a more romantic fashion to a girlfriend. We were persuaded to hold the experts in higher regard even as they were returned to a safe distance from the "heterosexual mainstream" (p. 15). The authors concluded the interaction portrayed in *Queer Eye* was "ritually tamed and rendered temporary" (p. 16).

As the media tell the Special Olympics story, once the competitions are over the athletes are nowhere to be found. Kids like Neil are barely there to begin with. For me this affirms that we should be wary of anyone who peddles the idea that we're "post" any social ill—or that we can ever get there. Even as we become more tolerant, and maybe more inclusive, we continue to return marginalized groups to spaces where we can deal with them comfortably and then pat ourselves on the back for growing so much. We just can't let Larry be Larry.

More troubling is the fact that the experience of disabilities favored by the news media shapes casual, spontaneous interactions with individuals who have disabilities. As Garland-Thomson (2001) explains, we have the power "to define normality and abnormality, full membership in the human community and marginalization in or complete exclusion from it." Case in point:

Sheila's dad was a voracious consumer of news; her mom used to complain that he'd turn on CNN in the morning and have it on all day - when he wasn't watching his beloved Phillies or Eagles or working on projects of various sizes and scopes around their house in New Jersey. He rarely watched anything else. I don't recall exactly if CNN was the catalyst, but Dad marked each of our visits with stories he'd seen or read (*Reader's Digest* was often cited) about children with developmental delays who suddenly, amazingly, overcame them, or showed hopeful signs of overcoming them. "And then he just started talking!" I remember him saying more than once. I realize now that he may just have been sending our way some misguided and incorrect, or possibly misinterpreted, media-generated encouragement. And it's seemingly in the DNA of most parents to offer advice without invitation. Then however it pissed us both off quite a bit, as though he wouldn't completely accept Neil unless and until a miracle happened. The articles were poorly sourced, we'd say. The journalist was just trying to score rating points, we'd say. Disabled people are constantly portrayed "as dependent on health professionals for cures or maintenance," as Beth Haller and Lingling Zhang (2017) say...we'd say. Two words: Jenny McCarthy, we'd say. It's taken our village a hell of a lot of work to get to this point, we'd say. This kind of thing just doesn't happen for kids like Neil, who have significant intellectual disabilities, we'd say. I felt as though he was instructing us to head home and immediately try the combination of therapies and cures, some valid, some from the crackpot section of the menu, that he saw in the story. To be fair - and as you may remember - I'm often the fatalist in the group, or I'm perceived that way. But I come back over and over to the advice from the neurosurgeon: he'll get there in his own sweet time. But for sure, Neil loved his grandma and grandpa; to this day, when the phone rings he says, "ama...apa," thinking that it might be one of them.

We had gone to New Jersey for Sheila to take a last look at her folks' belongings before the house was put up for sale. We had gently explained to Neil that grandpa, and now grandma, had died and that he wouldn't be able to see them again, but that they loved him very much and they knew he loved them. That they loved his visits. Grandma would disappear to a bedroom only to return with a plastic tub full of toys for him to play with. She would scare the hell out of us by shouting "where's the baby?!" anytime he meandered even a foot or two away. She would laugh when he moved her ottoman back and forth and express concern when he tugged at the drapes that covered the doors that opened onto their modest cement patio. Grandpa offered encouragement when Neil strolled the grounds, first in his walker, then hand in hand, then solo. When Neil moved up to sitting on the couch, grandpa would plop down next to him. We'd remember when grandpa would sing Irish songs to Neil when he was a baby. Later, he would poke his head into the open car window to say "I love you" and then stand in the driveway, waving as we pulled out while Grandma waved from the front stoop.

Sheila's attention and mine had been drawn away by something. I don't recall who saw Neil first, but there he was, in the middle of the room sitting on tucked knees, looking around the nearly empty room with the most heart-wrenching mix of sadness and confusion on his face. He had not touched any of the items strewn about the room. He knew that they were gone, that there would be no more visits.

Chapter Six

Packaged for Public Consumption

The Kennedy family's achievements, foibles, and tragedies have for decades been covered by reporters, at times with a tone that tends toward the sensational. Much of that coverage has appeared in publications that specialize in celebrities, like *People*. Journalists also have written extensively about the books released in 2015 by Larson and Koehler-Pentacoff. The latter's aunt, a nun from the Sisters of St. Francis of Assisi, took care of Rosemary while she was at St. Coletta's. So while the primary objective of journalists in covering Rosemary was to generate page views, clicks, posts, and tweets, they also managed to advance our understanding of what actually went on in Rosemary's life, despite the family's decades-long effort to "thwart the historical record" (Morris, 2015).

In fact, the family kept its "darkest secret" (McNeil, 2015a) until NARC in 1960 revealed her identity during JFK's run for President. Reporters had pursued few "fresh angles" (Liebetrau, 2015) in covering "the most famous dynasty in American history" (McNeil, 2015a). They were and for many of us will always be, "the nation's most glamorous family" (Dobbin, 2015). It was essential that the family maintain what today we would call "positive optics" if Joe Kennedy was to realize his dream of sticking his success in the faces of Boston's "Protestant elite" (Fabrizio, 2016).

The campaign to hide Rosemary's disability began almost immediately after she was born, when it became clear that the decision to delay her birth by two hours by pushing her back into the birth canal had stalled her "mental development" (Simon, 2015). Her "backwardness" (Gordon, 2015) was a "family issue from a young age" (Rich, 2016) as she failed to reach developmental milestones. Rose and Joe Kennedy wanted the public to believe that Rosemary was a typical young woman to protect their social status and later

71

to ensure that Joe Kennedy's aspirations for his sons would not be frustrated (Higgins, 2015).

Meanwhile, Rosemary was unable to "find her place in a family that prized achievement and success above all else" (McNeil, 2015a). Her "high-profile siblings" (Delcamp, 2015) were at times indifferent about the effort to include their sister in their lives and as part of their "social scene" ("Shocking Details!" 2015). Soon it was off to a series of boarding schools, none of which were informed about the extent of Rosemary's challenges. "A variety of medical treatments" followed, undertaken due to Joe and Rose's "mistaken belief that Rosemary could be cured" (Nowakowski, 2015). Ultimately though, their goal was to "keep her busy and out of the way" (Donahue, 2015).

Journalists contextualized, but did not excuse, the Kennedys' decisions, explaining that they grappled with Rosemary's challenges at a time "when a tremendous taboo surrounded disabilities" (Goldberg, 2014; Gordon, 2015), when children diagnosed with intellectual disabilities "wound up warehoused in institutions and forgotten" (Holohan, 2014; see also Carey, 2015). True, but the stigma and shame they purportedly felt had more to do with "plans to build a political dynasty" ("Rosemary Kennedy's Dad," 2015) than it did with concern for what might happen to Rosemary. In short, Rosemary was a "source of embarrassment" (Liebetrau, 2015) to her parents.

Despite ongoing pressure from her family "to perform" (Donahue, 2015), Rosemary "blossomed" (Gordon, 2015) when the family traveled to England so that Joe Kennedy could begin his service as U.S. Ambassador. She enjoyed a "few months of freedom" (Morris, 2015) in her "happy English idyll" (Morris, 2015). She captivated the British people and acquitted herself well in front of the King and Queen. It was, wrote a *New York Times* reporter, "the most satisfying time of her life" (Gordon, 2015). Once Hitler attacked England, the family was forced to return home; Rosemary's behavior worsened. She began to have drastic mood swings and seizures and throw violent tantrums (Gordon, 2015). Her "customary good nature," wrote noted historian Doris Kearns Goodwin (quoted in Weil, 2005), had vanished.

When she began to wander away from a convent school in Washington, D.C., Joe and Rose Kennedy became even more desperate for a nonexistent cure for their "rebellious" (Rich, 2016) daughter. They were consumed, these texts tell us, by a "dread fear of pregnancy, disease, and disgrace" ("Rosemary Kennedy Dies," 2005). Her sexuality was a "ticking time bomb" (McNeil, 2015a). Descriptions of innocent infatuations were rare, and quickly gave way to infantilization and what today would be called "slut shaming." Morris (2015) compelled readers to recognize that "on the verge of womanhood" Rosemary "had the mental capacity of a nine-year-old." Her parents were concerned that "her attractiveness and vitality coupled with her problems could make her vulnerable" (Simon, 2015). They desperately worried that during one of her forays she would be kidnapped by a "young man who flattered her" (Larson, 2015). Joe Kennedy was particularly troubled by the "chances of an unwanted pregnancy" (McNeil, 2015c), or more accurately on the damage an unwanted pregnancy might do to his sons' political fortunes. Staff at the convent school announced that Rosemary was "escaping to the local tavern to meet men" (Carey, 2015). Having concluded their daughter was "sexually dangerous" (McNeil, 2015c), and ignoring the procedure's staggeringly high failure rate, Joe Kennedy, acting with Rose Kennedy's input, not on his own as previous accounts suggest, arranged for the lobotomy.

Left with "a toddler's mental capacity" (Rich, 2016), Rosemary was "virtually hidden for decades" (Simon, 2015). Her siblings either didn't know or had been conditioned by observing the "Kennedy Code" (Donahue, 2015) to not ask about Rosemary's whereabouts. Displays of emotion were discouraged. Yet after JFK's visit in 1958 and her father's stroke in 1961, Rosemary was "rediscovered by her family, embraced by her family," at least according to Koehler-Pentacoff (quoted by Nowakowski, 2016). They began to "understand what had happened to their sister" (Powell, 2015). Eunice took the lead in reintegrating Rosemary and eventually managed her care. Rosemary visited her family at Hyannis Port and Rose Kennedy, after 20 years, finally visited St. Coletta's, only to have Rosemary "let out a primordial scream" and hit her "long absent mother" (Morris, 2015). She knew full well that Rose "had abandoned her" ("Shocking Details!" 2015).

Meanwhile, Rosemary's siblings, now "deeply, deeply moved" by their sister's experience, acted decisively to erase the stigma carried by individuals with intellectual disabilities and who suffer from mental illness. They "made amends" by making it easier for these individuals "to participate in life and integrate in communities in ways that seemed impossible" when Rosemary was young (Higgins, 2015). Journalists to this day assert that Rosemary was the catalyst for a broadened "national dialogue on mental health and disabilities" (Piereleoni, 2016; Mizoguchi & McNeil, 2016). More precisely, it was the injustice and tragedy to which Rosemary was subjected *by her family* that led them to undertake "one of its greatest missions," Larson told a radio interviewer in 2015 (Donahue, 2015). "How lucky for the nation that the Kennedy children then dedicated their lives to making a place for the marginalized, and in this busy go-getting world raising our consciousness around all issues of the differently abled," gushed a *Huffington Post* columnist (Marotta, 2010). Koehler-Pentacoff claimed Rosemary's work isn't done: "It's time. We need our own revolution—a Rosemary revolution—to really confront mental illness in our country" (quoted in Nowakowski, 2016).

That's it then? We now "publicly celebrate" ("Rosemary Kennedy Dies," 2015) our differences by taking part in Special Olympics and glance over the horror visited on the person who allegedly inspired the group's creation? "In a way, Rosemary Kennedy lived a life of service, didn't she?" Larson (2015) asked rhetorically in an NPR interview. She may not have "fit the family's political mold," said Tim Shriver, but Rosemary "still managed to help shape the clan's future" (Goldberg, 2014). One reporter actually concluded that Rosemary's "tragic tale culminates in an oddly happy ending" (Schlichenmeyer, 2015). OK, so...not the other thing...I see. She "taught a lesson no book, no military service could teach—the experience of feeling that you matter, that you are loved unconditionally" (Goldberg, 2014). His brother Andrew added, "You never know where the inspiration is going to come from, and what's going to move the needle. But she moved the needle in a big way" (Delcamp, 2015).

By being lobotomized. She should be the tragic hero of this media narrative, but she isn't. She was hidden away, packaged for public consumption, hidden away again, horribly damaged by her parents' unchecked ambition, reintegrated into the family, and finally recast as a "catalyst for change throughout the world," as Koehler-Pentacoff announced (Mizoguchi & McNeil, 2016). I came away thinking that for producers of media texts, Rosemary is still "the problem," as Beth Haller (2010, p. 40) might note, something that they had to overcome, to make the most of, even if that meant altering who she was. Yet a *Huffington Post* contributor was moved to argue that she wouldn't "judge or blame the Kennedys—judgment is a cruel trick to manipulate the past" (Welch, 2015).

While books by Larson and Koehler-Pentacoff and a surge in news coverage have broadened somewhat public understanding of Rosemary's life, these texts left me with the impression that she is still a mysterious, distant figure—absent from the creation of her life's story. Only in self-aggrandizing retrospect was she, as Larson claimed, "the center of this dynamic family" (Fabrizio, 2016)—for sure when she was hidden away at St. Coletta's or at any of the other schools. A *New York Times* reviewer correctly concluded that she continues to be "treated as an afterthought, a secondary character kept out of sight."

Thomson might argue that Rosemary Kennedy was and likely always will be an example of the *wondrous* rhetoric—a curiosity whose true self was never truly made available for public consumption. The Kennedys turned her into a role model, and tried to persuade us in what they thought were the most positive possible terms that *they* had been "rescued" from her learning difficulties, her outbursts, her flirtations. Rosemary was never rescued. It's a purely rhetorical choice—amplified by journalists—that mitigates or at least deflects the criticism the Kennedys in my view richly deserve for damaging their daughter. We have no way of knowing—certainly by way of these texts—what Rosemary felt about the course her life had taken. Instead, we are instructed to view her life as one of service. "This wasn't about deficit," Tim Shriver said, "it was about gift" (Goldberg, 2014). This establishes, of course, that Rosemary was viewed all along as have a "deficit," even as she was being rhapsodically eulogized as the family's "lifelong jewel" ("Rosemary Kennedy, 86," 2005). Even posthumously she was helpless, a victim—"the child who didn't and couldn't live up the Kennedy demand for perfection of performance" (Dobbin, 2015). While the texts acknowledge that her mild intellectual disability would these days be treated differently, Rosemary never was given the chance to overcome—to be *wondrous* as Thomson would say—as the athletes from Special Olympics so publicly are today. Soon we'll see a movie about Rosemary starring Emma Stone, who has already been criticized for being an able-bodied person playing a disabled character—still the "third-rail in casting" (Rich, 2016). So that's more distraction, more distance from what actually took place. Every photo that accompanied the texts highlighted the Kennedy's prefabricated nature; we saw kids lined up wearing matching striped shirts or dutifully surrounding Joe Kennedy. We saw book jacket cover shots of a beaming and smartly dressed Rosemary. There is criticism built into the narrative of Joe for sacrificing his daughter at the altar of political aspiration, but there is no criticism of him for having that aspiration. There is disgust and there is empathy, but this is *not* a cautionary tale—that might dampen our enthusiasm for the Kennedys.

VIRTUALLY SELF-CONTAINED

The same inverted rite of passage is easily detected in the narrative driven by journalists' accounts of the 2015 World Games. Special Olympics athletes were integrated into our lives at a time when folks with intellectual disabilities are still ostracized, despite what experts claim is our increased tolerance. Within the walls of the Los Angeles Coliseum and the other competition venues, they were allowed to break the rules, to act like athletes, to compete, to soak in the adulation and admiration from the crowd, to experience the trappings that come with athletic success. And then, with ESPN and Special Olympics International basking in the glow of positive publicity produced by the athletes' dedication, their hard work, their love of sports—their "ritually tamed" (Lacroix & Westerfelhaus, 2005, p. 16) efforts—they boarded buses and planes and headed home, to be seen again at the next competition and the next World Games, their access to the mainstream rescinded.

The plot for the Special Olympics narrative is right out of a Hollywood movie—or TV show. Which in different iterations it has been—think *Life Goes On* or the new A&E show *Born This Way,* which will be analyzed later. Courageous, determined athletes who have grappled their entire lives with their disabilities find a home, a second family, a means to express themselves in Special Olympics. They open up, they flower, they gain confidence. Their parents get on board, even if in the past they have, as in one case, "appeared to be in denial" about their child's struggles (Peter, 2015). At times, it seems that Ehrenreich's (2009) fear—that parents like better the version of their child who exhibits the "required emotions" (p. 22)—has been realized. The athletes experience "a degree of community presence and participation that is no different from that enjoyed" by nondisabled people, something Storey (2008, p. 134) contends has not actually happened. And for the first time they are individuals. Their athletic accomplishments are "theirs alone" (B. Kamenetzsky, 2015). Yet involvement in Special Olympics is often a family affair, with generations taking part—"passionately engaged for the long haul," as an organization official told a reporter (Nelson, 2015).

Meanwhile, Tim Shriver and the folks at Special Olympics International soldier on, preaching the organization's gospel of acceptance and inclusion. The oft-repeated message "resonates so powerfully because of the pain it is working to erase," explained a *New York Times* columnist (Downes, 2015a). With Shriver at the controls, the organization has "shouted a call for rights and dignity" (Downes, 2015a). The Games are "an integral part of the campaign to get people from all cultures and all walks of life to encourage the athletes and to elevate an awareness of their value to the community," Special Olympics President and CEO Patrick McClenahan told a journalist (Montero, 2015b). The athletes also inspire intercultural understanding. For one journalist (Bruno, 2015)—and one-time Special Olympics coach—the World Games was "an eye-opening experience" (Bruno, 2015). Merely watching the athletes causes "exhilaration for all to preserve and emulate here and around the world" (Bruno, 2015). Producing that exhilaration requires a Herculean behind the scenes effort by the event's organizers to ensure that the athletes, many of whom are not used to travel, safely arrive, participate, and depart the Games. Organizers focus on "streamlining the athlete experience in the most positive way possible" (B. Kamenetzsky, 2015). This includes providing basic health care and fitness screenings to athletes from developing nations or nations where people with intellectual disabilities are mistreated by officials and their own families (Bell, 2015; O'Neil, 2015a).

The athletes are the primary characters in the narrative, but they say little. What they do say is poignant, but is shoehorned by journalists into tales that affirm the hero—and "supercrip" themes. "It was fun," one athlete told a journalist (Trevino, 2015). "We were doing a lot of exercising. I made a lot of friends. They have been calling me saying, 'Ti-Ti, I miss you. I can't wait to see you." We were told repeatedly that the adulation that rained down on them from fans, coaches, and volunteers had "an astounding effect" (Bruno, 2015) on them, but besides the photos of smiling, waving, exultant athletes, journalists provide little concrete evidence of substantial impact. The unspoiled enjoyment experienced by the athletes rubbed off on the many celebrities attached to the World Games. Everyone from the First Lady to Olympic great Michael Phelps to music icon Stevie Wonder enthusiastically attested to the positive impact of Special Olympics on the athletes' lives—and on theirs. Make no mistake though—their presence was highlighted as a matter of journalistic convention. Celebrities always make a story more compelling.

The athletes' love for their fellow competitors, coaches, and their parents and siblings is "untainted," with "no strings attached" (Richardson, 2015). For every athlete, competing in the World Games is "the opportunity of a lifetime" (Wilson, 2015a). Journalists infrequently quote them, choosing instead to allow coaches, volunteers, officials, family members, and even their colleagues to gush about the bravery and guileless love for competition exhibited by the athletes. When athletes are given voice, they express unbridled joy and enthusiasm, but at times they sound like the canned, uncontroversial quotes about which sports journalists complain when they come out of the mouths of professional athletes.

Grateful parents who have watched for years as their children struggle with illness and physical limitations now marvel at their accomplishments and newfound self-confidence. Others were taken to task for failing to provide a loving environment in which their children could grow up. Some denied that their child was intellectually disabled. An athlete told a *USA Today* contributor that he "moved from home to home, family member to family member, because nobody in my family knew how to take care of me" (Peter, 2015a). Athletes are urged on by coaches who subscribe to the direct, no-nonsense approach favored by their counterparts in college and the pros. They claim to treat their Special Olympians no differently than they do their nondisabled charges. It's the discipline, the narrative indicates, that enables Special Olympians to make "the most of their circumstances" ("Some Special Olympics Competitors," 2015) and by competing redefine themselves (Bruno, 2015). They also lay the groundwork for the rest of us to change for the good our perception of individuals with intellectual disabilities.

Special Olympians are a welcome respite from the pampered, overpaid athletes whose exploits fill the sports pages. In the NFL or Major League Baseball, noted model and actress Brooklyn Decker, whose aunt has Down Syndrome, we don't often "see athletes hugging and consoling each other" (Gleeson, 2015). Special Olympians, she argued, have "an understanding for the human condition" (Gleeson, 2015) that the typical pro athlete lacks. Let's be clear though: the athletes want to win, journalists claim, but at the Games they are able to do so "without sacrificing their humanity in the process" (A. Kamenetzsky, 2015). As actress Brooklyn Decker explained, Special Olympics officials are not in the business of "giving out congeniality awards" (Gleeson, 2015). The goodwill and sentimentality engendered by Special Olympians "doesn't change the fact that when these athletes step on the field or between the lines, they're out to win. Period" (A. Kamenetzsky, 2015), explained an ESPN contributor. Covering the Opening Ceremonies for the

Los Angeles Times, columnist Bill Plaschke (2015) observed "no preening of recognizable stars." Special Olympians "are the only world-class athletes who want you to take their picture," he wrote. First Lady Michelle Obama told those gathered for the Opening Ceremonies that while the World Games might "lack the magnitude of the original five-ringed spectacle, it offers a unique camaraderie and atmosphere that is contagious" (Gleeson, 2015). It's a haven—"the most amazing place, a place we don't always find in the rest of the world," a Canadian track star told a columnist. "This is a place where we are all equal" (Plaschke, 2015), where "we can lift up our friends and neighbors," as the First Lady asserted. "[Y]ou don't get that everywhere," said one official (A. Kamenetzsky, 2015) observed at competitions. But that haven only exists for a short time. It's heartwarming but also daunting to suggest that the athletes will "take what they learned on the playing field into life where we have a long way to go" (Gleeson, 2015).

Special Olympics' athletes were not "props in a donor or volunteer's pursuit of redemption or in the attempt to rediscover their humanity" (Longmore, 2005, p. 506). The athletes may not have asked to be objects of emulation, but journalists heartily convey the gratitude of those whose lives they've touched, whose hearts they've opened. "There aren't a ton of opportunities anymore for families to sit down and watch TV together" (Lev, 2015) said an ESPN producer about the Games. "If we could do 24 hours of storytelling, we'd all buy in. Every story is incredible. The truth of the matter is, we should tell all 7,000" (Lev, 2015).

Elation on the faces of the athletes "captivates you" (Gleeson, 2015), said UCLA football coach Jim Mora, a longtime Special Olympics volunteer. "You spend time with the athletes here and you know you get so much more than they get" (Kunthara, 2015), said a Rotary Club official quoted on local television. The athletes, asserted former Special Olympics International (SOI) CEO Janet Froetscher, "have taught us more about life than we could ever teach you. And given more cheer in a world that could use more cheering" (Montero, 2015c). Apparently they exist to "motivate others to work harder and aim higher" (Fisher, 2015). With their behavior adjusted for public consumption, they are mechanisms for our enlightenment and introspection, touchstones on our path to self-improvement, playing a role they never sought. As referenced in an earlier section, existence of this theme affirms that the athletes can't just be admired or loved for who they are. But the experience empowers them—at least that's what we're repeatedly told (e.g. Gleeson, 2015).

An alternate reading of the narrative suggests the inclusion so vigorously advocated by Special Olympics officials primarily benefits *us*. Observing the joy on the faces of athletes "really makes you sit back for a second and be like 'you know, I really got to quit griping about my golf game, because it's a very humbling experience to be a part of this,'" comedian Bill Engvall told

ESPN (Mirecki, 2015). During the closing ceremonies, Froetscher told the athletes, "we deserve to have you in our lives." The world, she said, "is better when we include every one of you" (Montero, 2015d). *We* deserve—as if we've come so far, earned some credit for scraping a little of the rust off our brains. An "ecstatic" Paula Abdul, most recently a judge on the television show *So You Think You Can Dance,* gushed that she came to the World Games to be "inspired" (Gleeson, 2015). At a White House event commemorating the anniversary of the founding of Special Olympics, President Obama lauded the athletic prowess and entrepreneurship exhibited by "four-season" athlete Tim Harris. Harris walked up on stage, intending to hug the President. "Presidents need encouragement once in awhile, too," he said. "Thank you, Tim" (Koffler, 2015). The hug, it turned out, is also on the menu at the restaurant Harris runs in New Mexico (McGinnis, 2014).

A Special Olympian typically has beaten steep odds—and reined in inappropriate behaviors—to compete on the international stage, to have lives at one time "scarcely imaginable" (Thomas, 2015) to doctors and family members. "Despite grim projections from doctors as a child," wrote a *Time* contributor about a Special Olympics swimmer, "Chandler is just not an accomplished competitor, but a role model" (Koffler, 2015). Journalists enthusiastically recounted how athletes eclipse their limitations in order to play the role we expect. "It's wonderful," the swimmer's mother told a Los Angeles television reporter, for her "to be in a position where children look up to her as a role model, not someone with special needs" (Thomas, 2015). A first-person story by an athlete turned official born with Fragile X began: "Picture in your mind a little boy of 5 or 6 sitting alone in his room, obsessively lining up his toys in perfectly straight lines." The boy "would not look you in the eye, and would react inappropriately to the slightest physical touch" (Doring, 2015). One of the organization's first intellectually disabled volleyball referees didn't know she had a disability because, as a foster child, she was denied access to her birth records. Poor performance in school and homelessness followed. "Only after finally understanding her past was she able to get the help she needed and change her future," wrote ABC anchor Robin Roberts.

Even Special Olympians have to recover before they're allowed to be part of our world. Leave all that pity, all that negativity behind, journalists suggest. Finding the athlete within will put you on the path to acceptance and validation. Competition, in true American fashion, causes parents to want to unearth attributes in their kids that might have been there all along. For three years, gymnast Chelsea Werner was contentedly entering meets "even though in her earliest competitions she usually placed last," her coach recalled on the *Today Show*. And she didn't care. Didn't care? Eventually though, Chelsea came to understand "what the lower score meant." And as was the case with Andrew Peterson, she discovered her inner typical athlete. Together with her coach, she embarked on a "whole new journey of training her to understand if this is what you want to do, you have to work harder if you want to get a medal" (Stump, 2015).

Once she began to rack up national titles—once she "advanced to a level many though was never possible" (Stump, 2015)—Chelsea blossomed. Gymnastics—being an athlete—for the moment anyway, freed her from her disability. "What a princess," said her dad, who cited her "incredible personality, self-esteem, and just the pure joy" (Stump, 2015). According to her mom, Chelsea is "gymnast and loves life—very happy, very social, very outgoing." Their pride was underscored in the *Today* piece by showing them watching their daughter train under the watchful eye of her coach, who they hired when Chelsea's previous coach theorized she probably wouldn't make it past "level one for quite a few years" (Stump, 2015). The prediction didn't "sound right to us," so Chelsea's parents pulled out the phone and searched for a coach who would take their daughter on. Journalists have long lionized tough coaches who expect maximum effort and minimum pushback from their charges.

Thus, it is no longer enough for Special Olympics athletes to bravely participate, as the organization's motto demands; they now also must win. It is no longer enough for an athlete to gain self-confidence or see improvements in health. "Now the sport is a way for her to show others just how much is possible for other athletes with the disorder," explained a *Today Show* reporter (Stump, 2015). Chris Hahn, at the time the head of the U.S. delegation to the Games expressed concern that our athletes had "fallen behind their European counterparts because of inferior technical training" (O'Neil, 2015b). The World Games were "a call to action for the U.S. to improve its coaching" (O'Neil, 2015b). Special Olympics should also reconsider its practice of not publicizing how many medals were won by American athletes, Hahn claimed. This suggests that an elite tier of athletes has been created, leaving behind their more profoundly disabled counterparts.

It must be made easier for us to interact with them, and they must be in constant need of our intervention. I don't discount the possibility that it was only by competing in Special Olympics that these attributes emerged in Chelsea. But journalists would have a harder time explaining the emergence to us if it came about by, say, simply playing catch with her mom or dad—or walking up and down the stairs for two hours. The burden is still on the athletes to fit into society—not the other way around. The father of one athlete said his son "wasn't what you'd call a proper swimmer." Lifeguards feared he might drown. "He had his own way of doing a doggie paddle. They didn't know he had a special situation" (Bartholemew, 2015). Once he got involved with Special Olympics, however, he "discovered his inner dolphin" (Bartholomew, 2015).

So not all athletes with intellectual disabilities need apply. The narrative demands they have certain attributes or have the potential to overcome the genetic hand they've been dealt. Athletes who aren't able to mentor other kids or accomplish something on the field, don't deserve the love and respect—or as much of it—as their able counterparts. They have to kiss or bite their medals, raise their arms in victory, wave to the crowd. The father of a Special Olympian from Indiana summed it up as his son vied to be pictured on the cover of a national running magazine: "They said they were looking for a runner who was authentic, inspiring, athletic, passionate, unstoppable. I though those five characteristics very defined Andrew," said Craig Peterson (Blair, 2015). His son was nine years old "when the athlete within was born" (Blair, 2015). What would Andrew's life have looked like if it hadn't been?

Organizers took extraordinary steps to ensure that the performance of the athletes would do nothing to tarnish the city's image. For example, they "divisioned" athletes, grouping athletes into "flights" based on personal best performances provided by coaches, even if those performances took place elsewhere. They also implemented the "maximum effort rule" to ensure that athletes would perform as well in preliminary stages of competition as in the finals. Yet the athletes, said one official, "are not competing for charity or to provide the 6 O'Clock News with a series of feel-good stories, but to achieve at the highest level their bodies and minds will allow" (B. Kamenetzsky, 2015). In the same interview, however, the official stressed that the Games were "not intended to be a display of elite athleticism" (B. Kamenetzsky, 2015). Rules for the various sports were modified "to make sure all of the athletes competing are similarly skilled" (Montero, 2015a), in the words of one official. The goal, said another, was to generate "drama for the fans and the feeling among the athletes that any of them could win on any given day" (Montero, 2015a). An official in charge of finding horses for the equestrian competition said the goal was to "make sure every athlete is being serviced in a way that's fair" (B. Kamenetzsky, 2015).

It also helped if a Special Olympian was attractive. "With his GQ looks," wrote one *Los Angeles Times* reporter about an athlete, he is the "poster boy for the L.A. contest" (Bartholomew, 2015). The swimmer's "hazel eyes now twinkle for the L.A. Live jumbotron" (Bartholomew, 2015). An athlete who worked as an analyst for ESPN "leads by his example. And he has a million-dollar smile" (Peter, 2015). Thus, while Shriver and other Special Olympics officials repeatedly tried to highlight the differences between the World Games and other large-scale sporting events, journalists underscored the similarities—and did so against the backdrop of a spectacle that would have made Guy Debord smile.

Only by hosting a large scale event in a major city could Special Olympics officials maximize the "long-term effect" (Montero, 2015b) on attitudes toward folks with intellectual disabilities, the narrative suggests. Yet just as all my cousin Larry needed was a few football magazines to make him happy, at least on Former Los Angeles Mayor Antonio Villaraigosa, a member of the World Games organizing committee, asserted his city would "lead the way to provide more opportunities for the people who have been great athletes" (Montero, 2015b). Someday, he suggested, we would "see them in our workplaces and in our schools" (Montero, 2015b), as if we didn't now. It's like resetting the clock by implying we suffer from collective amnesia.

Where the *Queer Eye* cast had its loft, Special Olympians have a bubble. While they perform admirably inside of it, "the battle for hearts and minds, and for rights and laws" continues, wrote Lawrence Downes (2015b) of the *New York Times*. Safely inside the bubble, "you stop noticing the differences. The novelty wears off and it becomes clearer that the world is full of people of an astonishing variety of appearances and abilities" (Downes, 2015b). They are "brought inside by sport and its passion" (Plaschke, 2015). Still, as the athletes prepared to leave Los Angeles, "reality began to set for those who were not returning to the same amenities they enjoyed here, namely equality, protection, and acceptance" (O'Neil, 2015b). The head of the Pakistani delegation wondered if it would be better to give the athletes money rather than transporting them halfway around the world. It would be horribly unfair, he said, to "take them up to the pedestal and drop them back down on the floor" (O'Neil, 2015b).

Outside the bubble, life isn't as rosy. When the athletes escape the "ritual taming" described by Lacroix and Westerfelhaus (2005)—literally in the case of athletes from Bulgaria and the Ivory Coast who wandered away from their delegations as the Games wrapped up (e.g. Rocha & Hamilton, 2015; Zhang, 2015)—they were treated like an inconvenience. We're comfortable with their on-field performance, their bravery, their overcoming of odds, their dedication. But when they show fragility or act outside our expectations, it's almost as if their behavior turns criminal. We saw head shots and surveillance camera stills and footage; we heard and read breathless descriptions about police searches and when the athletes were found and reunited with their teams (e.g. Lloyd & Guinyard, 2015). Photos of the athletes sleeping under Red Cross-logoed blankets in the Loyola Marymount University gym called to mind a crime scene, or the scene after a natural disaster. All that was missing were the milk cartons. They are again made to seem pitiable—dehumanized, infantilized, as Longmore might have argued. They would be lost, stripped of their valorized social role. It's best to keep them in line, handlers nearby (e.g. Rocha & Hamilton, 2015), cordoned off, moving smoothly through airports, holding hands, focused on competition. It distracts them and us.

Perhaps the most striking element feeding this theme is the acknowledgement by Special Olympics that there is in fact a bubble, and that when athletes are not competing, they drop off the public's radar. "The glow" of World Games "has to last," explained Lawrence Downes (2015b) of the *New York Times*, "because the athletes will need it when they get home are become invisible again." The organization for almost 50 years has driven awareness and stimulated much good will—so effectively, Downes (2015b) claims, "that nobody has to take it seriously." Too many of us, he suggests, "still think it's a track meet." Even Tim Shriver admitted that "the perverse truth" (Downes, 2015b) for individuals with intellectual disabilities is that most of the money spent by nations on education and anti-poverty programs never makes it to them; it is spent "where results are quick and quantifiable," he said (Downes, 2015b). The intellectually disabled are still "willfully kept beyond the public's vision" (Downes, 2015b)—except when they are competing in a very public venue.

Still, journalists conveyed the hope of Special Olympics officials that from the goodwill engendered by the athletes would come increased tolerance and inclusion—and more acolytes to the gospel. Shriver told a reporter that 30 ministers of sports from around the world were first-time Games attendees. He maintained "a specific hope that they'll come here and become sort of converts if you will—believers—then go home and use that leverage" (O'Neil, 2015b) to expand opportunities for athletes with intellectual disabilities. Though perhaps not directed at the organization's critics, journalists provided opportunities for Special Olympics officials to assert that the organization does not abandon the athletes once large-scale events like the World Games have concluded. Timothy Shriver told the thousands gathered for the closing ceremonies that many "labor under the misconception that we are like the other Olympics, which is that there are Olympic Games and then they're over. Ours don't end" (O'Neil, 2015b). The organization remains convinced that "gentle persuasion and the attitude-changing power of sports" (Downes, 2015b) is the right strategy to open our hearts and minds, even though Shriver admitted that "the barrier, the attitudinal barrier, that this population is too different to matter" (Downes, 2015b) may not fall for some time, if ever. Despite the Sisyphean nature of the task, journalists indicate the group bravely pushes on—and should push on, should go on holding events from which they can benefit, rather than endorsing a more confrontational, revolutionary approach. Journalists have a long history of marginalizing vocal dissenters who dare challenge how things are done. Shriver at one point urged his charges to "storm the castle"—but "not militantly" (Downes, 2015a). Plaschke (2015) congratulated Special Olympics for coming up with an approach that tugs at our heartstrings but in our estimation also deflects criticism of the group and those affiliated with it. The innocence of the athletes insulates the group as it is0lates them. "There is no humiliation here," he wrote about the "isolated nightmares" that marred the lead-up to the opening ceremonies. "There are no losers here. There are not even any frowns here."

Journalists commented on the complicated logistics for the World Games, logistics exacerbated the vulnerability of the athletes and the fact they were inexperienced travelers. They did not have "the kind of sophistication with understanding how to deal with the challenges of travel" (B. Kamenetszky, 2015), said one Special Olympics official. Journalists cast medical professionals who volunteer for the Special Olympics Healthy Athletes Program (see Bell, 2015) as heroes charged with bringing basic medical care to athletes unable to obtain it in their home countries. Numerous stories detailed how the "army of volunteer doctors" (Rogers, 2015) who sign up for three-year stints as volunteers for the Healthy Athletes Program—"the world's largest healthcare provider for people with intellectual disabilities" (O'Neil, 2015a)—see lack of care, common diseases left untreated, no dental care, and evidence of horrible treatment. "Some of the most common fixes" are "also the most life-changing," an ESPN contributor noted (O'Neil, 2015a). Through the intervention of these professionals, athletes see clearly or hear for the first time.

"Tucked into a corner" of the USC campus, wrote an AP reporter, "is a makeshift medical clinic that seemingly sprouted overnight" (Rogers, 2015). There, doctors, nurses, and dentists labor "to ensure thousands of athletes go home with clean bills of health—or the closest thing to them that can be produced in a week" (Rogers, 2015). Optics are significant here; why couldn't athletes be cared for in existing facilities? It would added to the cost of holding the Games, but the tents and the lines convey the impression that these volunteers are working for a non-governmental organization in a war-torn or poverty-stricken part of the world. To make matters worse, the policies, or lack of them, and actions by officials in home countries that have resulted in some cases in a total lack of basic medical care are not evaluated or criticized. This only exacerbates the "island" feel.

The athletes' relentless optimism and gratitude for the doctors' care cancelled out communication difficulties. "It's a different world than what we're used to," a volunteer nurse told the *Los Angeles Times*. "Everyone is so happy. If I had to come up with a theme for the clinic, it would be 'hugs and high fives'" (Shepherd, 2015). A heartening description to be sure, but it again directs our attention away from why the athletes lack medical care in the first place. They wandered around Los Angeles like refugees even as we are encouraged to emulate other aspects of their personalities. Consider this description of the athletes' arrival: "[A] steady stream of yellow school buses, each adorned with the Special Olympics logo...continually jammed a small campus street as they disgorged" (Rogers, 2015). Soon, a tent in which dentists treated athletes "was filled shoulder to shoulder with athletes and their coaches." They were "chatting happily and loudly in a cacophony of languages" (Rogers, 2015). They leave with new athletic shoes, toothbrushes, glasses, hearing aids. "The saddest part," the nurse said, "is when we have to tell the athletes they aren't cleared to play" (Shepherd, 2015). The bigger goal, said Dawn Bainbridge, who led development of the program, is "putting them out there with everyone else doing the same thing everyone else is" (Bell, 2015).

Texts tell us that Special Olympics competitions are among the few spaces in the athletes' lives where they can experience true joy and acceptance. Organization officials and volunteers work tirelessly to create and sustain a valued social role for the athletes. It could be argued that it's still a bubble, even if it is constructed from "acceptance and equality" (Downes, 2015b). Within the bubble athletes aren't really accepted for who they are; like Rosemary Kennedy, they have to be transformed, worked, packaged, molded—given temporary membership in a class of people from which we get so many of our role models—in order to be accepted. Profoundly disabled kids aren't that malleable—their stories not sufficiently "incredible" (Lev, 2015) for ESPN producers. Special Olympians play a central role in a recruitment and fundraising; thus, engaging with them on their own terms is discouraged. Those terms have to sound like they're coming from any other athlete celebrating a win or making peace with a loss—and not causing trouble by piercing the narrative. For example, only the threat of negative publicity—and persistent parents—compelled Special Olympics officials to rescind their earlier decision to bar a young equestrian competitor from marching with her teammates due to her history of epileptic seizures (Tomlin, 2015).

The narrative isn't built for allowing them to be themselves. Even as we become more tolerant and inclusive, we continue to return marginalized groups to spaces where we can deal with them comfortably. Special Olympics events are venues culturally approved for public interaction with people who have intellectual disabilities. Events like the World Games are "communal, planned, and, in the end, ritualized," wrote disabilities scholar Paul Longmore (2005, p. 503). The Games have been deemed one of the "appropriate arenas for dealing with people defined as physically or physiologically anomalous" (p. 503). While the drive and spirit of the athletes is heartwarming, events like the World Games remind us of "the power dynamics between nondisabled and disabled people in both the institution and the larger society," as Longmore claimed. Nowhere is there evidence of these athletes partaking in the "normal rhythms of life," something for which Benjt Nirje (quoted in Kumar, 2013, pp. 671-675) so strongly advocated. We bear witness to their strength, are moved by their bravery and persistence, tear up at their moments of triumph, maybe pause to reflect on our own shortcomings during the teachable moment they provide.

And then, like the cast of *Queer Eye*, they go home. Kids with more profound intellectual disabilities are for the most part nowhere to be found.

Chapter Seven

By Any Other Name

In the colonial era, families cared for members with intellectual disabilities largely on their own. "Society did not become involved unless the economic stability of the family was threatened," writes Phillip Ferguson (2004, p. 43). When this happened, communities would shore up the families with food, supplies, and financial support, but cared little about disabled family members or about how disabilities affected other family members. This strategy was not only "fiscally prudent," it was "Providentially ordained," Ferguson explains (p. 43). Individuals who were just too disruptive were often "bound out"—provided a guardian and often a home by town officials.

Sociologist James Trent (1994) contends that until about 1820, we didn't really fear folks with intellectual disabilities. We teased them, pitied them, shunned them, labeled them "idiots," would assert they couldn't be educated (Dudley-Marling & Burns, 2013, p. 15; Ferguson, 2004, p. 46), and haughtily acknowledged they were "worthy of and receptive to Christian benevolence" (p. 8), but we at times saw their innocence and unaffected nature as a "refreshing contrast to the worldly excesses of an artificial and increasingly mechanized world" (p. 8). Yet as Rosenkrantz and Vinovskis (1979) noted, "coercion, control, and cost containment could easily overrule even the reverence for family stability" (quoted in Ferguson, 2004, p. 46).

What that often meant for the most profoundly disabled were long stretches of time spent in the almshouse—the "home for hopeless causes" (Ferguson, 2004, p. 46)—and later in asylums. By the middle of 19th Century, we had come to believe that institutions of all stripes were where "all types of devalued, or simply nonproductive, groups of people" (p. 46) belonged. The care was purportedly superior to the care they received at home—and more humane. With rare exception, this was not the case. Almshouses "quickly devolved into a system notorious for the cruelty of its treatment of those least able to fend for themselves" (Ferguson, p. 60). Ferguson further suggests that the intellectually disabled were caught up in society's growing disgust with able-bodied poor people. Poverty was the fault of the individual, who was seen by society as either lazy or incapable—as disabled (p. 51). "Pauperism was a moral choice, even a physical disease, as much as an economic outcome" (p. 52), Ferguson explained. Although the number of intellectually disabled inmates in almshouses declined during this period, and most intellectually disabled people actually lived in society (pp. 57, 58), we saw them as "inescapable burden" (p. 59).

Presaging the eugenics movement, intellectual disability quickly found a slot on the list of conditions supporting the "pseudoscientific linkage between heredity and a whole array of social ills" (Longmore, 2003, p. 45). Even folks with mild intellectual disabilities would come to be "blamed for poverty, vice, and crime" (p. 45). As with the poor, people with intellectual disabilities were blamed—and if not them, their parents, for their chronic condition (Ferguson, 2004, p. 60). Trent notes that intellectually disabled children were turned away by orphan asylums; they attended the schools for blind, deaf and dumb students until Samuel Howe in 1847 persuaded legislators in Massachusetts to furnish the funds to establish "for an idiot school" (p. 13). The Massachusetts School for Idiotic Children, later known as the Fernald School, opened the following year (D'Haem, 2016, p. 8). Howe had been moved to act after reading an article by John Conolly, chief physician at a lunatic asylum in England. A trip to two institutions in Paris in the early 1840s, during which he observed famed educator Edouard Seguin in action, convinced Conolly that "[t]here is no case incapable of some amendment; that every case may be improved, or cured, up to a certain point [is] a principle of great general importance in reference to treatment" (p. 13) of those with intellectual disabilities. Several states followed Massachusetts' lead in establishing schools to serve this population. But public recognition of the potential of individuals with intellectual disabilities to be educated was slow to materialize, Trent argues, despite the fact that the new schools admitted primarily students whose abilities would guarantee a "high success ratio," as Longmore (2003) contended (p. 45).

So superintendents, joined by students who had been "transformed by their efforts," (p. 15) took their show on the road to states that had not yet built schools for individuals with intellectual disabilities. They lobbied officials and philanthropists, had the students demonstrate what they had learned, and shared "techniques and administrative trends" (p. 16). Their promotional efforts, argued Trent, paved the way "for the emergence of idiocy as a social and cognitive construct" (p. 16). The "newly developed group of advocates" built their theory of how to train students around Seguin's work. Seguin believed that an intellectual disability "was the result of a flawed interaction of the will and the nervous system that affected the mind" (p. 46). This interaction left an individual "controlled by his instincts and separated from the moral world" (p. 45). Seguin designed a variety of techniques to "excite the will, to invigorate the muscles, and to train the senses" (p. 16), which until he worked with a child, had been "dormant" (p. 47). Applying his methods would tame "developmental deficits" (Longmore, 2003, p. 45) and by age 16 individuals with intellectual disabilities would be off to ply a trade or work on a farm. They would be reintegrated into their communities.

But this being America, government officials and the medical community quickly acted to pathologize intellectual disabilities. The quickest way to create a problem is to define it, as Susan Sontag might have argued. Levels of severity were soon established. Individuals with intellectual disabilities were said to be "passionate, filthy, self-abusive, animal-like, gluttonous, given to irrational behavior, intemperate, and possessed of all varieties of physical abnormalities" (Trent, p. 17). And thanks to improvements by the U.S. government in how the Census was conducted, there were more people to categorize and marginalize (Longmore, 2003, p. 45). Linus Brockett, a Connecticut reformer, asserted that an intellectual disability was "the direct result of violation of the physical and moral laws which govern our being" (p. 18). An immoral or depraved parent "inflicts upon his hapless offspring a life of utter vacuity" (p. 18), he claimed. Carefully orchestrated student demonstrations followed by grim reminders of what their lives had been like before enrolling in the schools—"making bizarre noises, masturbating frequently and in public, eating their own excrement, and abusing themselves" (p. 19)—heightened public fear of "moral degeneracy" (p. 19), which had been folded into the construct of idiocy. Enrolling them in schools reduced the threat and kept them away from the "worldly temptations" that awaited them in society. "Only under the guidance, care, and restraint of the institution could moral idiocy be controlled," Trent explained (p. 23).

Soon, the focus of reformers would shift from proving that individuals with intellectual disabilities could return to the community and enjoy productive lives to deploying them exclusively within the institutions. Trent summarized the emerging theory: "only under the guidance, care, and restraint of the institution could moral idiocy be controlled." (p. 23). And sustain the legitimacy of the institutions, Trent noted. Their success and the resultant publicity caused school officials to change their admission requirements to admit children and young adults with more severe disabilities. This meant implementing a regimen of "tedious, individualized training" (p. 28) conducted within "a family-like environment" and revolving around "minute-by-minute involvement" (p. 28) with their students. It also meant increased enrollment. Increased enrollment in turn meant experiencing a broader range of disabilities. So long as the schools kept on dispatching their more successful students back into the community, government funds would continue to roll in. Meanwhile, students with more severe disabilities, admitted to persuade officials and the public that the schools and their methods were legitimate, received less attention. Yet school officials persuaded lawmakers to allow them to admit more students who were grappling with these challenges (p. 29). Even as they continued to promote their ability to educate and reintegrate students with intellectual disabilities, Trent claims, officials were "preparing the way for custody" (p. 29). For his part, Howe publicly rejected institutionalization even as enrollment in his schools grew. But he also had concluded that individuals with intellectual disabilities would likely not be productive outside of the institution, in part because of a lackluster national economy. They must be cared for and educated, he said. This shift in rationale kept schools like his in business—and enabled them to expand (p. 31). But it was the shift in narrative that would prove more destructive: the nation now had to grapple with "the burden of the feebleminded" (p. 31).

It did so, Trent claimed, by medicalizing intellectual disabilities. In fact, all disabilities were subsequently seen as caused by "a biological insufficiency that could be ameliorated by what we now call professional intervention" (Longmore, 2003, p. 150). Paul Longmore (2003) succinctly summarized the shift: "custodialism replaced education" (p. 45). Educators were replaced by superintendents. At one time, Longmore explained, parents were permitted to withdraw their children from school. Superintendents then began to demand "exclusive authority" (2003, p. 45) over them. A number of educators nevertheless continued to argue that segregating children with intellectual disabilities was "obsolete and unjustifiable" (Dudley-Marling & Burns, 2013, p. 16) and that they would benefit from contact with other students in a typical classroom setting. Yet the asylum—"with its dependence on medical practice, medical institutional structure and medical paradigms" (p. 36)—replaced the school. What once were students now were inmates (p. 37). It was the individual's fault—not society's—that the individual's disability had to be dealt with. As Trent so compellingly put it, "A sick idiot fit a custody model better than did an educated and productive one" (p. 38). More important for our journey is Trent's observation that "physician superintendents" (p. 39) defined for the rest of us what it meant to have an intellectual disability.

By this point of course, the eugenics movement was in full misanthropic swing. Eugenicists wished to operationalize their findings to purge society of undesirable groups of people—including individuals with intellectual disabilities—by involuntary sterilization and euthanasia (see Gould, 1996). They endeavored to "recognize limits, segregate, and curtail breeding to prevent further deterioration of an endangered American stock, threatened by immigration from without and by prolific reproduction of its feeble-minded from within" (Gould, p. 189).

Measurement-happy scientists like Francis Galton, who coined the term eugenics, found themselves playing to an increasingly receptive audience by the end of the 19th century, notes Longmore (p. 36). After a period of allowing for the possibility that individuals with intellectual disabilities could share America's preoccupation with success (Trent, p. 133), we had come to believe that in only a handful of cases could individuals with intellectual disabilities function in society. "Without a head, one could not get ahead," as Trent (p. 134) so indelicately put it. The rest constituted a stifling burden on society and a threat to the stability of their families (Longmore, p. 151). Trent believes that a crushing economic depression, labor strife, the emergence of Jim Crow, our growing antipathy toward immigrants from Eastern Europe, and the rise of the "robber baron" also accelerated the transformation of intellectual disabilities from mere burden to "menace" by 1910 (pp. 137, 141). Armed with—and emboldened by—fallacious data generated by eugenicists, officials like Walter Fernald, for whom the Massachusetts school referenced earlier was named, could announce in 1912 that "feeble-mindedness is the mother of crime, pauperism, and degeneracy" (p. 151). They spread the gospel of testing with missionary zeal. Henry Goddard, the first scientist to encourage widespread use of Binet's test (Gould, 1996, p. 189), even came up with another designation just for the occasion: moron (Gould, 1996, pp. 188-204; Trent, p. 158).

The solution? Keep intellectually disabled individuals confined in institutions that the more able among them might possibly help to run (Trent, p. 143). And eventually nudge them out of the public schools, which would continue to test for intelligence as a way of differentiating "normals from abnormals" (p. 144). Ironically, as Stephen Jay Gould (1996) has noted in his groundbreaking book *The Mismeasure of Man*, testing pioneer Alfred Binet was worried—with good reason it turned out—that educators would use the results of his test "as an indelible label, rather than as a guide for identifying children who needed help" (p. 181). He believed that while "[s]ome children might be innately incapable of normal achievement…all could improve with special help" (p. 182). Binet had nothing but contempt for teachers who disregarded students with low scores. "We must protest and react against this brutal pessimism," he said in 1909. "We must try to demonstrate that it is founded upon nothing" (quoted in Gould, p. 184).

Sadly, those protests, if they did take place, didn't change the minds of most educators. Faced with a massive influx of students of all intellectual abilities caused by enactment of compulsory attendance laws, the nation's public schools focused on preparing students with intellectual disabilities for life in the institution (Trent, 1994, p. 144). Only those with mild intellectual disabilities were encouraged to attend. "The obviously impaired remained at home or were placed in institutions" (p. 146). Further, teachers for the most part did not adapt instruction in order to reach students with varying degrees of aptitude and inclination to learn. The first sighting of the "intellectually disabled kids hinder typical kids in class" argument occurred at about this time. Now labeled "mentally deficient," "backward," or "laggard," these students had become targets of scorn and ridicule from classmates. Following the lead of several European countries, our public schools began to establish separate classes, and turned to medical superintendents at institutions for training and guidance, a role they embraced—but largely for self-promotional reasons. They became fervent advocates for special education classes (Trent, 1994, p. 151)—but again, only as a prelude to eventual and lifelong institutionalization.

D'Haem (2016) claims that once in these institutions, intellectually disabled adolescents learned little, and did so in squalid conditions. Our contempt for them was alive and well. We see a clue in the title of the first special education text, *Laggards in Our Schools*, written in 1915 by Leonard Ayres, chair of a Russell Sage Foundation committee (www.russellsagefoundation.org) in charge of "Backward Children Investigation" (D'Haem, p. 3). The prevailing view was that educating individuals with intellectual disabilities was "a waste of resources." For others, they were a "menace" that had to be "removed from the general population so they would not reproduce" (D'Haem, pp. 3-4). The U.S. Supreme Court infamously agreed 12 years later, in its ruling in *Buck v. Bell*. The high court ruled that forced sterilization was legal; its decision has yet to be overturned. Writing for the Court, famed Justice Oliver Wendell Holmes contended that the nation often asks its "best citizens" to sacrifice for the common good. "It would be strange if it could not call upon those who already sap the strength of the state for these lesser sacrifices" (quoted in Trent, 1994, p. 198). Besides, most intellectually disabled women wouldn't know what was being done to them or why. It was a small price to pay, Holmes argued, to prevent the nation from "being swamped with incompetence." In an often cited passage from the opinion, Holmes concluded, "[t]hree generations of imbeciles are enough" (p. 199). By 1931, 29 states had enacted sterilization laws (Longmore, 2003, p. 46). Despite the realization by officials that it would be impossible to institutionalize the entire population of intellectually disabled people, the number of "inmates" increased dramatically (p. 46). Yet budget cuts caused by the Depression and our entry into World War II caused officials to realize that it might be cheaper to educate moderately disabled children than to institutionalize them (p. 49).

There were tiny hints of progress. Medical professionals in charge of institutions, uncomfortable with the success of eugenicists in scaring the public about the intellectually disabled, became advocates for "adjustment and adaptation" (Trent, 1994, p. 181) and for turning to the community as a source of services. Trent (1994) claims they were also daunted at the prospect of institutionalizing all intellectually disabled people (p. 181) yet wanted to retain their professional authority over the "feebleminded." By shedding the "menace" rhetoric, they were able to persuade the public that they were best equipped to care for those recast as "maladjusted perpetual defective[s]" (p. 181).

Research had revealed that the experience of an intellectual disability was influenced by environment (Longmore, p. 49). A few officials and educators realized that it would benefit intellectually disabled students to interact with peers who did not have disabilities (Dudley-Marling & Burns, 2013, p. 16). Yet the laws in place allowed "but did not require" (p. 16) school districts to provide an education to students with intellectual disabilities. In 1934, an Ohio appeals court in *Board of Education of Cleveland Heights v. State* ruled that children with an IQ of 50 or less could be excluded from school. "[A]s a matter of common sense it is apparent that a moron of very low type, or an idiot, or imbecile is incapable of absorbing knowledge" (quoted in D'Haem, 2016, p. 3 the court asserted. Still, parents, empowered in part by the Supreme Court's landmark 1954 decision in *Brown v. Board of Education*, began to advocate for their children. They demanded that the worst of the institutions be closed, that they be supplanted by community-based facilities, and that schools create classes for their kids (Longmore, 2003, p. 49; D'Haem, 2016, p. 11). They scored a key victory in 1971 when a Pennsylvania court ruled that the state's public schools had to provide an education to *all* students between the ages of 6 and 21. The court struck down a state law that permitted officials to back out of educating "uneducable" or "untrainable" students (*Pennsylvania Association for Retarded Children v. Commonwealth of Pennsylvania*; see D'Haem, 2016, p. 4; Dudley-Marling & Burns, 2013, p. 16). Activism also compelled the District of Columbia to offer "a free, appropriate education to all students regardless of the severity of their disabilities" (Dudley-Marling & Burns, p. 16).

In 1975, Congress passed the Education for All Handicapped Children Act, which required that districts educate disabled students in the "least restrictive environment"—according to their needs and not the label society had applied to them. Disabled students and those without disabilities are in class together, with disabled students in separate classes "only when the nature or severity of the disability is such that education in regular classes with the use of supplementary aids and services cannot be achieved satisfactorily," the Act states (quoted in McLeskey, Landers, Williamson, & Hoppey, 2012, p. 131). Before the Act, which was reauthorized in 1997 as the Individuals with Disabilities Education Act (IDEA), and then modified in 2004 and renamed the Individuals with Disabilities Education Improvement Act (IDEIA), only one-fifth of the country's disabled students attended public schools.

By the end of the last decade, the U.S. Department of Education reported that thanks to the IDEA and inclusion, three times as many folks with disabilities now go to college, and twice as many 20-year olds with disabilities have jobs (Haller, 2010, p. 87). All told, kids with disabilities account for 11 percent of our student population. Moreover, when it comes to covering disability, journalists devote the most space to disabled kids and to inclusion (p. 87). All well and good—but what is the experience actually like for students like Neil who are covered by the IDEA?

So here's the reality: We have a ways to go. While most parents support inclusion, they also remain concerned that teachers spend too much time with intellectually disabled kids, whose at times disruptive behavior they believe makes it harder for their kids to learn (Kimbrough & Mellen, 2012)—this despite ample evidence that the presence of intellectually disabled children in class does not hamper the academic performance of their nondisabled colleagues, and that in fact, the latter group benefits socially from spending time in an inclusive classroom. The same holds true for the kids with intellectual disabilities; one study found that they were "happier, more independent, and more motivated to go to school and participate in class" (Downing and Peckham-Hardin, 2007; quoted in Kimbrough & Mellen, 2012). Their parents worry, as we do, that they'll be isolated during the school day and might not get as much attention or instruction as their classmates. They also continue to believe that general education teachers just can't make sufficient accommodations for their kids. They even fear being stigmatized by the parents of kids who don't have disabilities.

Teachers are similarly conflicted. A survey conducted in 2008 revealed that while they endorse accommodating intellectually disabled students, the same teachers reject the idea of immersion altogether (Santoli, Sachs, Romey, & McClurg, 2008; quoted in Kimbrough & Mellen, 2012), especially if there's the potential for disruptive behavior. They often feel unqualified to teach intellectually disabled students (Braunsteiner & Mariano-Lapidus, 2014, p. 35). Like the parents referenced earlier, teachers recognize the social growth that can occur for both groups of students, but the folks who teach non-disabled students worry that they spend too much time with intellectually disabled kids. They also believe that intellectually disabled students aren't mastering too much of the curriculum and that, even if they were, there is often no way to accurately chart what they are learning (Downing & Peckham-Hardin, 2007). There's no time for both sets of teachers to collaborate on strategies that might make it easier for intellectually disabled kids to take part in the traditional curriculum. Some of the teachers who work primarily with non-disabled kids are frustrated with how little they are able to contribute to the activities and materials that intellectually disabled students experience while in the inclusion class (Kimbrough & Mellen, 2012). These findings seem to support the contention by experts that advocates for inclusion, though well intentioned, "have erred by placing too much emphasis on the place an education occurs and not enough emphasis on the quality of instruction and educational outcomes for students" (McLeskey, Landers, Williamson, & Hoppey, 2012, p. 132).

Students are only slightly more enlightened. They favor including students with intellectual disabilities, but only in art and gym class. They are concerned that their teachers in "academic" classes would focus unfairly on intellectually disabled students, resulting in lower grades. They're happy to hang out with intellectually disabled students, but only while at school. Forget coming over or heading to a movie (Siperstein, Parker, Bardon, & Wideman, 2007). Yet once again, in true "broken record" fashion, they see the positive social impact, the school experience enhanced by "providing diversity and giving them the opportunity to learn about people who face challenges different from their own" (Kimbrough & Mellen, 2012).

It's all about them, in other words.

And this halting progress only happens at schools that have embraced the inclusion model. When intellectually disabled students attend only special education classes, non-disabled students are more likely to bully the intellectually disabled students and less likely to defend them against bullying from their peers (Bunch & Valeo, 2004). Friendships far more often in schools that have implemented the inclusion model (Bunch & Valeo, 2004). It's heartwarming—but only to a point—that we've changed our language. We now say, for example, "barriers to learning and participation" instead of "special educational needs" (Braunsteiner & Mariano-Lapidus, 2014, p. 3). It's reassuring to know that capable, passionate people are working assiduously to promote a truly inclusive culture and attendant policies and practices. But there's a staged feel to it all. Boxes are ticked, goals are met, measurements made. But how well does this actually work? Where does Neil go during the day? During a week this past April, he spent a day in the gym and one in the library while the rest of the students in his school underwent mandatory state testing. Sheila once had to remind school officials that Neil's IEP required them to provide a "one on one" for him at all times. And he sometimes comes home with his diaper on backward—though I'm grateful to hand over a couple of his daily changes.

It's all pretty ironic given my approach to teaching—flexible, permissive, inclusive, built on a healthy respect for my students and a recognition of the experiences they bring on our journeys. Since I started at Drexel, I've invited my students to partake of Thanksgiving dinner with us here at the ranch; only two have ever taken me up on the offer, but I mainly want them to know I care. I consider myself a tour guide, there to nudge and steer them to self-teach, to learn with them. In a very limited way, I emulate the great educator Paulo Friere. No condescension, treatment as equals—I'm not sure my approach is effective, since I also don't believe in performance measurement, and rarely read my own performance evaluations, worried that I'll turn my classes into Yelp-driven bland and uncontroversial boxes on a checklist. I also tend not to think of what I do as an approach. I sometimes envy the structure and precision I see in the preparation of colleagues, but I am convinced that my flexibility encourages my students to strike out on their own.

But that doesn't excuse the times when I just completely drop the pedagogical ball with Neil, when I think about school as a place to stash him seven hours while we attempt to catch up, catch our breath, do our work, not have to tend to him every second, when I fantasize about a colleague's kid coming into my office, seeing the baseballs and mitts and telling me he or she likes baseball. We promptly head out for a game of catch. I'm consigned to watching escalator videos. I curate them extensively, but my grumpiness kicks in way too often. I resentfully attribute it to all the time I have to spend just tending to his medical needs. We talk about where the escalators he loves so much are located, and plan on visiting them someday. The Macy's on Herald Square in New York. The Namesti Miru subway stop in Prague. Our travelogue has expanded to home improvement stores across the country—provided they survive Amazon.com—to check out the latest and greatest in ceiling fans. "That's so smart!" I shout when he makes a connection or answers a question. And look at what I have taught him, I rant to myself: how to throw, how to catch. I want to be *seen* as having taught him, that what I've taught him has as much value, and that he enjoys it more, than recognizing numbers and forming sentences. So like the students who'll participate in Best Buddies but never invite a kid with intellectual disabilities to the family abode for pizza, I sort of abandon him once the bell rings, or once the breathing and feeding treatments are over.

I can barely look at him when I come back into the office from the kitchen after feeding the dog—and furtively acquiring a bottle of wine for us to split. I don't want him to get agitated, of course, but there's also a sizable amount of shame fueling the lack of eye contact. It's the paradox—one of many—folks like us face: you struggle like hell, every millisecond of every day, to properly care for your child without doing damage, either through ineptitude or anger, and yet you don't really want anyone else doing it, even when it is becoming clear that your ability to do it is slipping away, or was limited in the first place. Sometimes this struggle takes place internally—a week ago, Sheila volunteered to take Neil for a few spins on the Barnes and Noble escalator so that I could take a breath and perhaps peruse the magazines. Neil now melts down when folks use the escalator—more precisely, when there's a gap in usage. It's fine if a steady stream of folks heads toward us on the ground floor, but he much prefers it empty, as if he's in total control. Yet I almost broke down as Sheila lovingly took his hand and they ascended to the second floor. I don't want it to become their thing; it's *my* thing. It's our thing.

Thrown into that mix is age—creeping, destructive, strength sapping age. Oh, and pride and jealousy. I sometimes feel with a sour pride that it takes two or more people to change the dude's diaper and keep him happy when I'm not around. In those times, I have totally disregarded my beautiful wife's experiences with him, her perceptions of him, her feelings toward him. As I said, empathy can easily become the first casualty of life with a child who has intellectual disabilities.

And there's a line too about sharing it with my students. A few years back, we donated money to the R-Word organization. Our contribution brought us a blue armband on which was imprinted the organization's logo. I then ordered 50 more with the intent of giving it to the students in my classes. The topic of the class was free speech: I turned the distribution of the wristbands into an object lesson about political correctness, a discussion about whether the organization was guilty of trying to censor a society that had yet to become acquainted with trigger warnings. It led to one of the deeper discussions of the term; most of the folks in class gladly took the wristbands, and I saw them throughout the rest of the term. For that, I felt good. But as I mentioned, we're not really joiners, or even earnest members. Largely thanks to the time it takes to care for Neil, too, we're also limited to the occasional donation and event appearance. I felt like I was benefitting professionally from his experience, a feeling amplified by the fact that I couldn't share my conflict with him. I felt dirty. Yet at the same time, I've found that my classes are one of the few places where I can share these conflicts without judgment. Sure, it could be they're just being nice so that I'll give them As. But I like to think that by being inclusive and compassion-ate, my students feel that they can open up, that it's a different environment.

But if I'm so compassionate, how come now and then I throw something when or after my son thrashes around while changing his diaper? I have also concocted the fact that Sheila manages me like her employees, to fill my time, to constantly test my ability to multitask. And there I am, caught in my lie of being incompetent, of playing incompetent in order to build up the other folks in my life, to make them feel better about themselves. It might work as a teaching style, but it's pretty corrosive, at least to my self-concept and to my love for Sheila—as part of a relationship. I'm unable to make the negative thoughts go away, as I know they should, since they're unfair and absent of even a shred of empathy. Thus, in stretches I begrudge him nearly every moment of my time. I put on a good show in public, but, like the kids whose classrooms include kids with intellectual disabilities, it is all about me.

And the media are no help, at least according to Beth Haller (2010), who conducted one of the very few studies on news media coverage of inclusion. Haller explored the story of Mark Hartmann, then 9, whose behavior in his inclusion class at a school in Virginia—he "pinched, screamed, and threw tantrums" (p. 89)—caused administrators to remove him from the class and place him in a "mainstream" program which meant he'd see his inclusion classmates only for music, art, and gym. Mark's parents claimed the district didn't adequately train his teacher and aide. Citing how well Mark had done at his previous school in Illinois, they argued that "he go to school with his non-disabled friends" (p. 89). They refused to allow officials to move Mark to a special education class, but were overruled by a hearing officer appointed by the state supreme court. Mark's transfer was the first in the U.S. since enactment of IDEA. Undeterred, Mark's mom established residence in West Virginia so that Mark could be part of an inclusion program there. She and Mark traveled 250 miles there and back to rejoin the rest of their family on weekends. By this point, their case had become a national news story. A federal judge ruled in December 1996 that Loudoun County school district officials had not adequately trained its teachers to work with Mark. However, a federal appeals court reversed the decision, asserting that the lower court judge relied too much on testimony from advocates for Mark. The U.S. Supreme Court then declined to hear the case (pp. 90-91).

Haller's analysis revealed an equal number of themes for and against inclusion. Journalists were more interested in highlighting a debate rather than encouraging discussion, she found (p. 104). On the positive side, inclusion was described as having short- and long-term benefits for intellectually disabled kids and as cheaper than institutionalization. More important, coverage reinforced the idea that every child has a right to a free public education. Finally, journalists noted repeatedly how well inclusion has worked in other states (pp. 94-100). Then there were the "oppositional" narratives: disabled students were disruptive; their presence was at times "traumatic" (p. 101) for non-disabled students; they were a distraction from learning; and since some disabled students end up effectively segregated in inclusion classes anyway, inclusion might not be a valid approach after all. But despite the "either-or" or "tennis match" feel in the coverage, the Hartmanns were the catalyst for a slow but genuine improvement in public opinion about inclusion, Haller argues.

I'm not sure the pro-inclusion folks have been able to sustain public acceptance and understanding. First, readers rarely read or hear from the students themselves; this echoes what Haller found in her work on coverage of the Hartmanns. Parents are typically dogged—but also exhausted from having to constantly struggle and monitor what's going on in schools on behalf of their children. It's an ongoing search for the right environment (Bellamy, 2016). A student in Arizona changed schools six times in six years before finally finding a positive environment in which to learn, only to have the district decide to bus intellectually disabled kids to "specialized classrooms" which changed locations every year (Wasu, 2016). The student had enthusiastically announced to an Arizona reporter his love for the school and that he had made new friends. So one more time, parents had to go before the board at a meeting, hire a consultant, and consider legal action. And one more time, district officials declined to comment for fear of violating student rights to confidentiality, but added that they took parent concerns seriously and that they were committed to making decisions in the best interests of the students.

And what about the students—or "these types of kids," as a Special Olympics official in Vermont noted. They seem to be caught in a constant state of becoming—that is when they aren't being prevented from entering a classroom; more than half of students who have intellectual disabilities attend school in segregated classrooms (Bellamy, 2016; Freeman & Grindal, 2016). And when they are allowed into an inclusion class, they, not their counterparts, have to do the blending, adjust their behavior so that their classes aren't disrupted—all for what one school official called a "comparative experience of participation" (Johnson, 2016). But it's an experience imposed upon them, one that doesn't reference or respect who they actually are. We get only happy talk about what students who are not disabled get out of these interactions (Leahy, 2017) and how their stellar behavior can change a school's culture. The compassion shown to students with intellectual disabilities by Best Buddies participants had a significant impact on their classmates; they made it "socially acceptable to take small chances" (Leahy, 2017). Meanwhile, students with intellectual disabilities must aspire to act like their counterparts. "They aren't just there to take," said one parent (Leahy, 2017). It is their parents' read that they want to "feel involved and independent," to make a contribution, feel they are viable" (Leahy, 2017). It also helps if they can mask the differences between themselves and their non-disabled classmates so that an observer would not be able to tell them apart (Williams, "Ending," 2017). My critique is certainly colored by my wish that Neil was as able to participate and to comply as the kids referenced in these pieces, that he could voluntarily go to his seat in the classroom and vocalize his answers. But stories often feature students with intellectual disabilities off on their own islands, thrown lifelines only when teachers get around to it.

Data-obsessed district officials also strive—everyone strives. "It's important to create lasting change," said one, although I would add "or at least be seen in the act of doing so" (Silberman, 2016). Four decades in, they still try "to live up to the law" (Woodruff, 2016). "[B]ig challenges" remain as officials and educators address questions "about how well those efforts are working" (Woodruff, 2016). Canned, reporter-friendly quotes abound. We still talk about the need to correct "longstanding misconceptions regarding the capacities of students to thrive" (Freeman & Grindal, 2016). We still have overworked, overwhelmed—and at times oblivious (Allard, 2017) teachers and therapists—and not enough of either, thanks to burnout-driven resignations, standards of measurement that hold intellectually disabled kids to general education standards (Grida, 2017), and new and persistent budget constraints. One Virginia teacher moved from classroom to classroom in her elementary school rather than have the students come to her—and spent time "beating herself up about being late to her next student and lesson" (Williams, "Ending,'"" 2017). Many of the teachers are talented and dedicated, but if they rabblerouse, question authority, go outside the accepted tactics and techniques, they risk being disciplined. Others are zealots who have "waxed poetic" (Allard, 2017) about the benefits of inclusion but who often fail to recognize that it just isn't right for some kids. And some teachers still flatly oppose the concept. "[T]he more extreme those edges are, academically and behaviorally, the more my instructional choices become dilemmas," a Vermont teacher asserted, "where I have to choose between two incompatible, mutually exclusive objectives, where the only other alternative is that I fail to satisfy either" (Berger, 2017). So the "disruption" theme identified by Haller is alive and well.

For others, inclusion isn't inclusive at all. "In the rush to include everyone," wrote a *Washington Post* columnist, "no one created an option for kids like my daughter, who don't benefit from either inclusion or separate special education setting" (Allard, 2017). But what a rush it is; champions push back against skepticism, against sporadic funding. TED talks are created (Williams, 2017). Educators from other countries visit and marvel at how much all students benefit from inclusion, how all students are respected (Cline, 2017). Probably deserving teachers receive awards for their skill and for their advocacy on behalf of students with intellectual disabilities (Sklar, 2017). Journalists gush about Project Unify, developed by Special Olympics, which "mixes sports and education to engage students with and without disabilities in athletics and leadership opportunities" (Nanez, 2016). The program's success draws admirers from all over the country to check out games and observe an environment "where teenagers have been taught that everyone is different and everyone is able" (Nanez, 2016).

I'm jumping around a bit on the timeline, but this swirl of optimism, zeal, and frustration brought me back to our tour of Neil's high school in the summer of 2016. We were led around by his friendly, peripatetic associate principal who did everything in his rhetorical power to assure us that not only would Neil be safe and be cared for, he would thrive at the school. One mother and father arrived separately; it was clear they had split up. We wondered how many couples had split thanks to the pressures of raising a child with intellectual disabilities. Neil chugged through the halls using his walker with the kind and firm assistance of his paraprofessional, a man about my age with a ruddy complexion. Neil ran over his foot a few times, changed directions suddenly a few times, but he patiently guided him around. We talked at length with his teacher, who has since become a valued member of our village, thanks to her weekly Tuesday visits. We visited the classes where Meadowood kids will land during the day—auto shop, the radio-TV studio, marketing and communications. Sheila and I confessed to each other afterward that we didn't think Neil would actually choose any of those classes—except gym of course. That he loves. During our stop there, he spent a chunk of the time bouncing a basketball against retracted bleachers and laughing at the noise he made, still under the watchful eye of his para. But he did great. The other kids were so big, we thought—the same thought we had when he started middle school, and the same thought we have whenever we look at pictures and videos of him. Until recently, that is, since he's packed on some weight and added the mustache. We met the school nurse, and avoided eye contact with his fifth grade teacher, who was there for the proceedings (this reference will be fleshed out in the next chapter). We noticed again that parents gravitate toward certain teachers, despite the fact that, in this case at least, the teacher likes to do the put-upon act, spewing out what a bother her charges are and making subtle, delivered out of the side of mouth cracks about her kids.

And she won Teacher of the Year.

We talked about job opportunities for Neil after he graduates and begins the state's transition program. He loves shredding paper and delivering the mail, but would he be able to a job for more than 20 minutes at a time? And would an employer treat him well, especially if his attention—and he—wandered like that? Successful transitions to employment, like inclusion on athletic teams, are frequently highlighted by journalists, with the attendant gushing quotes from organizers and officials as the students happily embrace their vocations.

But maybe this is my own prejudice talking—shouting for attention along with my fear and my selfishness. I've seen Neil make amazing strides. Less than a month ago, he fist-bumped successfully and sat in the back seat of the car without his booster seat, both for the first time. He loves school—particularly the aforementioned gym and swimming. By Friday, he's exhausted, but in a good way. So maybe I should ease off. Maybe it's not the teachers and officials who are lacking.

Chapter Eight

The Homecoming Court

Enactment of the IDEA didn't mean that scorn directed at intellectually disabled people magically went away. Proposals to establish group homes are to this day met with resistance, some of it quite vicious. Or that we've all banded together to support inclusion. Despite the inroads made by disability rights advocates, our embrace of the medical model of disability—based on the idea that "labeled people have real and objectively quantifiable deficits, located in their bodies and minds" (Smith, 2010, p. 8)—shows few signs of giving way. Teachers, behaviorists, therapists, and officials endeavor to fix intellectually disabled people—to help them acquire "skills needed to function *normally* in a *normal* environment (italics in original)—at least as far as possible" (Dudley-Marling & Burns, 2013, p. 18). Teachers intervene and accommodate—they exclude intellectually disabled kids from deeper discussions, talk to older disabled students as if they are much younger, dissuade them from interacting socially with their nondisabled peers, and disregard the students' interests when it comes time to find a job (Jorgensen, 2005, p. 5)—all while insisting students strive to overcome their disabilities. They're still too often characterized as the "problem" (Dudley-Marling & Burns, 2013, p. 18) They are asked to do this without disrupting their classes, taught too often by under qualified teachers. Earnest attempts are made to improve their social and communication skills. Yet if they fall short—many are still subjected to the same standardized tests as their peers (Braunsteiner & Mariano-Lapidus, 2014, p. 33)—they still may be excluded or have their participation in inclusion classes curtailed, as has happened to Neil a few times over the years.

It would be wonderful if educators embraced a social constructivist perspective, whose adherents argue that learning "does not reside in the mind of individuals as much as it dwells in activities and cultural practices situated in the context of human relations and institutions" (p. 22). Educators who operate in this mindset concentrate on what the intellectually disabled person brings to the table—the meanings they have made from their experiences. Like his stellar middle school speech therapist, they go in thinking that a person like Neil is capable of learning—that he can do so competently. They are well aware that "it takes a community of people doing just the right things in the right time and place for a student to be identified as disabled" (Dudley-Marling & Burns, 2013, p. 22). It's not enough to modify curriculum, co-teach, or to change the seating arrangement in a classroom to accommodate a wheelchair or two. Yet it's still up to the disabled student to try and "fit in" (p. 26). Normality is still the desired state. Of course, this would require ditching standardized testing, among other reforms that would take decades—not to mention a complete paradigm shift—to implement. But what a world it would be: treating these young people as being capable of learning, using person first language, not talking down to them or dumbing down curriculum, including them in all conversations about their performance in school, focusing on their strengths, recognizing their personalities, and empowering them to take part in the "mainstream of school and community life" (Jorgensen, 2005, p. 9). That begins with or depends on giving them the tools and the instruction they need in order to communicate.

Like most families with school-aged kids, we observe an after-school ritual—several actually. Neil's bus arrives in front of our house at about 3; one of us walks out to assist him off. He's taken of late to squeezing in a nap on the 20-minute or so ride from his high school to our house. As a result, we often have to pop up into the bus to help his trusty aide and driver wake him and coax him to disembark. Coaxing is sometimes necessary on days when he doesn't nap. We receive a brief report about his ride. Neil now looks for his friends is as he gets on and off the bus. Since the bus, during the regular school year at least, carries kids with special needs, there is a sense of community.

We walk carefully across the front yard, making sure we step on the three square pieces of slate in the garden (the number jumped to four after a misstep split one of the pieces, and then to 20-plus when that piece shattered), stop at the porch, take a careful step up, and head for the door. After the weather turns colder, I take off his jacket. Neil nearly always heads immediately for the stairs, climbs to the landing and waits for David or one of his babysitters—or one of us—to partake in an hour of climbing and variations on Step-Ball before heading off—usually under protest—to do his breathing treatments and have his dinner.

As he waits, I drop his backpack next to Sheila's chair. She reads any and all communication from Neil's teacher, school officials, and the district as I go back to the stairs or crash back at my desk. She summarizes the day's events, hitting the highlights (worked on his shredding job or pushed the cart carrying menus to the cafeteria) and less than highlights ("Uh oh—Neil pulled a little girl's hair, Daddy"). Within seconds, our dog inserts himself between Sheila and her desk and begins to whimper. Turns out our dog has to announce to the neighborhood and any wildlife that's breached the suburban sprawl that "the boy" has come home. He does the same thing when Sheila or I come home. While the dog is out, we sign permission slips, review works of art, toss wet or soiled clothes in the wash, and remind him about upcoming activities that he particularly likes (You're going *swimming* tomorrow, Mister Neil!). If it's a David day, he's already taken Neil's pulse and temp, checked his lungs, and been dispatched by Neil up the stairs.

We pull out Neil's worksheets. In the past, they have featured examples of stamping (his name in rectangular blocks on the page, or brightly colored dots placed within in a letter or number; number recognition exercises; and one-page treatises on periods in history, with keywords pasted or stuck to the page to highlight key concepts. We—or maybe just I—think that there's very little chance that Neil completed them by himself, or without help. We definitely think this when a neatly colored item comes home in the backpack. Maybe he sits still long enough, I think, to observe and enjoy tracing one's hand to produce a Thanksgiving turkey. Otherwise, it's hand over hand or a scribble or two of his own. While he will from time to time sign birthday and Christmas cards for relatives and friends, it's usually a fight—he's never liked holding a pencil or crayon—so we forge his signature. We're investigating the purchase of a name stamp. Sheila and I recap stories from the worksheets and compliment him about his improving number and letter recognition and his stamping.

We have to quickly get in our commentary and congratulations though, since Neil will move along with dispatch to tearing up his work. We have given up persuading him to ponder them. We've managed to save a few pieces of art; a green owl peeking out from between two trees and a Pollockesque turkey are pinned to our office bulletin board. And I saved on my computer the fact sheet we wrote for him about the Mayflower (on which the aforementioned Abraham Pierson and his family sailed to America in 1639). But most of what Neil doesn't tear up is tossed into the recycling bin three or four days after they come home at the latest. Like many parents in America, we would be hip-deep in archival material if we saved everything he did or had a role in doing. But his work occupies precious little space in the dozen or so memory boxes we've created during our time together.

Having Neil attend inclusion classes in a public school opens for us one of few what for now I'll call (awkwardly) a "window of typicality." For one thing, Sheila and I get to revisit our love of school, or aspects of it anyway. We are energized—emboldened—by the promise of a new school year. We mainly like to shop for school supplies and Sheila for clothes for Neil. Our love for the latter is not diminished in any way by our shared opposition (I'm a longtime opponent; Sheila has come around) to school uniforms. As we cruise Target each year, I'm saddened sometimes by the fact that we don't buy Neil a typical complement of supplies: notebooks, pencils, glue sticks. He gets a new backpack and perhaps a new folder in which his teacher sends home the aforementioned forms and work, but that's about it. I'm also saddened by the fact that Sheila has for the most part given up buying Neil math and vocabulary workbooks. Yet it also should be noted I am never saddened by the 1996 Staples ad which concludes with a gleeful father riding across the frame on the back of a shopping cart as the holiday classic *It's the Most Wonderful Time of the Year* plays.

As Neil has gotten older, fewer worksheets have been sent home. I miss not getting them. This year, his teacher has added a "My Day at School" sheet to our communication, with stamped (by Neil) indications of whether he had a good, bad, or "OK" day, whether he was happy, mad, or sad, whether he ventured outside the school or stayed in class, did or didn't finish his work, and whether he earned a "Bee Buck" for being "cooperative, responsible, and safe" per rules established as part of the district's adoption of the Positive Behavior Support (PBS) program. Check out this description: "PBS is an approach for assisting school personnel in adopting and organizing evidenced (sic)-based behavioral interventions into an integrated continuum that enhances academic and social behavior outcomes for all students" ("The Meadowood Program," 2014). Somewhere George Orwell is smiling.

A lot of Neil's activities these days are of a vocational nature, in the hopes that he'll be able someday to hold down a job. Lately, he's been delivering menus to folks in the cafeteria, although his route was modified somewhat because he hasn't yet developed the stamina to complete his route (his high school is much larger than his middle school). He's also sorted mail, put dirty laundry in his middle school's washing machine (and taken it out of the dryer), pushed a cart loaded with juice and other drinks to the cafeteria. He's visited a local university medical school with his inclusion classmates, has racked up nearly a dozen perfect attendance certificates, and was named by his Meadowood friends to his new school's Homecoming Court this past fall. We both were a bit nervous about him receiving the honor. I had *Carrie*-like images of him being made fun of while up on stage.

Neil looked dapper in his navy blue sweater vest and blue and green plaid shirt. He seemed excited about the event, but wanted to hit our hallway stairs as we made our way out to the minivan to head to the school. Then he wanted to go into the main building instead of heading up to the stadium. He was then fine going up the steep hill to the field and waiting for Sheila to return from parking the car (she drives nearly everywhere now because Neil has refused to stop pulling from the right rear passenger seat at her hair and the collars of her shirts). He waited somewhat patiently near the stands as the first half quickly passed, perking up when folks would walk up and down the nearby stairs into the stands. I hadn't seen live football since we went to a Temple game three or four years ago. I now and then went into play-by-play mode, commenting several times on the staggering size difference between Neil's team and their opponents. Sheila just wanted the evening to go well.

The young woman selected as ninth grade Homecoming Queen smiled broadly in our direction as the ninth grade assistant principal introduced her; she resumed talking with her friends, then with about two minutes to go in the half, whisked Neil away in his stroller chair. We worried about what the kids might be saying to him as he sat by the end zone fence as the half wound down. By half's end, with his team down by more than 30 points, he had been moved across the field, and was enjoying what was going on. Mostly he was enjoying the young woman's long brown hair. But he was happy, even if the other chief source of that happiness might have been fans walking up and down the bleacher steps. Sheila and I rushed up the ramp to snap a few photos after he moved across the field to in front of the grandstand as the marching band—20 strong—and cheerleaders did their thing.

It turned out that Neil was voted in by the entire ninth grade class. We were stunned—and proud, but I was more relieved. I use these occasions to judge how much he's actually wanted. The very earnest assistant principal told us several times at the game how much he's loved and how he's thriving at the school. That, I'm sorry to say, is sometimes enough for me. And I don't know if that's because I don't believe he'll learn more, or that his cognitive abilities will improve. I just want him to be safe and happy. I'm not much further along than my folks were, I guess. After my mom's two terms as PTA president, her involvement and interest in my education dwindled a bit, though she did make a hell of an Owl (from *Winnie the Pooh*) costume for me one Halloween and acquitted herself with aplomb and dedication for a couple of years as a Cub Scout den mother; dad's struggling business, and her decision to assume control of his books and payroll, swallowed up a lot of her time. But by the time my brother was in high school, we were pretty much on our own. This approach has morphed in my own teaching into allowing my students to find their own path through our material, with me serving as self-effacing tour guide. I do wonder though how much Neil's actually getting out of his anatomy, algebra, and English classes. So far, it seems as though his communication technology class is his favorite. The kids head to the high school's radio station studio. Even if he has his eyes opened a little, or he picks up something, or makes meaning of the experience in his way, then that's cool.

The IDEA requires school officials, ideally in consultation with parents, to create and annually revise an Individualized Education Plan (IEP) for all students with disabilities. The process begins when parents receive written notice about the need to meet. Actually, the primary objective is to determine whether a student continues to be eligible for services. If officials and parents agree that the student is eligible, the IEP is then developed or revised. Parents in our district also complete a Priority Skills Form, on which they list their goals for their children.

That's the law. The experience is annually unsettling. It was at Neil's first IEP meeting that we were informed that based on testing, Neil would be labeled "severely mentally retarded" for the state's purposes. He climbed the ladder to "trainably mentally retarded." Today, he has a "moderate intellectual disability," so at least the terminology has become a little friendlier. We get underway by signing in. Officials are required under the IDEA to offer us a copy of the Notice of Procedural Safeguards. We aren't required to accept it. They joke about killing trees; we joke about our files bulging with copies, about being able to wallpaper a room—or two. We recognize, if not appreciate, the intent, the law, the ritual, but we usually toss it into the recycling bin.

It's not that we wouldn't leap into the fray if we felt that Neil wasn't being treated well. It's just that the rest of the gauntlet we endure each day just to take care of him prevents us from taking a deeper dive into the law's nuances. The district's psychologist batted leadoff with her triennial evaluation of Neil. A list of Neil's physical and cognitive challenges was read. Everyone around the table is fully aware that he needs continued services and therapies, yet we all have to agree out loud so that it can be duly noted and the funding from the state secured. He'll spend less than 40 percent of his time in his inclusion classes. This year, the psychologist was particularly officious as she recounted visits with Neil to assess his behavior. His inclusion class teacher complimented him for being quite social and noted that he sat through the aforementioned dissection, but wasn't permitted to use the tools. Neil loves to people watch and is able to communicate what he wants—most of the time it's going to gym, or to get his backpack and jacket in order to head home...or somewhere. Neil's speech therapist reported enthusiastically that he can now sit for 30 minutes at a table in a group setting without getting upset (for the record, during summer school in 2016, he was up to nearly 50 minutes). Before the meeting, she shared with us a video of Neil interacting happily with a classmate. "They were playing!" she announced.

Neil is quite capable of understanding and following requests. When you ask him to back up from the top of steps so that he won't fall, he complies. When you ask him to rise to his feet because he's about to have a snack, he does. When ask him to turn off his DJ Master Keyboard, he carefully depresses the switch. He's become more cooperative and continues to benefit from exposure to his inclusion classmates, she said. His temper is still an issue, though, and he can't stand still for too long without fidgeting or acting out. But much celebration takes place when he successfully uses his device to communicate, she said happily. The team wondered if it made Neil sad or uncomfortable to see everyone else eating lunch while he had nothing. We reminded them of the fight he put up years back when teachers and paras tried to feed him, but were open to the idea of letting him sample some ice cream or yogurt or something his colleagues cooked in class. The nurse reminded us that we'd need an order from his doctor to make this happen.

His physical therapist hit on what became the meeting's main theme: potential. He has so much talent, she said—several times. It was her goal to tap into it. The team had chronicled more drops while Neil was in his gait trainer traversing the hallways on his delivery job. It was disconcerting to hear that Neil would no longer walk through the school without the gait trainer. We were also a bit saddened at the news that he had been laid off from his menu delivery job and had resumed shredding. He likes it—especially the sound made by the machine. We offered that he might just be tired since he has to cover more ground. Rather than explore new prompts, we thought offering him a chance to rest might be a solution. During catch, he can now trap a ball to his chest with one hand, something we've been working on at home. She urged us—as had her predecessors—to discourage Neil from sitting in a "W" position. Persuade him to side sit or long sit, she said.

The discussion of his drops took me back to his eighth grade graduation ceremony held in June 2016. We sat near the back of the auditorium after handing Neil over to his caring and skilled eighth grade teacher, Fiona. One of the area's few theatre organs played as the kids marched in. Neil and his Meadowood classmates were at the front of the line, and took their place in the front couple of rows, stage left, so that they could have easy access to the stage when the time came to receive their diplomas. He then marched steadily in his walker across the stage, even pausing to shake hands with the principal - and even after the teacher charged with reading the students' names changed gears and started with kids whose last names begin with Z because they traditionally have had to wait. There was genuine applause for Neil and his colleagues, although from the family behind us it took on more of an "isn't that nice they allow kids like Neil to participate" quality. But two of their kids went after each other for most of the ceremony, so they likely have their own battles to fight.

It angered and I regret to say disappointed me to see him using his walker as he navigated toward the stage. I knew why: officials didn't want to prolong the ceremony. I'm a teacher, and love attending graduations, but they run long. But we worked so hard to instill the confidence in him to walk— and had to do it all over again during fifth grade. He walks from his chair to the escalator, from our Florida Room to the steps, and can, if he's fascinated by or enamored with an object or person, practically run to it or them. And now, the real reason: he had achieved something! And it was one less thing to cart around. It would be a step backward to have him use it at home. Sheila patiently explained that it gave him more freedom. Ha - freedom! He's used the walker we subsequently ordered for him exactly twice; it sits in our garage under some tarps. We wrapped up the day with some escalator time at the bookstore. Flashed the martyr creds by rushing back from the magazine racks, but we had a lot of fun. And then? He whined all the way back to the car. And we had our first attempted driver asphyxiation, as he yanked from the back seat on my seat belt. I dialed up my vacant, only slightly exasperated look, but kept cool as Sheila bravely dove in to stop Neil, only to have her hair yanked again.

Some belated backstory: we've had promising and soul-crushing experiences with Neil's teachers as he's made his way to high school. The former sportswriter in me couldn't help but note that for a while, the promising experiences took place in even-numbered years (K, 2nd, 4th) and the soul-crushing experiences in the odd-numbered years (1st, 3rd, 5th). I thought of the San Francisco Giants, who won the World Series in 2010, 2012, and 2014. Neil's kindergarten teacher is a calm, patient, encouraging young woman who left teaching in the ensuing years to become a behaviorist; she now works for Dave, a jargon-happy practitioner with a low, burbling voice that he rarely directed at Sheila. He always asked me first what I thought of a plan, policy, or idea.

In first grade it was Jackie, a thin, caustic woman who reminded me of the actress Kirsten Johnson (*3rd Rock from the Sun*). She paid only intermittent attention to Neil. Second grade brought Laura, whom Neil had in pre-school. Loving and compassionate, she always had Neil's best interests in mind and believed—though not to an uncomfortably zealous degree—that he had potential. More important, though, she appreciated him for who he is, potential be damned. In third grade it was Frankie, though she left midway through the year to have a baby, taking her fetish for sticky notes and her gratingly peppy demeanor with her.

We hit the mother lode in fourth grade with Karen, a bright-eyed, enthusiastic relative newbie who loved Neil from the get-go. Visits to Neil's class were loud but fun; her compassion for and interest in her charges was obvious. We received long, descriptive notes about his days. She hung out with him here at the house so we could go on dates. She was properly skeptical of the time he spent in his inclusion classrooms. I'm not sure what the opposite of mother lode is, but we hit it in fifth grade with Alice, one-time Teacher of the Year and by our count an acolyte of the program's principal. During the summer between fourth and fifth grade, Neil fell and scraped his knees during an inordinately, unsafely long walk through a neighborhood near the school. He had just learned to walk on his own. The fall undid his progress. We went back to holding his hand all the time. But in an attempt to apple polish for state regulators, Alice and the behaviorist turned Neil into an experiment even as he slowly regained his confidence. Alice was allowing him to drop to the floor sometimes more than 100 times a day. She rated his behavior as "try harder" on the daily summaries. As punishment for his recalcitrance, she didn't let him go swimming or take part in other favored activities.

We had Neil checked out by an orthopedic surgeon, who found no permanent damage. While we waited to be seen, Neil walked all over the module in which the doctor was based, dropping only a couple of times out of exhaustion. "Believe me, it was a boring day of walking up and down the same hallways," Sheila explained in a note to Alice. The doctor advised that Neil's heel cords be stretched during the day to facilitate walking. He warned us surgery might be necessary if Neil's cords remained so tight. The physical therapist—the same person who charted Neil's drops on graph paper that looked it was made in the 1960s and later exploited Sheila's deep love for Neil at an assembly celebrating a successful playground fundraiser—flatly refused to do it, claiming it was a medical issue outside her purview. She later had the audacity to tell the doctor in a letter that "the staff is concerned about the affect (sic)" the dropping "may have on his knees."

We observed the experiment at school (without Neil seeing us) and developed a "behavior plan" with the team that revolved at the time around looking straight ahead and not acknowledging Neil when he dropped. I discovered during a later visit to his classroom that his paraprofessionals were an uncaring bunch and that they sometimes punished Neil by separating him from his colleagues and putting him behind a screen—this on top of the fact he was spending large chunks of his days in the hallway. Not exactly the "least restrictive environment," we thought. Our breaking point came when he came home with a deep and ugly bruise on the inside of his left knee.

It was Neil's bus driver who about a month before Christmas 2012 floated the idea of reuniting him with Karen, his fourth-grade teacher. Sheila and I had talked about placing him in a school for kids with special needs. We invited Karen to attend his IEP meeting the following January. She gladly agreed, but asked that the invitation come from the principal. She was later disciplined for her trouble. We had wondered if Karen would earn official wrath for coming to our aid and defense. Coming out of the meeting, we demanded that his heel cords be stretched, that we receive a full report about drops and missed activities, not just about how often Neil in their view disrupted class and had to be removed, that he be allowed to go swimming, that we approve any disciplinary action taken during the school day, that the staff ramp up their kindness, and that we hold bi-monthly progress meetings. They balked; they played the Teacher of the Year card - and told us that there "lots of pieces to the puzzle." They claimed that the fifth grade inclusion team was "nicer" to Neil than the folks in Karen's class, though we knew that to absolutely not be true. I had gone one day, at Alice's frantic request, to reinsert his feeding tube button only to find him sequestered behind a divider - something we had agreed would never happen. The behaviorist muttered and the principal tried to work her iPad. We had no other choice: as is our right under IDEA, we threatened to sue the district unless they either moved Neil to Karen's class or pay for us to enroll Neil in another program. They caved - or as our notes confirmed, "acceded to our wishes."

A week or so later, Karen resigned. She had tired of the stifling bureaucracy, the failure to innovate, the treatment of her charges as the "problem." We wondered if they had been skeptical of her methods for some time—the methods that had helped Neil so much. We were happy for Karen, but also—in my case at least—a little pissed off. How dare she leave our Neil? And we were concerned that there would be blowback for Neil. But my anger passed; we've stayed in touch with Karen, who's gone on to earn a master's degree and find a less compromise-dependent career path. The teacher assigned to complete the year was the same one who completed third grade—she liked Neil and treated him with kindness.

Compared to elementary school, middle school was a relative breeze. His time there seemed to pass quickly. One day we were taking the tour and the next he was headed up on stage past the theater organ. He had three skilled and caring teachers, a host of friendly paraprofessionals, and a diligent school nurse. To avoid having Alice again, Neil was assigned in eighth grade to the seventh grade teacher's class. He made new friends, though he missed the kids he'd been with since kindergarten. Despite the formalities, our most recent IEP meeting was encouraging; we spent most of the time exploring ideas to help Neil thrive; we squeezed the required review of the plan into the last 20 minutes or so. A second school psychologist was a little data collection-happy, but she's enthusiastic and is more willing than her predecessors to find constructive ways to redirect Neil to activities other than those he initiates. We explained his love for escalator and Slinky videos. The assistant principal teared up at one point while explaining how much Neil is revered. Far more than at any other point in our journey, we have the "buy-in" (Dudley-Marling & Burns, 2013, p. 21) so valued by those who study implementation of inclusion. On the way to our annual debriefing at a local restaurant, I mentioned more than once that I felt Neil had found a "home." We vowed—again—to make Neil's actual home a less restrictive environment.

But the whole endeavor is still predicated on the idea that Neil is deficient—that those deficiencies have to be addressed, ameliorated. As in middle school, his classroom is windowless and is located a bit off the beaten path. Sheila pointed out that the former might be a good thing, since Neil would try when unobserved to pull curtains and blinds and check out airplanes. Approaches that wander from the norm are not tolerated, at least not publicly. Iconoclasts are left to keep the authorities at bay and try to do the right thing. To hide in plain sight. Respect Neil, recognize that we all have created—and cling to—the definition of "disability" and act accordingly, but when the authorities come around, do just enough to make sure they think you're complying. For the iconoclasts, this has to feel like an episode of *Hogan's Heroes*.

What if we just dropped the presumption of deficiency?

So it gives us very, very little solace that we've progressed from involuntary sterilization and mercy killing to institutionalization to segregation to inclusion (that often hides segregation). And now Donald Trump is President, a man who mocked a disabled reporter during a bigoted campaign that reporters belatedly labeled as such. He nominated U.S. Senator Jeff Sessions of Alabama to be the nation's Attorney General, a man who in 2000 asserted on the Senate floor that the IDEA and related laws have "created lawsuit after lawsuit," have resulted in "special treatment for certain children," and are "a big factor in accelerating the decline in civility and discipline all over America" (Cherkis, 2016).

Suddenly, trying to "fix" Neil doesn't sound so oppressive.

State Medicaid officials in June 2016 refused to cover the cost of an Accent 1000 communication device for Neil, claiming that it wasn't medically necessary and that the device he's used since third or fourth grade, a Springboard Lite, was still adequate, despite the fact it isn't made anymore and that replacement parts for it are nearly impossible to find. We quickly filed an appeal, and let our friendly but overly concerned with box-ticking Medicaid representative, who has since moved on, know that we were pushing ahead. She set off to find information about a three-point harness for us to use in the car to prevent Neil from snatching Sheila's hair and abruptly pulling my shoulder belt as I tried to drive.

Neil's cerebral palsy has left him unable to communicate verbally; he has mastered only a few signs. He is unable to let us know when his Cystic Fibrosis symptoms are causing him discomfort or when he is feeling ill or has been hurt. A few years ago, he had broken a toe but pressed on until we finally noticed a limp and took him for an x-ray. During fifth grade, he suffered a serious bruise on the inside of his right knee as the result of a fall during one of those dangerously long walks arranged by his assessment-obsessed teacher and monitored by burbling Dave. He was left to suffer until we discovered the bruise while changing his diaper.

Our appeal hearing took place in mid-October 2016, on the ninth floor of the company's gleaming, well-appointed headquarters in Wilmington, Delaware. Sheila and I calculated the value of the lobby furniture and took in the commanding view of the city and the surrounding area as we mentally prepared for the meeting, having already spent an hour talking and snacking in an eco-friendly coffee shop. The owners clearly prided themselves on community involvement; their food truck was parked outside the window in front of which we sat. Sheila excels at anticipation; she maintains a number of arguments for any situation, and constantly revises them. I made jokes about the quality of our temporary security photos and cited barely relevant media examples of what we're going through, believing that my actions lessen the tension. Remember that episode of M*A*S*H where Henry Blake is put on trial for treason? You get the idea. I don't how she stays with me.

A kind, soft-spoken employee fetched us from the lobby and escorted us to a distant corner of the ninth floor where we found the cramped conference room in which the meeting was held. The room's size and location should have tipped us off about how much importance officials assigned to Neil's case. We walked past rows of empty cubes –some inexplicably labeled as such—and signs about preferred workplace conduct that pertained to almost no one.

Joining us at a rectangular table clearly made for a larger space were a nurse, a representative for the state, and an appeals analyst. The company's medical director (a board-certified physician) and a second nurse joined us on speaker. The appeals analyst smiled for the entire proceeding. Her voice, lilting and devoid of bass, caused me to think of the singer Kristin Chenoweth—and that the analyst with a few acting lessons could play true believer bureaucrats for a living. After forced introductions and awkward handshakes, she summarized why we had gathered that morning. The perfunctory feel was familiar, at least to me: parents of kids with developmental delays spend a lot of time defending their parenting ability in front of assembled experts armed with laptops and conventional wisdom.

Sheila cut the appeals analyst off as she asked why we believed Neil needed the new device, especially since he used it to a quarter of its capacity because of his cognitive delays. Her beautiful face showed a mix of frustration, anger, and disbelief. She began to cry as she told of Neil's struggles to communicate and why the Springboard Lite was no longer any help. She went at the true believer like, well, a loving and concerned mom. I've never been prouder of her, although the competition for that accolade has over the years has been heated. She led with the fact that clearly these folks believed that Neil was "too dumb" to use the more advanced device.

My task was to fill in the specification and historical blanks. For once, I was organized and thorough. In front of me on the table I neatly arranged highlighted pages of his school speech therapist's detailed and emphatic letter of support. In boldfaced type, she asserted, "The Accent device is not a gaming system that is part of his leisure activities; the Accent device is the most appropriate speech generating device that allows Neil to communicate effectively." I rolled calmly through the problems with the Springboard Lite and then backstopped Sheila's passionate contention that the Accent 1000 had in a short time enhanced our life with Neil. The analyst and one of the nurses summarized our argument on their laptops for bureaucratic posterity. But we did get a few looks of true sympathy as we passed around the old device in its banged up faux leather case—so sympathetic that we thought they exceeded the recommended daily allowance of sympathy dispensed to appellants. The rebels.

The doctor and nurse barely weighed in, asking only if the Springboard Lite had ever been refurbished. We said it had—once, to lengthen the battery life. Even with the refurbishment Neil's therapist gets only a couple of hours in before it dies.

And then it was over—we were out of there in under a half-hour, optimistic about our chances.

We received word a day later that Medicaid had upheld its earlier decision. No Accent 1000 for Neil. One of the nurses voted to cover it, apparently shocked at how we've been forced to make do with the old machine, and we hope amazed at the progress Neil has made despite it. A day later, we sought help from one of our U.S. Senators, who coincidentally has been fielded complaints from other parents whose kids have developmental delays about unreasonable treatment by Medicaid. A kind representative from the Senator's office recommended we go ahead with plans to seek a hearing with state officials. And so we will. We also vowed to start the process over if the state appeal didn't go our way. We also learned that the nurse representing the state at the first hearing voted for us; she was amazed that we were making do with such a cranky, limited device. And his former speech therapist miraculously located another device on which he could continue to train until our appeal reaches its next stage.

More troubling to Sheila and I were the assumptions about Neil's capabilities evident in the denials. Neil is an intelligent young person whose right to communicate in a socially acceptable way must be honored. As his Meadowood speech therapist said, "every person has the right to build relationships and to feel competent to share information with another person." The Accent 1000 is far easier than the Springboard Lite for Neil to use, especially given his motor skill deficits. The unit's size is more conducive than the Springboard Lite's to engaging in conversation. The increased range of on-screen word options means Neil is less likely to get frustrated and start pushing the buttons without purpose, as if it were an iPad or a toy.

The Accent 1000 has a longer battery life than the Springboard Lite; comes with a desk mount that makes it more stable for Neil to use; its screen clarity is better; its visual display background can be changed to provide increased contrast—and less missed hits; it has more icons than the Springboard Lite and a full activity bar that changes when a subject or verb button is pressed. It has a capacitive screen which doesn't depend on the force applied by Neil to activate. Due to his cerebral palsy, Neil's fingers hyperextend, making it difficult for him to exert force on the button. The longer it takes Neil to activate a button, the faster he gives up trying to communicate. Finally, the microphone on the Springboard Lite that allows the therapist to record a voice output to accompany a depressed button no longer works. This is important since Neil likes escalators and stairs—these aren't found in a typical set of icons; not being able to record them would further dampen his motivation.

Until we were able to set up the two-week long "test drive," our Springboard Lite-based interactions with Neil were painfully brief. But with the Accent, he was able to tell us for the first time that was thirsty and that he needed to go to the bathroom. We sat on our stairs and cried as Neil showed off his newfound ability to communicate. It was like his world—and ours—opened up a little. We finally can envision the day when Neil will be able to communicate in environments outside the school and home. We may no longer need to guess at what he's feeling or what he needs. His therapist agreed; Neil was for the first time in her four years of working with him "motivated to use the device to express his needs, his wants, his feelings, to make comments, and to direct others in various situations at home, at school, and in the community." With less frustration for Neil has come a reduction in the amount of dropping to the floor, crying, yelling, hair pulling and pinching we've experienced when Neil is upset.

While our experience with Medicaid has been beyond frustrating, we are at the same time saddened at the thought that other kids with challenges like Neil's but whose parents don't have the time or inclination to engage in a protracted bureaucratic battle—or who lack insurance coverage—might never get as far as we have. The company's conduct was in direct opposition to the "Least Dangerous Assumption" paradigm that guides, or should more often guide, instruction of individuals with intellectual disabilities. In proposing the paradigm in 1984, scholar Anne Donnellan argued that "educational decisions ought to be based on assumptions which, if incorrect, will have the least dangerous effect on the likelihood that students will be able to function independently as adults" (quoted in Jorgensen, 2005, p. 4). The assumption of officials that Neil is, as Sheila so accurately characterized it back to them, "too dumb" to use the new device is without question a dangerous one. If a student struggles to learn, Donnellan asserted, it is the fault of the teacher. "[T]he quality of instruction should be questioned before the student's ability to learn," wrote disabilities scholar Cheryl Jorgensen (2005, p. 5). Teachers have to be taught—persuaded, cajoled, even browbeaten—to believe that students like Neil can learn. It's been our experience that only a few actually do.

But we continued the fight - and lo and behold, we won this past February! State medicaid officials agreed to pay for the device, though it took nearly two months to actually put it in his hands. It was a long, cluttered road, as are so many of the roads that lead to solid care for Neil. We enlisted the aid of two Legal Aid Society attorneys who already were working with several similarly frustrated parents. Neil's former and current speech therapists generated colorful, cogent, and detailed talking points on Neil's behalf.

They turned out to be unnecessary, as did their appearance at our final hearing. That's because Sheila handed the ass of Medicaid's officious, buttoned-up doctor right back to him. She clearly, unmistakably was on her "A" game, as a source within Medicaid contacted by the rep for the Accent 1000's manufacturer had recommended. The rep told us she had spent nearly 500 hours advocating on behalf of parents. It was "the same story all over Delaware," she told us.

For the record, Medicaid's doctor claimed he had not received the information about Neil's hyperextension and the fact that the battery didn't hold a charge. I was ready to go; I had made extensive notes, had the papers spread out in front of me. I was rehearsing in my head - and then the attorney asked Sheila to speak. I was so incredibly proud of her, and yet pissed and jealous at the same time. I wanted to prove to the world that I could do it, that the image they all of me as a fumbling, head constantly on a swivel incompetent was wrong. As mentioned, Neil's therapists said little, but their moral support was palpable. It seemed as though Medicaid's attorney was in actual pain having to sit there. Yet at the same time he exuded smugness, as though he knew the hearing would go their way, as so many probably have. But they didn't have Sheila on their side. She left it all on the field, as I teach my sports journalism students never to write. At times in tears, her beautiful face swollen thanks to an out of the blue infection that days later would land her in the hospital, she was our son's champion. Thankfully, she recuperated from the infection, thanks to her resilience, her strength, her doctors, and the support of our village.

Chapter Nine

Other Voices

As I mentioned earlier, I share a great deal of our experience with my students. As I began writing the book, two - Morgan Weiss, then a sophomore, and Sadie Pennington, a freshman - expressed interest in conducting research and contributing essays. While veering off in this way is unorthodox, their stories - and the stories contributed by the people who responded to an invitation to participate we distributed in 2016 - compellingly flesh out our story, giving it even more ballast.

IT'S JUST ONE CHROMOSOME, BY MORGAN WEISS

On a very rainy and windy Monday morning in January 2017, I accompanied my fifteen year old sister, Stow, to the Children's Hospital of Pennsylvania (CHOP) on a trip to get an abdominal scan for some pain she was having. She had been getting pain in her abdomen for months, but no doctor, scan, or test could produce any answers as to what was going on. The pain prevented her from eating, and I felt like I was watching my baby sister slowly wither down to skin and bones; I went home often to try to force as much food in her mouth as I could. My family and I were all worried, confused, and anxious to hear any kind of solution or answer a doctor could give us.

This visit was about the third or fourth time I had ever been in CHOP, but the first time I felt like I was truly experiencing what CHOP is all about. For anyone who has never been to this hospital, it is one of the most beautiful, uplifting, and humbling establishments ever created, but it's also one of the saddest places to walk through. It was the first hospital in the United States to focus exclusively on the care of children and has been the home of many medical discoveries and innovations that have both improved pediatric medicine and also saved countless children's lives ("About the History," p. 1).

There are medical departments in that hospital that house studies and treatments I have never even heard of or imagined existed. CHOP is designed and decorated to make children feel more at ease during their visit or stay; most of the wings are different colors and the walls are decorated with stickers, pictures, and words like "princess."

In my previous visits I felt as though I was just visiting the hospital; this time, I felt like I was walking among the confused families, the moms and dads and siblings who just wanted answers and for their children to come home and just be children again. They were just like us, and I felt their grief. Before, I had admired the cupcake stickers, the trains running through the lobby and the nurses who were too nice to be real people, but this time they were all a little less enchanting. Watching my sister uncomfortably adjust herself to accommodate the port in her arm made my heart sink a little, and I saw how the decorations are distractions from whatever your reality is. I'm lucky I was there for a one day visit, but I was surrounded by families who won't be leaving for days or weeks, siblings whose time left with their brothers and sisters is shortening every day, and parents whose children have mental and physical disabilities that prevent them from ever walking or functioning on their own. How could stickers, bubbles and trains make that any better?

When we made it to the general waiting room to be registered I was overwhelmed by the amount of families waiting to be seen and I tried my best not to stare at anyone. As my mom walked to the desk to sign in, I scanned the room to find a good place for my sister and me to sit. The first face I saw as I looked around was an adorable little girl, maybe two years old, dressed in pink and smiling in her dad's arms. As soon as I made eye contact with her, her smile grew and "hi" repeatedly rolled off her tongue as we both waved to each other. I walked to the other side of the room to get a tissue before sitting down, and as I walked back towards her she began to reach out to me, making noises and smiling. Her dad noticed and said, "There she is again!" I sat down across from my new friend, admiring her energy, charisma and bright personality. She lit up the whole hospital for me. I would have never guessed that she had Down syndrome if her appearance hadn't given it away.

As we were waiting for my mom to finish registering, Stow and I waved to the little girl and admiringly watched her eat her snack. My sister looked at me and whispered "She likes you... Morgan are you crying?" I was. I had just completed, or so I thought, my chapter about Robert Lewis and how his story and its coverage exemplify the issues surrounding media coverage of disabilities. I barely have any personal relations to anyone with Down syndrome so I don't often have the chance to interact with people or children with Down. So when I saw this girl, this beautiful, happy soul, so many emotions rushed through my mind. When I saw her, she put a face to the stories and the people I'd been writing about; she gave my work, my writing, and this book a whole new meaning for me. Out of everyone I encountered that day, she was the person who made everything in the hospital seem a little happier. As she hugged her dad tightly and watched cartoons, I couldn't imagine ever trying to portray her as anything less than what I am: human.

I tried to hold myself together as my mom walked over and sat next to me. I poked her and whispered, "Look how adorable that little girl is," and the reply I received was, "Aw, she has Down syndrome." Now, keep in mind that my mom loves and makes friends with everyone and is one of the most knowledgeable and both socially and globally aware people I know. She didn't respond that way because she hates disabled people (in fact, she's probably read more about mental disabilities than I have), but because it's practically programmed into our minds to look at people and automatically begin to categorize them. For people with Down syndrome, the category in which they are placed in society is so far from where "normal" people are placed.

That moment made me realize just how misinformed we still are about disabilities and Down syndrome - that includes me. I probably would have responded the same way my mom did if I hadn't been researching and writing about Down syndrome and disabilities. I started to really question why, if this child's facial features were my only hints towards her having a disability, then why do non-disabled people have this idea that people with Down syndrome are so different from us? It's because when I hear or think "Down syndrome," stories from the news rush through my head, stories that differentiate "us" from "them" far too often and far too dramatically. That brings us to Robert Lewis.

Basketball players can be characterized by their height, keen hand-eye coordination, and long limbs. To be successful, they have to be able to focus for extended periods of time, jump, and sprint. Based on these characteristics, most people would not think that someone with Down syndrome would be categorized as a basketball player. Down syndrome is usually distinguished by below-average height, short fingers, reduced muscle tone, and difficulty concentrating, walking, standing, and even sitting. This contrast alludes that someone with this disability, someone like 19-year-old Robert Lewis, cannot be categorized as a basketball player. Lewis, however, during his high school's Senior Night basketball game, proved that although people with Down syndrome can be pointed out or distinguished by what meets the eye, the power of what lies beneath, the power of the heart and soul, is what truly determines how a person can be categorized.

Robert Lewis was the manager of the soccer, football, and basketball teams at his high school, Franklin Road Academy, in Nashville, Tennessee. Lewis, who has Down syndrome, was told by his coach, John Pierce, four days in advance that he could dress for his team's Senior Night game. Franklin Road Academy would be playing against University School of Nashville, the high school Robert Lewis' brother, Matthew, attended and played basketball for.

It was February 5, 2016, and Franklin Road Academy was up by 20 points against University School of Nashville with one minute left to play. Pierce decided to put Robert in the game so that the high school senior could have some time on the court. The opposing team's coach, Mike Jones, put Matthew Lewis in the game to guard Robert so that the brothers could be on the court together. Robert took a three-point shot - he missed, but his brother continued to encourage him to try to score a basket despite being on opposing teams. Then, with ten seconds left in the game, Robert sank a three-point shot to help lead his team to victory. After the buzzer, the gym erupted with cheers as everyone rushed to the court to celebrate Robert's shot, his teammates lifting him into the air triumphantly.

"I feel good about how much people love and care about me," said Robert. "This is a thing I will remember" (Holohan, 2016).

Until recently, Robert Lewis would not have been allowed to play basketball, let alone attend a normal school. In terms of the acceptance of Down syndrome, society has come a long way since the condition was first identified. Down syndrome is named after a British physician, John Langdon Down, who first referred to the syndrome as "Mongolism" in 1866. Dr. Ananya Mandal says that Down "used the term 'mongoloid' to describe the condition, due to his opinion that children with Down's syndrome shared similar physical features to people from the Blumenbach's Mongolian race" (Mandal, 2014). It was not until 1959 that Jerome Lejeune, a French pediatrician and geneticist, discovered that an extra chromosome is what characterizes Down syndrome. The term "Down syndrome" itself was not even accepted or used until the 1970s, which may have been a result of the negative spectrum of opinions surrounding the condition and the treatments that were practiced on people diagnosed with Down syndrome at the time.

People with Down syndrome were denied basic human or civil rights throughout American history, even up to the 1980s. They were deemed "less than human." A Down syndrome baby would be "warehoused" in an institution, as he or she was considered to be too much of a burden for any family. These institutions lacked basic accommodations such as plumbing and were centers for abuse and neglect; the National Association for Down syndrome describes the former institutionalization of people with Down syndrome as them being "locked away so that the rest of society could not see the horror of their lives." With limited help from the media, misconceptions about Down were perpetuated by institutions. In 1924, the State of Virginia began allowing the sterilization of the intellectually disabled, and several other groups, without consent. Not only was a state government stripping people with Down syndrome, and disabled people in general, of their rights, but the government was also brazenly communicating that a person with a disability is such an encumbrance to society that he or she should not even be able to procreate.

There was also the establishment of an organization called the Council for the Retarded Child in Ohio in 1933; roughly a dozen similar groups would be created in different states throughout the following decade. In contrast to Virginia's law, these organizations were unquestionably a positive step towards integrating people with Down syndrome and other disabled people into what most consider to be "normal" or "everyday" society; however, the organizations created to help and include disabled people were still segregating, devaluing and dehumanizing those people by categorizing them under the demeaning title of "retard." Determining what defined a "good citizen" at any point in American history can help with understanding the rationalization behind how different groups people were treated during that time. Author Janice Brockley (2004) notes that in nineteenth and twentieth century America, parents raising intellectually disabled children were doomed to fail because one of the most important outcomes of parenting was widely believed to be raising "upwardly mobile competitors for the workforce," which is obviously a more challenging goal for someone with a mental or physical disability. A good citizen would be raised to become an independent adult who would eventually be able to take care of himself and contribute to society by working (Brockley, p. 130); otherwise, that child would be a waste of time and resources that could be used to raise children who had the potential to become self sufficient.

From this perspective, it's easier to understand why parents were discouraged by their children having Down syndrome. They were being told that their children would never achieve middle-class status or be able to survive on their own and, sadly, that was true for a long time in America. Once a disabled child's parents were gone, there were very few people who would want or even know how to help them. Even in the 1950s, renowned psychiatrists were arguing that people with severe disabilities should "prepare for a life of complete dependency" (Brockley, p. 131). With this pressure from professionals, the motives behind placing disabled children into institutions become clearer despite their tragedy. Parents were not necessarily disgusted by their children and their needs but were more likely afraid of the path ahead; institutionalization was often embraced as a solution for parents of children with severe disabilities because of fear that those children were at a higher risk of falling into poverty and were more susceptible to abuse (Brockley, p. 131).

Many media outlets in the nineteenth and twentieth centuries put the pressure of raising a disabled child on mothers. The job of a father was to provide financial support for his family by working, which means that fathers spent less time with their children than mothers. Over the course of American history, the way society viewed and talked about parental roles in the household changed, but the emphasis on the priorities of the mother remained. In the 1890s, women were no longer believed to be able to raise children with just their "emotional and moral gifts" and therefore needed scientific guidance; however, childcare was still primarily a mother's concern (Brockley, p. 132). All of these views were established, maintained, and changed over and over because of media. Publications in the twentieth century warned that mothers, especially of disabled children, were the root of various family issues. Professionals suggested that a disabled child's progression towards independence might be hindered by an unhappy mother because she is more likely to seek fulfillment through her child's dependence upon her. Fathers of disabled children were also considered to be less capable of fulfilling their duty of preparing their children for independence and success, and their own emotional needs may go unsatisfied because their wives are tending to the needs of their disabled child (Brockley 133).

By the end of the twentieth century, the "denial of reality" shifted into "virtue and an obligation" (Brockley, p. 156). Parents of children with disabilities, especially mothers, were no longer criticized for loving their children "too much," but were encouraged to give their children as much love and support as possible; however, this turn also meant that parents could be criticized for not doing enough. Professionals and the media were now increasingly stressing the responsibility of parents to not only give their disabled children more affection and help, but also to be social and political advocates (p. 158). Brockley argues that the media's criticisms of parents have not progressed, only changed, and that the largest shift throughout American history has been from the idea that parents are not obligated to care for a disabled child to the long list of obligations that those parents are now believed to have. She says that all of the judgment towards parents, however, "has failed to change the underlying reality that American society depended on individual parents to fulfill the difficult task of raising children who were socially stigmatized and rejected" (p. 157). While the media has continued to criticize people for their parenting techniques and decisions, society has also failed to address or acknowledge the difficulty of raising a child in a world where he or she is still viewed as an outcast and a burden to his or her family.

One woman, along with the help of her husband, was able to initiate some change in how America sees Down syndrome. Kay McGee and her husband, Marty, worked tirelessly to help both people with Down syndrome and their families after the McGee's own daughter, Tricia, was born with Down syndrome in Chicago in 1960. Although the normal route to take during the time would have been placing Tricia in an institution, Kay and Marty took their child home. Almost immediately, Kay began to get in touch with professionals and other families who were raising children with Down syndrome, creating what would eventually be known as the National Association for Down syndrome, an organization that "would always recognize the great value of individuals with Down syndrome and of parents helping parents." Over its lifetime, NADS has consisted of parent support programs, local support groups, temporary foster care, and several educational programs ("History of NADS," 2017).

One significant influence on America's acceptance of disabilities is how they are covered and discussed on TV, online, and even in conversation. I explored coverage of Robert Lewis and Down syndrome by media outlets from February 2015 through December 2016. For folks with Down like Robert, the key issues with media coverage lie within misunderstandings of the disability. People tend to think that Down syndrome is characterized by stupidity and an inability to function or to amount to anything that a "normal" person could. In February 2016, Robb Scott, the father of a boy with Down syndrome, recorded his tearful message about the beauty of the disability after hearing a conversation in a grocery store. He overheard a father tell his son that Down syndrome is "an illness of 'not knowing anything.'" Scott decided that if he wasn't going to confront the father directly, he at least needed to share his response on the Internet. His video received countless positive comments and responses, making Scott feel as though society was telling him "it's okay" (Dunlap, 2016).

Media coverage of Robb Scott's story is a positive step towards spreading awareness that people with disabilities are not so different from us. The article about Scott in the *Washington Post* (Holley, 2016) illustrates his frustration without bias and includes his quotes about Down syndrome being a gift and how having a son with Down syndrome is the best thing that has ever happened to him. There are still pieces in the media, however, that cover news about people with Down syndrome in a way that makes them seem incapable and as deserving of segregation. One article on CNN was headlined "How a Model with Down syndrome made it to the Catwalk," which describes Madeline Stuart's journey to becoming a model (Stuart, 2015). Stuart's story being covered by one of the world's largest news organizations is a positive step, but the title insinuates that she ended up somewhere that people like her normally should not be. This article, along with many of the other articles about people with Down syndrome, is proof of the changes that have yet to transpire in society concerning the mindsets surrounding disabilities.

Almost every article I read from the last two years that highlights an achievement made by a person with Down syndrome insinuates that they are accomplishing something that they normally shouldn't accomplish, or that they would not be able to accomplish if they were not being handed victory or success. The stories range from Lewis being handed the opportunity to score a three-pointer to a soccer fan with Down syndrome being "given the privilege" ("Eleven-Year-Old," 2015) of scoring a half-time penalty kick at

New Douglas Park in Scotland. Another article posted on CBS Sports talks about a high school wrestler who planned on surrendering his undefeated record so that a student wrestler with Down syndrome could experience the happiness of beating him and ending his streak (Dicker, 2016). The gesture is kind and thoughtful, but like the other news stories, it perpetuates the idea that people with Down syndrome are incapable of lone achievement. Don't get me wrong, giving children with a disability the chance to succeed and thrive is wonderful and the kindness should not end, but portraying the accomplishments of people with Down syndrome as the product of their neediness is not helping their cause. The media makes it seem as though these people only achieve when society allows them to, and although it's nice to see people with Down syndrome appearing in the news, the stories should hopefully evolve into coverage of people with Down syndrome accomplishing things on their own, without sounding as though everything must be simply handed to them.

In many of these stories, the focus is on the kind acts made by the people who don't have Down syndrome even though the story isn't supposed to be about them. An article posted on Fox News in March 2015 ("Players Leave Court," 2015) describes Desiree, a middle school cheerleader with Down syndrome being rescued during a basketball game by the players on her team. During the game, the young boys heard people in the stands teasing Desiree and walked off of the court to stop the bullies. This refreshing act of kindness, though a wonderful example of the importance of community, was misrepresented in Fox's article as an incident involving several selfless middle school boys and their distressed, disabled classmate. Almost the whole piece, minus four short lines, is about how brave the boys were. The player's support of Desiree is definitely commendable, but not more commendable than the bravery shown by Desiree just for continuing to stand in front of all those people while being bullied in the first place. This article could've been about the adversity people with disabilities have to face day to day, but instead was turned into yet another piece making everyone but the disabled person seem like a hero. Another article posted by NPR (Chappell, 2015) was closer to highlighting Desiree's bravery, quoting her when she told her dad that she still loves the bullies even if they don't like her back.

This brings us back to Lewis. His story is incredibly heartwarming and uplifting; in the end, Lewis seemed thrilled just to have been able to be a part of his school's success. So, why end the story there? Are we merely reporting on the events that will make everyone say "oh look, that sweet little Down syndrome boy was a hero for the day," or do we really want people to read the article and say, "wow, people with Down syndrome are truly heroes"? Why do we have to call it a miracle throw or a "special touchdown" (Criss, 2016), why can't it just be a throw or a touchdown? I want to hear the rest of Lewis' story, not just the story of one special night, because the rest of his achievements leading up to and following that basketball game are equally commendable and heroic. Our perspectives on Down syndrome should not be defined by the moments when a camera crew and a journalist catch a person with Down syndrome doing something that they typically wouldn't be doing. The media should publish stories that feature children like Lewis if their accomplishments would also get a child without a disability featured in the news. Of course shaming disabled children because they look and act differently is going to segregate them from their peers, but placing disabled children on a pedestal because they are different is still segregating them, just with a different intention.

If Lewis' team was not winning with limited time left in the game, his coach would not have put him in, and there would not have been a nationally recognized news story. If Lewis' brother had not allowed him to score a basket, he would not have made that last three pointer, and, again, there would not have been a nationally recognized news story. Or, at least, that's what we can take from the articles about Robert Lewis' memorable night. One article posted in July 2016 represents how a story about a person with Down should be done. The piece is about two friends, Sam Suchmann and Mattie Zufelt, who came up with the brilliant idea of filming, directing, and starring in their own zombie movie. Rather than speak for the boys, Jennifer McDermott of the Associated Press actually let them be the voice and set the tone of their own story. McDermott (2016) focuses on the boys' characters and passions, the qualities that make them individuals, not their appearances and the things that classify them as a people with Down syndrome. She quotes the two more than she quotes anyone else, which works to her advantage because Sam and Mattie are pretty hysterical. She writes that the boys can be seen chugging soda throughout their film because it's one of their favorite things to do, and includes a quote from Mattie saying that his character is "a straight badass" in the movie. Those who have helped the boys aren't praised; nobody says the duo couldn't have done it without the help of someone else. They aren't called brave for making a movie "despite their Down syndrome." McDermott shows that they are people with character, passions, and unique personalities who are capable of doing anything they want to do, but without the dramatic language used in other pieces like the Lewis articles. Robert Lewis, Sam Suchmann and Mattie Zufelt all did something worth celebrating, but the difference in their media coverage is that Robert, along with many other people in the news who have Down syndrome, was not allowed to be his own hero.

If we as a society want to include, love, and accept people with Down syndrome, or people with any disorder for that matter, we have to start recognizing them as individuals who each have something special to offer. Lewis might not look like a basketball player, but he proved to everyone that self perception is what counts during the last couple of seconds, not what everyone perceives you to be. Robert Lewis is a hero, not because the Internet says so, but because he saw himself as a basketball player before any news story said he was one. Society cannot keep categorizing people who are disabled based on what their capabilities are believed to be, because people like Robert Lewis will clearly continue to prove us wrong. We must stop thinking in terms of "us" and "them," because we are all one in the same. After all, it's only one chromosome.

THE BEST DAY, BY SADIE PENNINGTON

My brother Ian received a Starbucks mug from my Aunt Rose the last time we got together as a family. It had the words "best day ever" written on it in gold letters with texturized confetti popping out on each side of the graphic. When Ian pulled it out of the bag my entire family erupted in exchanges of laughter and familiarity. Of course Ian would receive a mug that had those words on it. After all, Ian is famously known in my family for having the best days. Ever. You wouldn't believe another human could have that many good days, and Ian makes it look easy.

Ian is a 28-year-old man from New Jersey with a stout body and big circular glasses. He lives on waffles, bagels, peanut butter & jelly sandwiches, and instant coffee that he heats up in the microwave every morning. His favorite artists are Taylor Swift and Selena Gomez, and will sing his heart out when he sits at the computer with his headphones perched on his small head and the volume at full. Ian is designated Fire Chief at home, always making sure to unplug my power strip when I leave for school or turning the toaster notch all the way down just in case, by some chance, the idle toaster could ignite a fire. He is the weekly source of entertainment at my grandma's retirement home, lighting up the eyes of every Crane's Mill resident at dinner time when he vivaciously engages in conversation with my grandma and her friends. Ian is my ideal joy ride companion because he compliments the contents of my mix CD'S and doesn't hesitate to belt with me during "Send Me on My Way" by Rusted Root. He is someone I can always count on for a pep talk and a gushy, all-encompassing hug.

Ian is one of my three siblings, and he has Down syndrome.

Down Syndrome is the result of pure chance. My two genetically normal parents (though I could dispute their normalcy in other areas) produced a baby with an extra copy of Chromosome 21, and with that came a myriad of challenges and abilities that Ian and the rest of my family face head on, day in and day out. And when I say head on, I literally mean head on. People with Down Syndrome have distinguishable facial features that stamp them as different from the get-go. They have flat faces with small noses and upward slanting eyes. They also stand short, with protruding tongues and abnormally shaped ears.

Ever since I could crawl, I was able to recognize that Ian was different from the rest of my family. He had specific behavioral patterns that even I could tell were out of the ordinary, despite my ranking as the wide-eyed baby of the family. In most situations, he would start out irritated and stubborn, throwing temper tantrums when he didn't get his way. But somewhere in between the foot stomping and screaming, he would surrender to the almighty forces of mom and dad. In his moment of defeat, he held the power to completely alter the mood of the room with a single smile. Once he realized that he wasn't going win the battle, he would let out a little giggle and return to his lighthearted yet intricately sly ways.

When I saw Ian happily sitting at the breakfast table enjoying his waffles, he was really plotting his next move to dump an entire gallon of milk on my brother Cole's head. He is constantly testing boundaries, walking the fine line between what would melt my mother's heart and make her laugh, or send her into a reprimanding rage. Most of the time, Ian would successfully pull off one of his pranks and put a cheek throbbing grin on everyone's face. And even in the times where his humor went too far, he knew exactly what to do to make the room dismiss his wrong doings and fall in love with him again. That is the kind of energy Ian has. Ian's Down Syndrome demands a good kind of attention, an attention that requires compassion and patience and so much love.

I try not to look at Ian's condition as a disability, but rather him possessing a different set of *abilities*. Yes, Ian can be very strong willed and stubborn at times, especially when one suggests that he doesn't go for that third PB & J sandwich for dinner. He needs daily reminders to brush his teeth, put on deodorant, and change his socks (we all do, sometimes). And because he can't ride a bike or drive a car, he depends on my family members for transportation and companionship. He is unlike most 28 year olds in that he can't fully function as a healthy adult by himself. He relies on the assistance of my family to do things that you and I can easily achieve by ourselves. But what he lacks in things that come easy to most of us, he makes up for in his unique abilities to comfort, inspire, and make others smile. I mean, who else can say that they've received an anonymous slice of cake at a cafe for jubilantly dancing during a jazz set? He is such a positive and loving force in my life and always has my back. Ian can look at me with his bagel-shaped glasses and know when I'm feeling stressed, offering words of encouragement until I feel better. In fact, he often won't let me leave a room until I vow to him that he did a good job consoling me. He wants everybody to experience a "best day ever" as frequently as he does. It's hard to convey Ian's character through text because he is so animated, so full of life. But for these purposes , I'll try to convey his personality best I can via black type on a white piece of paper. Here is a list of Ianisms I've compiled through my 20 years of observations:

When someone in the family offers to shave him after a week or two of neglect, he will always protest with his line "I'm keeping it because Jesus had a beard."

If I try to sneak a sip of beer at a family gathering, he takes it out of my hand and reminds me that I'm underaged, but assures me that my time will come soon enough.

After he's had a drink or two, he claims he's getting "focused" which is his code for a little tipsy.

At the very mention of the Chinese delicacy Peking Duck, he will do a little hand gesture fashioned to look like a duck is peaking out of water. He always does this motion with an accompanied squeal...we aren't sure when or how this started, but that's Ian for you.

Any time he comes into or out of a room he'll hug you or put a hand on your shoulder.

If one of my family members asks him to bring the butter or ketchup to the table at dinner, he will come back with relish or a spatula - anything to conjure up a laugh.

Most important, he has an obsession with doing the right thing that I'm not sure was instilled in him through any of us. That's not to say that we haven't taught him great values, but somewhere along the line Ian became a custodian of justice and morality, almost out of nowhere, and I think that comes from having a pure heart.

And as with most brother and sister relationships, I want Ian to accomplish every goal he sets, no matter the size. In order to lead my best life, I know that I need to maintain good friendships, do something productive every day, and work towards goals both big and small. I hate to see others minimize or completely silence Ian's dreams just because he has Down Syndrome. Ian is a human, my brother, one of my best friends. I want everyone to see his potential and worth the way I see it, abundant and deep. What is life if not just setting goals for ourselves and working towards them? We all need to feel a sense of purpose and belonging.

One challenge that comes along with having a family member with special needs is the speculation that surrounds our lives. How difficult is it to care for Ian? What is his quality of life like? Can he even form complete sentences? People seem to have preconceived notions of what it's like to have Ian in the family. I often observe others tip-toeing around the fact that he has Down Syndrome, as if it is some heinous crime to bring it up...like it's a fragile topic that, if approached incorrectly, can offend or antagonize. Yes, he has Down syndrome, but he also has blue eyes and brown hair and has a great sense of humor. Him having Down syndrome does not solely define him, just as me being left handed doesn't solely define me (though studies have shown people who are left handed tend to be more unique and creative). And if it's not a person being overly cautious of them offending me, they act as if my family and I are doing God's work, as if we rescued a litter of blind and deaf kittens from a Kill Shelter or penned the Emancipation Proclamation. Heck, some would like to give my family a Nobel Peace Prize if they could. But why isn't there an in between? Why can't people see my brother as 1/6th of the Pennington family, not "the one with Down syndrome." When I asked my Dad for his interpretation of how others interact with Ian, one thing in particular stood out to me. He said that "the one defining factor that overcame everything else was this one monolithic truth; if we, his family, didn't or couldn't fight for Ian, then who would? He didn't ask to be born with an extra chromosome, we had to be his warriors, we couldn't afford to wallow in the what-ifs and half-truths. We had to be fierce, have indestructible resolve, and not give a whit about what anyone else thought about any of it." And that is precisely the attitude I've been employing in my life with Ian.

Perhaps a reason why I have these one-off and misguided interactions with others when it comes to my brother is lack of knowledge and exposure to the Down syndrome community. One way in which people form their expectations of those with intellectual disabilities is through mass media's skewed depictions. In TV shows and movies, characters with Down Syndrome are often one dimensional, serving as comedic relief or vehicles for heartwarming and uplifting themes. Their five second cameos as the "token disabled person" can't even begin to tell the narrative of the differently abled, triumphs, tribulations and all. Due to the lack of representation of people with Down syndrome in mainstream media, limitations are automatically imposed on their abilities. Movies rarely give them a chance to share their stories and talk about the ambitions, goals, hobbies, hidden talents, and so on and so forth. Whenever there is a depiction of a person with Down syndrome on television or in a movie, the audience sees them as "the one with Down syndrome" instead of "Miranda, the artist who loves Brie cheese" or "David, the cashier who holds the title for longest consecutive pogo stick jumps." Instead, their disability is their character. These depictions lack depth and perpetuates the idea that people with Down syndrome are low functioning, needy, and intellectually stunted.

As I mentioned before, I have three siblings. Their names are Cole, Mae, and of course, Ian. Cole and Mae both have dreams and aspirations, Cole wanting to travel the world while artistically capturing the bizarre and enthralling, and Mae wanting to lead the charge in reforms to state funded disability services. Ian is no different than my other two siblings on the big ambitions front. He wakes up every morning and makes breakfast for himself, getting ready for the long day ahead of him. He does his own laundry every Monday, makes his bed and maintains his room, and works at his home office in hopes of opening his own technology driven data business one day.

Throughout his life, he's had an abundant amount of dreams, whether it's owning his own farm in the backwoods of Mississippi or making the *Billboard* charts for his covers of Taylor Swift songs. His aspirations are bold and present, and if you would let him, or X developmentally disabled character on X show talk about these goals, you would know that they too possess this basic human trait. There is a serious problem of misrepresentation of Down syndrome, among many other disabilities, in the media. I am calling for a total shift in the attitudes of individuals when comes to differently abled people. We should no longer "other" and isolate, undermining their desires to lead a normal and productive life. We should no longer laugh at their expense and use them as a reference for stupidity and simplicity. We should no longer ignore the fact that we can make our society a more accepting and loving place by opening our ears and hearts to those with different abilities.

Born This Way, an Emmy-award winning docuseries chronicling the lives of seven individuals with Down syndrome, is a good place to start in my quest for change. When I first heard about this show, I was excited for the Down syndrome community because we were finally given the microphone to share our collective story. I was hopeful that this would have a positive impact on the public opinion of those with intellectual disabilities by breaking down barriers and shining light on what it means be differently abled. This was an opportunity to expose the big truth that the public was not yet ready to face: people with intellectual disabilities are just like you and me. However, there was a big part of me that resented the fact that TV producers were capitalizing on this. I had my reservations about Hollywood being involved and how big of an influence it could have on the overall story told. After all, *Born This Way's* producer, Jonathan Murray, also produced and co-created *The Real World*, *The Challenge*, and *Bad Girls Club*, some of the most pathetic and embarrassing examples of reality television. I was nervous that this depiction of Down syndrome would still be askew, just in a different direction. Maybe they would highlight the uplifting, triumphant, and marketable aspects of having Down syndrome and gloss over some of the unsavory parts to tell an easily digestible story. I was fearful that while the Down syndrome community finally had a chance to share our story with the mainstream media, and that A&E would completely misrepresent us. A&E had a huge responsibility in having the platform to tell this story, and I commend them for providing an accurate, all encompassing, and sincere representation of differently abled people and the lives they touch.

Born This Way focuses on the lives of seven different young adults with Down syndrome, each of them boasting unique talents, senses of humor, and varieties of personal expression. In season 1, we meet suave Sean, a self proclaimed "ladies man," nurturing Christina who is a good listener and even better friend, caring Rachel who wants everyone to get along, articulite Steven who is also a big movie nerd, headstrong Elena who brings vigor to any room, jazzy John who has a thriving rap career, and determined Megan who owns her own business. These are the faces of Down Syndrome presented to the mainstream media, and the stories they told throughout the course of the show are now in the public's collective consciousness. I couldn't be happier and more proud to be a part of this community, and am so grateful that A&E did such a good job showcasing the Down syndrome experience. As I was watching *Born This Way*, I kept a notebook of things that I saw in the show that resonated with me or echoed my experience of having a brother with Down syndrome. Without fail, in intervals of 5-10 minutes, I would scribble things down like "there was a time when Ian had the same reaction as Sean" or "I'm very pleased they brought up the stubborn eating patterns of those with Down Syndrome". In general, there were so many things that I'm glad the show discussed, and countless moments where I caught myself laughing, crying, and nodding my head in agreement and familiarity of experience. Yes, the show utilizes the "feel good" agenda that I discussed before, one I was worried about A&E exploiting. However, as I watched the show and reflected on my very own experience, I realized that you couldn't tell the story of Down syndrome without that notion.

The cast of *Born This Way* met through Leapz and Boundz, a special needs community center in Southern California. Leapz and Boundz provides a place for people with Down syndrome to hang out, have fun, and socialize with other people. One struggle that my family faced after Ian graduated high school was finding a good day program, job, or any other structured plan for him that would fill his day up and give him a sense of purpose. Ian saw that my sister was moving to California to take a position at Habitat for Humanity, I was moving two hours away to attend college, and my brother had signed on to teach English in Thailand at Assumption University. He recognized these major life changes in all of us, and expressed to my parents that he too wanted to start writing the next chapter. Ian graduated from our town's Vocational Technology school in 2010, and it wasn't until recently that he found a program that was the right fit for him *and* financially supported by the government. Hopefully that gives you some idea of how much of a process getting seemingly basic resources for Ian is - playing years of phone tag with the Division of Developmental Disabilities in the Department of Human Services so he could qualify for funding to get a support coordination agency to work with my family and find a program.

I'm happy to report that Ian meets with a life skills coach twice a week and takes part in our local Jewish Community Centers special needs program once a week. He is also involved in a program called The Social Scene, what I see as Northern New Jersey's version of Southern California's Leapz and Boundz program. Ian is happy in his new set up, and I am relieved that he is finally getting the interaction and social stimulation that he once got when he was enrolled in school. I am glad that *Born This Way* features the utility of, and even the necessity for, the Leapz and Boundz center. These types of establishments are imperative to not only those with developmental disabilities, but their families too. I am so happy that Ian gets to enjoy a social life like my other siblings and I do. I think it's really important that Ian he has an opportunity to make friends and interact with people outside of our family. With the addition of these programs to Ian's schedule, most of his weekdays are filled up with activities that get him outside of the house. I've seen an improvement in his overall mood and health, and I am thankful that my sister assumed the role of liaison between testy and unreliable governmental agencies and my busy and often impatient parents.

In the first episode, we meet Megan, who primarily lives in Colorado with her mother but moved to Southern California to film the show. She has dreams of permanently moving so she can live close to her *Born This Way* friends and lead an independent life. She also wants to move to California to expand her growing business, Megology, which specializes in one of a kind hand tie dyed accessories. Megan's vested interest in expanding her business lies heavily on the fact that she's using her profits to pay for college and look for her own place. However, Megan's mom is hesitant in agreeing to let her reside independently. She feels that Megan doesn't know how to do things that are imperative to solo living, like grocery shopping, cooking, and laundry. Megan's mom even cites herself as the biggest reason why Megan doesn't have these skills, because it's always been easier to do things for her instead of taking the time to teach her. She regrets taking the easy way out when Megan was growing up, because it now hinders her plans for increased independence.

We also meet Sean, a sassy and stubborn twenty two year old who lives with his mom, dad and pet Turtle named Speedy. Like many others in the cast, Sean's biggest goal is to achieve independence, which he defines as procuring his own apartment. Perhaps Sean wants to escape the doom that his mom imposes every morning as she tirelessly tries to wake him up - he's infamously known for not being able to get out of bed in the morning. Sean and his parents often butt heads about these living arrangements, for Sean wants to live in an expensive Bachelor Pad with tons of square feet and luxury kitchen appliances. In Sean's defense, what single twenty two year old man wouldn't? Sean's parents urge him to set the bar lower and bring him back to reality, explaining that living in an apartment costs a lot of money, and that things of this size take a lot of time and effort. Sean, being the headstrong man that he is, doesn't want to hear any opposition to his big plans.

Whether it's Megan's mom, who doesn't want to prematurely leave Megan by herself, or Sean's parents, who are weary of the logistical implications of a move, families of those with developmental disabilities need to make tough decisions about the future of their loved ones. This is something that my entire family must start considering in the next couple of years, for it affects us all. Though Ian hasn't voiced his living preferences, I know he could very well want to live on his own in the near or distant future. When my parents downsize, will Ian move with them? Is he independent enough to live on his own? Would a group home be a better fit for him? Should he come live with Mae, Cole, or I? Tackling these big questions can be challenging, and I can sympathize with the families on *Born This Way* in not knowing what option is best and proceeding cautiously when faced with decision making.

Luckily, Sean and Megan's parents meet them halfway to come up with solutions that are satisfactory for all parties involved. After filming wrapped for the first season of *Born This Way*, Megan and her mom returned to Colorado so they could be in a comfortable environment for Megan to master the life skills she needs to live on her own. And as for Sean, in season two he finally moves into a modest yet fully equipped bachelor pad with castmate Steven. Though the future is uncertain for Ian, I want him to decide what he wants on his own and have my family accommodate his wishes to the best of our ability. When I asked my siblings about the possibility of him living with one of us, my brother Cole said he would "like to take Ian abroad and do a little traveling with him. I don't want him to stagnate at home, I want him to enjoy the richness and depth of the human experience. I want him to of course be happy, but that goes without saying--what I'd like to see him do is fulfill some of the goals and dreams he's put forth, like being involved in business, penning an article....getting into the music scene...In the near future I'm happy to go on drives like we always do, but in the semi distant future I'd like to invite him to live with me somewhere other than New Jersey. Or at least take a long road trip and expose him to different worlds and really allow him to be immersed in new cultures. He's got the same thirst for adventure that the rest of the family does and I'd like to support that to the best of my ability." And that is how I think it should go, too. Let Ian live as much of an independent life as possible while still being by his side to offer assistance if necessary.

Love, relationships, sex, marriage, babies...all part of the human experience, including those with developmental disabilities. *Born This Way* showcases a variety of opinions and preferences when it comes to this topic. Christina, a compassionate and level headed cast member shares the story of her relationship with Angel, a man who also has Down Syndrome. Angel and Christina have been in a committed long-term relationship for nearly five years and even share a promise ring to express their devotion, but only after Angel got the O.K. from Christina's dad. Admittedly, the episode where Angel planned an intimate dinner with Christina where he would offer up the promise ring really put a dent in my tissue box supply. It was such a warm moment seeing Christina so genuinely happy with Angel's proposition. Others like Sean and Steven are still searching for their "Mrs. Right," but admit that they're only attracted to women who do not share the experience of having a developmental disability. In a very candid moment, Steven confesses that he typically veers away from women with Down Syndrome because they are mostly concerned with love and marriage, but he "thinks more about sex than marriage." Megan, on the other hand, is navigating the muddy waters of a long distance relationship while she's in California filming the show and her boyfriend back home in Colorado. She expresses a strong desire to get married to Brendan, her boyfriend of seven years, and eventually have babies with him. However, her mom cautions her that caring for another human takes a lot of time, sacrifice, and hard work. During a solo interview, Megan's mom also admits that she is fearful of Megan having a baby because she knows that she will end up having to care for it- as if she has two children instead of one. My heart hurts when Megan's mom shares the realities of motherhood, because Megan so desperately wants to become a mom. We can't fault her for that, after all that is a pretty common human desire.

All seven cast members have compelling perspectives on love and relationships, just like my friends do. I have one friend who has absolutely no interest in getting married or having kids because she finds them irritating and sticky. I have another friend who is already picking out baby names and nursery wallpaper. As for me, I'd hope to have a family one day but spending my income on me, and only me, seems pretty appealing too. My family is always curious to see where this love game will take Ian, because we know that he is interested in women but rarely expresses admiration for specific people (besides Selena Gomez, he's very upset about her unrequited love). In fact, Ian is set on "staying single forever" but I'd like to think that one day he could find a companion through The Social Scene or his day program at the JCC. I've always been a sucker for fairy tale endings. I think he is the captain of his own ship in this regard, and I'll be happy for him in whatever he decides just like I'm happy for my two siblings that are currently in relationships. Part of me admires Ian's ability to confidently say that he wants to stay single forever, because he isn't reliant on another person to make him happy or "complete" him. I wish I could employ the same kind of independence and self-fulfillment in my own life. The different agendas of love and relationships vary from human to human, and it's no different for people with developmental disabilities.

The last episode in the first season of *Born This Way* is titled "Don't Limit Me" which is based on a speech that Megan wrote and performed for the Douglas County School District. There is a particular line in her speech that most eloquently sums up what I've been trying to say in the last 13 pages: "Set high expectations, not impossible expectations. There is a difference, you know. You will learn a lot from me. Good teachers teach and learn from their students. I will teach you a lot about yourself. I will teach your students about people with disabilities. If you DON'T LIMIT ME. We will teach our school how to be an inclusive community." We are conditioned by the rules that society, the media, and culture give us on how we should act, how we should determine success, who makes the grade, who fails the grade. Ian has taught my family to question those rules and consider who we are and what we believe in by a different set of rules. I am able to manage my life through this lense because I grew up with having Ian in the family. People often impose limitations on those with disabilities because they don't know any better, because the only exposure they've had perpetuates the idea that they are limited in what they feel, what they can do, and how they express themselves. In turn, we are imposing limitations on ourselves by passively shutting out the entire spectrum of what it means to be human. *Born This Way* is documented proof that people with Down syndrome are vibrant, strong, independent, accepting, vulnerable, innately rational, frustrated, frustrating, and loving. I am thankful that the world can see a person with Down syndrome on television that is not characterized by their disability, but characterized by their personality traits, passions, and motivating forces. Ian, and the entire cast of *Born This Way*, has taught me that we all possess our own unique set of possibilities and limitations and in the end it's about finding that spark that ignites our own internal flame that matters most. Don't limit yourself by limiting others.

Chapter Ten

Other Voices, Continued

The 15 parents from across the U.S. and Canada - and seven members of Sadie's family - who graciously responded to our invitation to share detailed narratives about their experiences faced the same conundrums, and much much more. Keep in mind that we weren't attempting to generalize or make blanket assessments of behavior.

Many respondents meticulously plan their public excursions. A respondent from Florida likened heading out to an "expedition" for which her family had to be prepared "for all possible contingencies," especially when they were journeying to a new destination. Less planning was needed when an excursion took them to a familiar spot. "We need to be sure we have his backpack with a change of clothes, his sound-dampening earmuffs, and at least one toy," wrote our sixth respondent. The respondent and her significant other no longer have to discuss the plans, "because the process is routine," she said. Some asserted they didn't factor in the possible reactions of others when making plans. "I rarely cared too much about other people's reactions to my son," noted our seventh respondent. "I am careful about going anywhere too crowded or overwhelming for him, but I don't stress too much about making plans to go."

Other respondents have developed elaborate mental checklists. "What goes through my mind is: I hope he can handle the lines. I hope no one makes a comment that I am forced to respond to. I hope no one touches my son so I don't get arrested. I hope no one takes a picture of my license plate and decides they need to call DCP&P (New Jersey's Division of Child Protection and Permanency) because of witnessing a behavior and my response that they don't understand," explained a respondent from New Jersey. A couple from Chester County, Pennsylvania said that therapy for their 29-year-old son has eased his travel anxiety, but his parents still have to nail down "who is going to handle going through security, the plane, the confusion and noise, the restrooms." Visits to the homes of friends and family take place after they establish or recall whether he'll have to deal with their pets and after they figure out if he "will eat when he's there or just stay in their basement."

A mom from Western New York volunteered a poignant, heartfelt monologue. After estimating noise and conversation levels and determining whether she and her husband should pack extra clothes in case their son, who has Down syndrome, doesn't make it to the bathroom, the gymnastics in which many parents like them (and like us) engage is revealed:

> . . . can we leave the bag in the car or is the parking too far away so we have to bring the bag in with us? Who is going, all of us, or just one of us, does his twin (typical) brother want to come or would he rather stay at home or would he rather stay home?

They wonder if they'll encounter dogs, which their son is afraid of. Then it's onto technology:

> Do we need to bring his speech device/iPad and if we do, who is going to be in charge of it so it doesn't get lost. And will he be distracted by too much by the fact that the iPad has YouTube and Netflix on it to use for communication and/ or focus on what we are doing there.

The respondent noted that they should have the device with them at all times "since his speech is unintelligible to people who don't know him." But there's a tradeoff, she wrote: "the distraction factor is high which leads to it not being useful." She and her husband "end up taking it away and translating for him." And there's a downside: they are unable to reinforce for their son how to use it, and lose an opportunity to teach others that "yes, you can have a conversation with them just like 'real' people."

They wonder if the outing "will be successful, will it be welcoming, will it be awkward." They wonder, as we sometimes do, if one will get mad at the other for "trying too hard" or "calling attention to our group." The couple argues about places that for now they never visit with their son. Topping that list is Walt Disney World. "One of us is in no way ready to go there and live with that stress for even a long weekend while one of us thinks the window may be gone and is really ticked that our kid might not get to see this magic place where all his friends live," the respondent wrote, without specifying who was who.

In one case, it was the child whose anxiety governed the decision to head out. "Our son is 13 and HE (*respondent's capitalization*) has noticed that people stare at him," explained a respondent from British Columbia whose son has Down syndrome. "I couldn't even dismiss his comment," she wrote.

It is true - "people do stare at him. We now avoid crowds for this reason - he starts to get paranoid and very anxious if there are many people around."

A few respondents claimed they didn't plan and weren't concerned with what awaited them in terms of public reaction upon arrival. Passage of time often lessened the concern, at least in the case of the parents of a young man with Phelan-McDermid syndrome. Still, they do talk about "some people's reactions." When their son becomes excited, his mom "will affirm his excitement so others can understand," she said. Other folks avoided certain places altogether. "I need to know exactly what I have to buy at the grocery store, preferably already mapping out the trip to make it as quick as possible," explained a respondent from Minnesota. "We choose not to go out to other places knowing his behavior means no one, not us, him, or the people around us, will have a good experience. At least not for another few years."

This is on top of just getting through the days, which typically include appointments of various stripes. Sadie's sister Mae explained that since Ian is now of out of school, her role has changed from "interpreter" to "conductor." Gone are the teachers and specialists who used to help the family. "Operating the train through the congested railways of post-school life takes a lot of energy," Mae said. "There's no outside force propelling everything forward in the same way as when Ian was in a school setting. It's now completely up to she, Sadie, her parents, Clare and Gerald, and her brother, Cole, to stay in touch with a stocked roster of doctors and care coordinators. "Keeping the timetables ticking forward ticking forward by remembering where you left off with each person and what you have to do next takes a lot of organization and endurance," she said.

Like me, her dad went through an extended period of self-pity after Ian was born. I'm not sure mine has ended, so we should connect and talk. He initially saw Ian as "a drag on the entire family, robbing us of our vitality, wealth, and any hope for a 'normal' life." Vanity also colored these relationships. "How could I, a 'superior being,' have such a flawed offspring? How could we suffer the embarrassment of not having a 'normal' child," he asked. Ironically perhaps, his demeanor produced in others what he called "faux pity." He resented their reactions, believing that they came away from interactions ons with Ian thinking "wow, I'm really glad it wasn't me that suffered this lifelong misfortune."

Eventually, "one monolithic truth" changed the script: "[I]f we, his family, didn't or couldn't fight for Ian, then who would." Family members embraced the "warrior" role; "we couldn't afford to wallow in the what-ifs and half-truths," Gerald asserted. "We had to be fierce, have indestructible resolve, and not give a wit about what anyone else thought about any of it." Once they became Ian's defenders, "[t]he sun started rising again, food suddenly regained its flavor, jokes were funny again, [and] the future seemed like something I wanted to contemplate with optimism," Gerald said, along with the realization that there was "a whole community of people out there just like us, and they had somehow figured it out and were there to genuinely help us do the same."

The 13-year-old son of a Delaware respondent visits sites in the community - the grocery store, fast food restaurants, even the bookstore that houses his favorite escalator. As mentioned earlier, his IEP requires that he have one-on-one supervision. The respondent's two daughters accompany their mom and brother on family trips. "I always have to give people mean looks," she wrote, "because they are surprised by (my son's) high-pitched sounds" made "when he gets excited or is singing." At home, new locks ensure that her son can't get out of the house, as he had repeatedly in the past. "I feel like we are on 24-hour lockdown," she wrote. Fortunately, "as he gets older, he gets better with not running out of the house." The respondent wistfully explained that she is "too exhausted to continue explaining" about her son's autism. Her response of choice these days? "[M]ean looks."

A feeling of separation pervaded the responses having to do with family interaction. For us, they have two parts: the part where Neil tolerates hanging out with people, checking out the scene - if it's not a family member's home - hanging out while we catch up, and then heading for a set of stairs if one is available. Christmas means two hours on the multiple sets of stairs at his aunt's house, followed by an hour at the dinner table where he can see the stairs and subsequently pines, sometimes aggressively, to be back on them, two more hours on the stairs, an hour or so for present opening which features even more pining, and then more time on the stairs. Easter goes roughly the same way, except for some time on his aunt's glider.

With family interaction came pet theories and misinformation dispensed earnestly and just as often with arrogance. The respondent from Minnesota explained that when her mother learned her grandson was autistic, "she asked when he could start taking the pills and how long it would take to cure his autism." Her parents had also concluded that his autism "was a symptom of me working outside the home." Blame was also placed on our respondent from Delaware. "Some great aunts, and great great aunts, are very talented at saying the right things while STRONGLY (*respondent's capitalization*) implying that if I were a better Catholic and more diligent about praying my rosary and attending daily mass, my son would not be so challenged," she explained. From the in-laws of our western New York respondent came blame both for her ("it's always a problem with the eggs") and their son, who hesitated for some time to marry. "You waited too long and got too old," she recalled them saying. While the in-laws now show more compassion, the respondent has so far been unable to put the first round of comments behind her.

Even when their children were treated with kindness, respondents felt varying levels of stress. Their descriptions often had a "work in progress" feel. Family members at times were portrayed as working on warming up to their children or as being friendly now after not being friendly in the past. Respondents had to prepare for family visits with the same degree of skill and alacrity as for public excursions, and were always on alert for behaviors by their kids that might make others uncomfortable. "It still can be very stressful," noted our New Jersey respondent. "When he makes loud noises and funny sounds we try to hush him as it is inappropriate during parties." We consider ourselves quite lucky that our family members don't do this, even at solemn occasions like the funerals of Sheila's parents. Just recently, a young boy, may 8 or 9 years old asked if "anything was wrong" with Neil as he happily climbed a set of stairs - and later as he turned the steering wheel on a large model train - at a local children's museum. We've had numerous similar exchanges. We explain that he's happy, that those are his happy sounds, and that he communicates differently than other people.

A few respondents seemed to be happy with even the most perfunctory of interactions. "We are lucky for the most part, said our Chester County respondent. "Family will acknowledge him and ask how he is but that would be about it" aside from the occasional inquiry about the activities in which her son is involved. Then there are the parents who choose to scold and judge. The respondent from British Columbia speculates that her parents are "embarrassed" by her son. "They don't understand that his behavior is communication, and instead choose to threaten him or pull him by his arm to get him to 'listen' to him - neither of which we approve of," she wrote. It reached the point where her parents no longer babysit her son, and only see him when the respondent and her husband are present.

A little personal growth by a family member happens now and then. Sheila and I put these in the category of "little victories," or *parvis proeliis* for you Latin fans. While most of the cousins to the young man with Phelan-McDermid syndrome don't interact with him, one has softened with the passage of time, the young man's mom reports. "When his family came to the east coast for a baseball tournament, he gave" her son "a special team pin." It took a near-death experience for Minnesota respondent's father to spur he and his wife to ramp up their respect for the respondent and her children. "[W]hile they don't always honor my requests or my specific instructions for how to interact with my son," she explains, "they do respond to the best of their abilities and they try to appear as though they are not patronizing me."

A few families are paragons of acceptance. "We all know that" her son "is our "grouchy old man," said a respondent from New York. "He will say 'Buh-bye!' when we have people over because he doesn't want people in his space." Her son makes it a point "to escape from large gatherings and will "cover his ears when someone is talking to him." Yet the family is fine with it. "We all know he is who he is, and love him even with his attitude and sass," she wrote. A respondent who declined to indicate where she's from was even more emphatic, defiant perhaps: "We honestly never even think about anything related to any of our children before we go to family gatherings," she wrote. "The children in our entire family are treated exactly the same. If anyone feels differently about our son we would never know it." Members of our College Station, Texas respondent's family are similarly generous and understanding. "Because he gets overwhelmed so easily," she wrote, she and her husband limit themselves "to smaller gatherings, and places where we can 'escape' to a quiet place should he need it." Her father's birthday in 2016 was celebrated "with a relaxed meal at home with just my siblings and parents, rather than a large, chaotic party.

Attention does not always mean understanding, however. Our Florida respondent noted that while her family showers equal amounts of attention on all of the children, they "don't always understand the amount of care we must take with him." At times "they take for granted the ability to move about quickly or change plans. Our life moves at a slower, much more planned pace," she explained. Other families feign acceptance and then revert to ignoring the child. "They make a fuss over him and cook him his favorite meals and at holidays buy him things they know he will like," said the respondent from western New York. "But they also tend to let him sit there with his iPad or DVD player." Other children in the family do not include her son in play "unless we intervene or suggest it or facilitate it some way," which at times means she and her husband playing too. Their son, who is a teenager but is the size of an adult, will sometimes join in with the younger children, but his parents "have to be there to intervene/supervise because he really doesn't understand that he is the size of a man and could hurt the littler kids."

Aunts, uncles, and cousins from the other side of her family run the behavioral gamut. One set is wonderful with her son. They're "always happy to see him and spend time with him" and "will babysit if we need them to or take him to swim practice or dance if we ask." The apparently status conscious second set of relatives "kind of try too hard" when they interact with her son. "[I]t sometimes comes across as fake," she said. When they have cared for her son, he's been injured "or done something crazy like to in their bathroom and try to use a razor because they don't think they really need to supervise him." Even though her son is scared of dogs, they allow a cousin's dog at family gatherings, claiming it is "friendly." In one instance, her son's fear of the dog prevented him from making it from the basement to an upstairs bathroom in time. They cleaned their son and left the gathering early. Her husband eventually told the aunt and uncle about what happened "and asked if the dog could be excluded" from future gatherings or that they could be notified if the dog was going to be there.

Sadly, the occurrence turned into a hot "topic of conversation" within the family - and apparently with friends of her aunt and uncle. They all now believe that their son is not potty trained. "They were much more upset about the rug (in the basement) than the fact he was scared," the respondent recalled, and contended that *she and her husband* "made too much of a fuss about it." Since her in-laws died, they don't see the final set of aunt and uncles that often - "and that is fine with us," the respondent asserted "They don't 'do' Down syndrome," according to her husband. Her mother-in-law would buy the boys matching shirts for family photos, but the aunt and uncle had a limitless list of stall tactics to keep their son literally out of the picture. "He's busy, don't bother him, he doesn't have to be in the photo if he doesn't want to," the respondent noted. When she, in true Elizabeth Warren fashion, persisted, "they would try to put him on the end so they could crop him out." The respondent figured out what was going on and moved her son to the middle - but they were ready for her. "[T]hey would try to put their kids on the end as far away as possible, so they wouldn't have to sit near him." The aunt and uncle would roll their eyes at her "like I was the problem. Gifts for her son were often wildly inappropriate. "[H]e would always unwrap a toy that was suitable for a 6 month old even though he was very obviously beyond that," the respondent explained. Her son is unaware of their insensitivity. "[H]e runs to give them big hugs and kisses and they make a phony fuss over him," she said, "but it's very obvious to everyone but him that they would rather he didn't hug or kiss them." Oh - they only send his brother birthday cards. "Hello, they are TWINS *(respondent's capitalization)*," a clearly frustrated respondent noted. She speculated her aunt's unease may stem from the fact that she aborted a fetus which doctors confirmed would have Down syndrome "because she couldn't have a baby that wasn't 'perfect.'"

And then there are parents who simply withdraw - from the public, from their families. Her son's behavior - "he likes to go through people's homes, turn off/on lights, open all doors and look and sees what is there and open their refrigerators" for example - and the resultant criticism from family members caused a Delaware respondent to limit their outings to "certain areas" in her mom's home. Neil sets those limits for us; it's usually stairs, rooms with ceiling fans and maybe the swings, but that's about it. Like us, the respondent longs to connect with her family more frequently: "There are so many times when I miss family gatherings because I cannot go," she explained. Her son returns home from his group home for the holidays, "so no holiday celebrating for us. [We] have our own parties at home." Sheila reminds me not to cause Neil's world to shrink; he recently tipped over his dresser, narrowly missing his hands and legs. After making sure he was uninjured, I abruptly took it out of his room to prevent a replay, though I did explain why. He didn't seem to mind; he was enjoying slamming it against the wall before it fell. Still, this means that the only piece of furniture in his room is his bed - a single sized mattress shoved in a corner - and a bookcase anchored with long screws to the wall of his closet.

While some respondents noted increased compassion and enlightenment from family members over time, it still is a mixed bag. In some cases, one, two, or a few relatives will show compassion, while the rest do not. Yet a Colorado respondent's mother "lives close by and is probably (her daughter's) best friend. She consumes all of her grandmother's time during visits. She "connects much better one-on-one with adults," her mom said. "She has a harder time when she is with peers because she is not able to play at their level." The respondent from Minnesota said a family member who once insisted on eating out has "realized that this is not as much of a treat for our family as it is for him." Too much love isn't always a good thing, noted the respondent from New York. "My family is beyond compassionate, to the point that some of them (ahem, my mom) treat him with white gloves and not like the four year old he is," she wrote. It's fine that they want to protect him, "but I want him to be treated like other kids his age." For example, her son, " like any child who is allowed to get away with things, can easily get away with being bratty, and that's inappropriate." Our New Jersey respondent feels it's reasonable to expect that her now 18-year-old son act with a "certain amount of maturity." It's "natural," she said, "for people to look at an 18-year-old, 5-10 boy and expect him not to jump, scream, or hit."

Several respondents wished that relatives would send a little actual help their way along with all that love. "Many family members say they will help but I do not ask and they do not ask if I need help," said a Delaware respondent. We can attest that sometimes you just need to get out, if only to grab ice cream at a local creamery for the first time in years or hit the farmer's market for the first time period. Compassion doesn't get you out the door. Most respondents understand distance makes it impossible for relatives to help. "They can't help out with day to day stuff from over 100 miles away," said another Delaware respondent. Still, "family members who are relatively close in proximity may not call to check in or offer respite care," explained a New Jersey respondent.

And then there are the relatives who simply vanish. The New Jersey respondent's uncle married a woman who never was kind to her son. "She did not want (her son) involved in their wedding ceremony," she recalled. They weren't invited, and now are estranged. The Minnesota respondent has relatives who declined to read the books about her son's disability she suggested in the hopes the rust might be scraped from their brains and hearts. Their intransigence has introduced even more tension into the respondent and her partner's relationship with the family; their "very different" political views had already made them outliers. Some relatives like to preen publicly about accepting a relative with an intellectual disability. "My in-laws like to post inspirational crap on Facebook about people with Down syndrome, but have never ever spent time" with the son of our British Columbia respondent. "They seem to like the 'idea' of having a relative with a disability, but aren't interested in their lives."

Being open and honest about a child's experience doesn't cause light bulbs to illuminate, claimed the respondent from western New York. Her sister suggested - chided her is more like it - that she identified "a little TOO (*respondent's capitalization*) much as a parent of a kid with special needs." The respondent was incredulous. "Well . . . that IS (*respondent's capitalization*) who I am. Or at least a pretty giant part of who I am. As if we can change that or turn it off. What am I supposed to do otherwise - just pretend he doesn't have a disability?" So she took the bold - and rare - step of trying to educate her sister. She told her sister about the time a child with special needs grabbed her hair while she waited in her dentist's office to be seen. The respondent wasn't injured, and the dentist's staff apologized profusely. The child's mom didn't see what had happened, and the respondent asked the staff not to tell her. Her sister was amazed and angered that she had said nothing to the mother. What followed made me wish I was as brave: "I told her, no - look, this is the reality: If a kid is doing behaviors like that, he is doing them at home and at school and in the grocery store and EVERY-WHERE (*respondent's capitalization*)," she recalled. "HIS MOM KNOWS (*respondent's capitalization*) and she is probably freaking out about and stressed and worried and losing sleep trying all kinds of strategies."

She was probably taking fire from all quarters: "The teachers are telling her, people at church are telling her, the bus driver is telling her, probably she and her husband are arguing about what to do about it. BELIEVE ME, SHE IS WORKING ON IT (*respondent's capitalization*). The time in the waiting room might have been "the only 30 minutes she has today or MAYBE EVEN THIS WHOLE WEEK" to read a magazine or to text "or to just BREATHE (*respondent's capitalization*)," she asserted. "[T]here is no way in HELL (*respondent's capitalization*) that I am going to ruin that for her." It could be that her son was simply trying to say hello - "DID YOU EVER THINK OF THAT? (*respondent's capitalization*)" the respondent asked her sister. While the light bulb did in that moment go off, "I don't know if it's something she kept with her. It's not their life, they're not living it, so I can talk about it 'til the cows come home, advocate and educate but until they walk in our shoes they're really not going to get it totally." But she remains hopeful - and grateful: "I do appreciate it when they try!!!" As referenced throughout the book to this point, Sheila and I rarely, if ever, make a separate effort to educate people about Neil's challenges or altering their worldview. We don't fit the advocate's profile, to be sure, and Neil's care takes up a lot of time. Yet we admire the respondent's fearlessness and her vociferous defense of someone she barely knew.

Most of the respondents cautiously cited increased public acceptance of folks with intellectual disabilities. A few asserted that they have not experienced anything but acceptance. One practically announced that she and her family "live in a compassionate area," but acknowledged that she was "sure this is not the same elsewhere." Others noted - correctly in our view - that awareness does not always lead to acceptance. And a child's age plays a key role. The Chester County, Pennsylvania respondent sees more compassion "since autism is so widely publicized," but it helps that her son now is nearly 30, is working, volunteers in the community, and is better behaved. "It was much harder when he was small," she noted. During a gym class he took at age 10, he mimicked the actions of the boy in front of him. The boy's mother demanded that the respondent's son be kicked out of the class "because he made her boy uncomfortable" - we hope you're flashing back about now to our discussion of inclusion classes. Missed "was an opportunity for the child to learn compassion" by assisting her son. Yet one of the respondents from Delaware, as well as the respondent from Montgomery County, Pennsylvania, had nearly the opposite experience. People have become more compassionate since her son, now in his early 20s, was a baby. Now though, "my son is a grown, bearded man..not the cute kids he was at 7 or 8," she wrote. "There is still not a lot of tolerance for quirky behaviors coming from adults. Society is very focused on 'kids with autism.' Kids grow up."

The respondent from British Columbia took a decidedly dimmer view. "I'd say there is a real fear of 'other' and a push lately toward a more homogenized world," she said. Her son too is older, which means fewer "'aw, he's so cute' comments." She cited "greater discomfort with a teenager with a disability." She loves the demographic diversity of her hometown, but claims "the drawback is that there are many people new to our country who have never seen anybody with a visible disability before and some people gawk and openly stare." It's the age of the people out in public that most resonates with the respondent from western New York. "Some people are great and don't make a big deal of us moving through the world with them," she said. "I notice this more with younger people - kids, teens, 20s, and sometimes people in their 30s. They will always say hi to him in the store, give him a high five, generally not be shy of interacting with him - he loves to say hi to everyone when we are out."

Older people are, well, less kind. They "will often pointedly ignore him or make a disgusted face at him or something like that," the respondent recalled. "They will get annoyed when it takes us longer to go up the escalator or put our groceries on the belt or huff a little and ask 'the air' why on earth are we letting him scan the groceries at the self-checkout, it is taking so long." And then there are those folks "who go overboard with the compliments and (are) gushing to show how enlightened they are." Once in awhile, she will encounter a family with a child who has special needs - they "get it," she said.

"Actually they don't have to say it, you can tell by how someone acts and how genuine they are that they get it."

Companies and organizations have fallen in line - motivated by federal law of course, but also by a burgeoning sense of responsibility. "We have enjoyed sensory friendly shows on Broadway and at the movie theaters," said one of our New Jersey respondents. She added that her family has had "mostly positive experiences" at Disney parks. People are typically friendly, although now and then she still hears reports of folks being asked to leave shows - and airplane flights - for purportedly "disruptive" behavior. At Disney World, it's other attendees who cause the most trouble. "These experiences have included staring (even without a reason) and using a handicapped stall or bathroom that I needed for my son," she said.

The media have deepened misperceptions of behavior, said Sadie's dad, Gerald. They "paint all of these touchy topics with a broad brush," offering primarily "oversimplification of the real people, all one-dimensional and usually some gloppy *Huffington Post* version that bears no resemblance to the real world version." There is still a way to go to erase from the public's mind "the frightening 1970s institutional version" of care for the intellectually disabled. It might be too much to ask of the public to grasp the differences between Down syndrome "or any of a host of conditions that make our kids different from theirs." Still, exposure and providing points of contact are good things, he said. "I think the work that has been done lately on shows like *Glee* have been helpful and not pandering in an overly solicitous manner to a crowd that just wants to check the PC box." Sadie's sister Mae had similar reservations. Exposure, she said, "is the best way to normalize something." But folks with intellectual disabilities are "never the central character in a story." The audience sees them as "'the one with Down syndrome' instead of 'Becky, the cheerleader' or 'Tom, the drummer.' Their disability is their character," she said.

Our comfort level - not the child's or the family's is of paramount importance. "[T]hey think that every child with autism is like the *Rainman* movie," a Delaware respondent said. "They don't understand about aggression, tantrums, safety, and security." Reactions to she and her son run a maddening gamut. "I have experienced people shaking their head when they hear (her son) walking down an aisle. I have seen people give me mean looks when he has a tantrum because he is frustrated that he can't tell me what he needs, wants, or is in pain," she explained. Headaches cause her son to bang his head on nearby surfaces. "Some people think, 'should I just put him in an institute and let someone else, a stranger, raise him.'" Others overstep their bounds by offering worthless advice. "Like, 'what do you think caused his autism?'" she said. "Or 'why don't you try this, or try that?'" As if she already hasn't tried everything; boy, can we empathize with her on this point. Sadly, despite fundraising and lining up a second job, she is unable to afford a promising therapy for her son. Insensitivity has caused her to stop talking with coworkers. Thus, she and her son spend even more time in their "bubble."

Thus, it warms the heart a bit to read that there are some kind people out there. An attendant at a carnival allowed the son of a New Jersey respondent to ride the carousel for free as many times as he wanted. "That really touched our hearts because we did not even think she would have noticed him in such a busy crowded line," the respondent wrote. The son of another New Jersey respondent received extra time with Disney characters and a walk with Goofy. The young man from Chester County had learned to tolerate traveling by plane, but it helped if his family was headed to the beach. On the way home from what turned out to be a sightseeing vacation, "tears start to fall from his eyes and he says 'no Bahamas'?" his mom recalled. "An astute flight attendant sees this and tries to comfort him. He offered him treats and very kind soothing words." The respondent from Minnesota - a college professor - said that when she shared her son's autism diagnosis with a student who also is autistic, "she congratulated me and told me all of the awesome things about autistic kids! (*respondent's emphasis*)." Surprised by her student's reaction, the respondent cried. At least one person "didn't think his life would suck being autistic."

Some in the respondents' villages went the proverbial "extra mile" to engage with their kids. A preschool teacher in Texas read extensively on her own and accompanied the respondent to a Temple Grandin lecture to better connect with the respondent's son. "She has allowed several therapists to observe my son on site at her school. Each therapist has always commented to me afterwards about how well she knows and works with him, and was impressed by her questioning them (the therapists) about how better to work with him," she recalled. That included honoring his fascination with geography by spending more time on it in class. But her son moved on to kindergarten; he struggled to adjust. So his former teacher "let us come and spend every Thursday afternoon with her after school, and let him come back in the summer," his mom said. Administrators at the school attended by the Colorado respondent's daughter are "so kind," she reported. "They go to her class and carry her to the nurse's office" when she needs a rest. "When she wakes up, she gives each of the front office workers a hug and they give her a snack and take her back to class."

More news coverage and "feel good stories," as the Montgomery County, Pennsylvania respondent called them, was cited more than once as a possible source or inspiration for this compassion. Greater societal awareness and push back against discrimination - both of which have stalled it seems during the first months of the Trump administration - has meant more kindness, however perfunctory or misguided it at times may be. But this progress doesn't lessen the impact of the hurtful reactions to these kids. Some simply stare or look on in disbelief. A nurse asked the Florida respondent about her son, "was he born like this?" One of the Delaware respondents recalled a woman saying to her son, "Oh my, you're too big to be screeching like that." Some are over with quickly, but sting nonetheless: a New Jersey respondent recalled her son being yelled at by a store clerk after he threw a juice box. When her son was diagnosed, the respondent from Minnesota caught flack from the speech therapist, who "basically told me she couldn't believe I didn't notice it before. She never implied I'd hurt him by not getting help sooner, but she made me feel like a fool."

When a New Jersey respondent's son was 7, he and his mom were at the store. Around his neck he wore a T-shaped chewy tube threaded through a string. It was a "comfort item." Her son fell. "An older woman, in her 80s, stepped forward," she recalled. "I thought she was going to help my son up off the floor. She snatched the chewy tube out of his mouth and told me he was too old for such foolishness."

Sometimes contempt comes disguised as concern with a dash of judgmental. The respondent from western New York bemoaned the fact that so many people reject her son because he's unable to follow society's rules. But when she went to buy new glasses, he was calm. The respondent picks it up from there:

> The person at the counter wouldn't look at him directly; she kept looking at him out of the corner of her eyes and turning her head away from him, while at the same time telling me what a 'wonderful' person he was and how 'blessed' and an 'angel on earth' and 'sure to get into heaven.'

The respondent asked the clerk how she reached these conclusions, especially given that they had never met before. "She just gestured with her head to my son. I didn't even give her the chance to show me any eyeglasses and I'll never go there again." Something similar happened to us when in 2012 we visited Cooperstown, New York and the Baseball Hall of Fame. I wandered into a shop that sold a bewildering array of custom bats. Sheila and Neil, then 10, waited outside. Sheila made Neil smile by twirling an umbrella. As I looked at the bats and revisited my fantasy of playing first base for the Mets, I overheard one of the employees make a disparaging remark about Neil's happy noises, clearly audible from the sidewalk. "Who is that?" said one. "That's my son," I half-proudly, half-angrily - OK, three-quarters angrily - announced. I hung up the bat and walked out. I caught a sheepish look from one of them as I did.

But nothing - at least for me - tops the reaction fielded by the Newark, Delaware respondent at a local pizza-themed restaurant. Her son was playing in a ball pit with another boy. They were enjoying themselves. The other boy's father saw them, went over, "grabbed his son by the elbow and

YANKED (*respondent's capitalization*) him out of the pit, shouting 'Get out of there. They shouldn't let things like that out in public." Stunned and pissed off, the respondent nevertheless remained calm, as she was alone there with her kids. "If there had been someone there to take the kids home I would have spent the next few months in jail for assault."

It's little wonder then that so many of the respondents have curtailed their activities, as referenced earlier. Some make minor adjustments to the schedule, especially if the venue, the event, or the noise might overwhelm their young charge, if siblings were part of the journey, or where keeping up with him or her would require more than one person. "But we would never take him out. He loves to go out!" said one of the New Jersey respondents. For some, other medical concerns make the decision for them, as was the case for the Florida respondent, whose son struggles with immunosuppression. The Colorado respondent's daughter has to sleep after suffering seizures. When a seizure occurs right before they head out, plans have to be altered or abandoned. She once suffered a seizure atop a play structure. "When things like this happen, it makes me hesitant to take her places where I can't be right by her at all times," the respondent said. "But I don't want to shelter here to a point where she can't learn or grow. I don't worry about what other people think; I just worry for her safety." Another respondent acknowledged that reactions from others bother her. "I am afraid that his behaviors will cause others to look at him differently," she said. Even more paralyzing is the fear that a pregnant woman - or one considering having a baby - would see her son's behavior and decide then and there to abort a fetus that has Down syndrome. "It's a bit over exaggerated," she admitted, "but I don't want to take any chances."

It helps us if a venue has an escalator or a set of stairs - the Newseum in Washington, DC has a stellar set - but that means we don't experience what we came for, or experience it in carefully choreographed bursts. The respondent from Newark, Delaware forgot her son's intolerance of noise when for his 21st birthday she bought him tickets to see his favorite stand-up comedian. "12,000 people at the Wells Fargo Center for Jeff Dunham was too much for him," she noted, "My 17-year-old daughter watched the show while I walked the halls with my son." Top restaurants are out too. "There are just some things best left undone," she said. It can be particularly painful if a child doesn't appreciate being stared at; such is the case with the British Columbia respondent's son. "We won't go to family gatherings or other parties if we feel people aren't going to be friendly or understanding." As a consequence, she concluded, "[w]e tend to have a very small social circle and really don't have many friends."

Respondents acknowledged minor and major changes to their own behavior when out in public with their kids. It's necessary, said the Chester County, Pennsylvania respondent, "to be somewhat milder in public." For her family, this means avoiding places "where I know he won't be success-ful" that, and lots of practice. It took nearly a month of sitting, and later a month of standing in a church parking lot before her son was ready to attend a family christening. "I'm definitely aware of how I am perceived when I am out and about," said the respondent from Minnesota. "I think there's a strug-gle there of managing your own public face and managing less controlled environments for your kids." In fact, that desire to manage drove most of the behavioral shifts. The respondent from western New York admitted that she puts on her "'happy' face a lot when we are out, even if I am tired or in a bad mood or not feeling well, because I don't want people to assume it is because of my child or [to] reinforce any negative stereotypes." These changes have become standard operating procedure, though they do compel at least one respondent to now and then "look at other kids in the mall and imagine how simple our lives would be too if our son was like that."

We do too. Ninety percent of the time (probably 95 percent in Sheila's case), we are proud, compassionate, accepting parents. But every so often we ponder a life where Neil could tell us what's on his mind, where the time spent on his care could be spent at the piano or on the baseball field, where he wouldn't pinch or pull hair. My journey back to reality usually includes a stop of contrition where I wish his body wasn't so ravaged by CF. "I make a concerted effort to display love and joy with my son when I am in public because I have noticed that others will cue off of my responses to him," said the respondent from Florida. For example, "[i]f I act embarrassed or ignore him, so will other people and so will my other children."

The "love and joy" she and the other respondents experience are genuine to be sure. The goal always is to ensure the child's safety, even if that means "shushing" a child now and then. "He thrives on routine and consistency," said the Texas respondent, "so if we changed how we interacted in public, that would upset him." Now and then this means "acting strangely in public, but that's okay." Or more than okay in the case of the Newark, Delaware respondent. Some time back, she had taken her son to see the animated version of *The King and I*. Near the end of the film, the King brings Anna onto the dance floor. Just then, "my son stood up, took my hand, and dragged me out to the aisle to dance," the respondent recalled. "Was it typical? No. But was it doing any harm?" The small crowd that day was not bothered by their dance. "After the credits, two much older ladies approached us, compli-mented him on being a gentleman, and [told] me that we had made their day," she said. Her conclusion? "Quirky is odd, but it's not always bad."

Words to live by. As is empathy. The respondent from British Columbia said she makes it a point to "nod and smile at other parents out there to show my compassion toward them, and ask moms if they need a hand if their child is having a tantrum or they look like they have their hands full." It is our fervent wish that folks recognize that every now and then we can't always sustain our public behavior at home. The Colorado respondent acknowledged that her responses to her daughter's tantrums have included "a pop on the butt," locking her in her room "until she wears herself out," and spraying "water in her face to try and snap her out of it." Another admitted that her patience with her son, who has Down syndrome, has diminished, especially since the birth of her second child. "I still work on being more 'compassionate' when he has a meltdown in public," the respondent said. Still, she feels "like people look at me like I am a horrible person 'yelling at the Down's kid.'"

And then there are those respondents who have decided essentially to tell the public to get over itself. "I stopped apologizing for my son's behaviors a long time ago," asserted a New Jersey respondent. The sounds he makes, singing loudly, and touching things are "what he has to do to be able to navigate his surroundings without melting down completely. It doesn't matter to me what anyone thinks." Citing her own "Jersey Girl" attitude, the Newark, Delaware respondent said, "I do what want or need to do; the rest of the world can think what they want." Still, respondents constantly evaluate their own performance and search for ways to engage their children while out in public. Positive reinforcement - and lots of it - candy, snacks, iPads - whatever it takes. But sometimes even endless reflection and effective tactics are no match for a child's behavior. A Delaware respondent recalled her son's lengthy tantrum after a doctor's appointment. He reacted badly after she tried to pull up his pants and took him aside after he urinated on the sidewalk outside the hospital. He struck both she and her mom. Security rushed over to help and stayed with the respondent while her son calmed down. "Now we make sure, when we arrive, we use the bathroom, and when we leave, we use the bathroom again," she explained. This new ritual is complicated by her son's need to use the faucet and sink in the bathroom for long periods - nearly an hour and a half in one case. Nevertheless, she is more affectionate toward her son in public "so that people see he likes hugs and kisses," that "he is not all bad."

At times these strategies take the form of either overstating or understating a child's challenges. "I might understate challenges when I'm taking to friends, acquaintances, or some relatives because I don't think they are really interested in hearing anything but my son is doing fine," said the respondent from Chester County, Pennsylvania. Others engaged in advocacy on their kid's behalf. "[W]hen my son was 6 or 7, I felt like I had to be the 'Down syndrome' cheerleader with everybody," recalled the British Columbia respondent, "so they would think more highly" of folks like her son. Eventually, the lobbying exhausted her. Now, "I simply only confide in others who 'get it' - e.g. other moms or those who work with people with disabilities."

But the respondent from western New York pushes on, talking about her son's disability at the outset of any relationship - "like let's get this out of the way," she said. "If they react badly, then I gauge whether I want to put the effort in to educate and advocate." If the person is "unfazed" or shares their own relevant experience, "then maybe I can let them in our inner circle. Which is very small. Let's face it, it's miniscule." It would help if more folks recognized and accepted that she can't leave her son at home. "So I might overstate things in the beginning just to make sure people don't get ticked at me later when I have to bail on plans," she said. Unfortunately, some folks simply stop asking her to socialize. One of the New Jersey respondents used to go one further; she carried an "Autism Card," giving it to "cashiers, store employees, or anyone who just stared too hard." Eventually though, she realized that "my son is not anyone's business really and autism is just what he has, not who he is." But the desire to see a child accepted by his or her peers can be unwavering. Thus, one respondent continues to believe she must overstate her son's capabilities "to ensure that he has friends, which I don't think he personally cares to have many of." Once, a friend tried to show her son something on an iPad. Her son "threw his head back" and "started yelling because he didn't want to be bothered." Embarrassed and frustrated, the respondent recognized that his actions made everyone uneasy. "I know he can be such a good boy and is better than that . . . but sometimes I wonder if he 'can' be," she said.

Sometimes just a slice of internal peace is the goal. "I always understate my child's challenges because I guess in my mind, I do not want to think that things as bad as they really are," said a Delaware respondent. The main impetus, though, is ensuring that members of her family don't worry too much about her. Her son asks repeatedly to do nearly everything - throw something in the trash, put salt and pepper on his food, put his bowl in the sink once the meal is done. She soft-pedaled the repetition "because I do not want them to think it has gotten that bad, but in reality it has." On the other hand, overstating her son's challenges in meetings with school and governmental officials ensures he that receives much needed services. Like us, she fought a protracted battle to obtain a communication device for her son. Unlike us, it took years, not 18 months. Her son now attends a school whose staff is more responsive to his challenges and where he is learning to communicate. "But, of course, the school waited until their staff was getting hurt in the classroom to approve the decision," she said. "It was not bad enough that everyone in my family was getting hurt" thanks to her son's aggressive behavior. "It should not have gotten this bad and he should have received better services years ago" to help him.

Trying to pry loose money from insurance company vaults isn't the kind of story that triggers a journalist's Spidey-sense, the respondents argued. We see families trying to coax their kids onto airplanes or to ensure that a wheelchair makes it onto the plane. "They show the trials and tribulations which is good, but sometimes make it seem as though all autistic people are the same," said the respondent from Chester County, Pennsylvania. This maddening consistency produces similar responses from people, she said. "I don't know how many times people ask if my son was like *Rain Man*, because that is all they know." A Delaware respondent concurred: "Not everyone is autism is Bill Gates or Sheldon Cooper," she said. "[T]he media still needs to be taught that autism and developmental delays are NOT (*respondent's capitalization*) a mental illness, as stated in lots of news stories these days." What we don't see, at least according to the respondents, are stories about children with more severe intellectual disabilities. "One thing that is often missed is the socioeconomic disparity of people with disabilities," said the Minnesota respondent. "The array of people with disabilities is huge and the media has done very little toward helping people understand this."

We also rarely see or read about the experience from the perspective - the actual perspective, not one that sustains a pre-existing narrative - of the person who has an intellectual disability. We might become more compassionate if the media could get beyond *Born This Way* and other stories "that show how difficult they make life for everyone else," she said. Also missing is any consideration of how a child's disability actually affects caregivers and family members, said the Texas respondent. "There is never a real, true story about the real struggles of home life," said one of the Delaware respondents.

A New Jersey respondent picked up on the *Rain Man* theme: in television shows and movies, "those with intellectual disabilities are just so cute and clean with savant type abilities, Never do we see a person with muscular issues in the face and jaw or body. We would never see someone with an open jaw, unable to swallow their saliva. We would never see a person who needs toileting assistance, or a person who needs diapers."

Like Neil.

The Delaware respondent offered a similar assertion. "In the *Rain Man* movie, I only remember him having a mild tantrum." In addition, she said, "they mostly showed all the great things that he could do, like calculate numbers, and [that he was] a genius at remembering events." I nodded in agreement and let out an internal cheer or two when she expressed her hope that a movie would someday be made on her son's life "that would show the other side of his silent world."

Non-profit organizations paying inordinate attention to individuals with less severe disabilities characterizes the experience of the respondents. Some don't have any connections with non-profits, while the respondent from Minnesota said she and her family hope to launch one. Fundraising with groups tends to be exaggerated, focused on the 'superstars' with Down syndrome," said the respondent from British Columbia, "and not the challenges and experience of regular people with Down syndrome." One of the New Jersey respondents pulled her son from Special Olympics because she felt the group favored "participants who are higher functioning and more independent." The organization's promotional materials "seem to imply that anyone with intellectual disabilities is included." The organization would likely counter that this is indeed the case, but I agree with the respondent that the public face - and the media coverage - does sometimes skew toward folks with less severe disabilities, as referenced in a previous chapter. Today, her son plays in the Miracle League, a nonprofit that empowers kids of all abilities to play baseball. The respondent wrote warmly of the group's "simple message of letting participants experience the fun of baseball." It "promotes a sense of family," she said.

One of our Delaware respondents, who works for a non-profit that advocates for families of kids with special needs, said that exaggeration is standard operating procedure. "Is the work of these non-profits well-meaning? Absolutely. Do we always get it right? Of course not. Do we sometimes claim credit for correlation while implying causation? That's how grants get funded. Do some grant-funded programs cherry-pick participants to ensure a higher degree of success? Of course - again, that's how grants get funded, and re-funded," she explained.

It helps if parents are running the show, said a New Jersey respondent. "We have had the least success with nonprofits and agencies where policies have been developed by intellectuals with many letters after their names who have no clue what the day to day experiences are for the families they serve," she said - and I take no offense. She doubled down: "It seems the information they depend on isn't valuable if it wasn't obtained in a textbook written by an individual with many letters after their name or presented in a workshop hosted by an intellectual with many letters after their name," she said.

I still don't take offense.

And sometimes there are tradeoffs. One of the Delaware respondents said she was involved with an autism-centered nonprofit. Her son attended a camp sponsored by the organization until the fact he still wears diapers made it impossible. The group mandates that the kids be high-functioning and that they are able to communicate verbally. Yet the group also used her story of how her son had wandered away from their home on several occasions as part of its advocacy for legislation that required insurers to cover autism-related expenses. And she is still paying for therapy provided before the bill was signed into law.

But as is the case with Neil's time at the Mary Campbell Center, the son of the western New York respondent has had exceedingly positive experiences with non-profit groups. "He's found a lot of love" with an organization that provides dance classes for kids with special needs, making friends both his age and older. "We parents have bonded too; since he is one of the youngest I call them my 'early warning system,'" she said. The group does deploy success stories in order to secure funding, "but I think they are pretty good about being respectful and not exaggerating things," she asserted. "I will tell them if I think they are getting too over the top." That layer of oversight is why they put parents on their board of directors. A summer camp attended by her son gives her the same feeling of comfort. "The staff is fabulous. I can't say enough about them; they really love our kids," she said. It's particularly reassuring - and heartwarming - "when you pull up to camp and counselors come running to greet your kid shouting his name." Because we arrive at the Mary Campbell Center early in the morning on camp days, the volunteers don't usually run out to greet us, but they do a fair imitation of the *Cheers* gang when we arrive.

So once again, it's a mixed bag. Signs of progress. Glimmers of hope. But also leftover bigotry, intransigence, and indifference. It would be a more compassionate world if more of us - myself included - could be moved to the epiphany experienced by Ian's dad: "[I]t all comes down to the people in your life and your relationship with them; everything else is just window dressing." Ian, he said, "is the truest expression of what it means to be human; vulnerable, strong, innately rational, loving, frustrated, frustrating, accepting, needy, independent, resilient, and comforting."

Chapter Eleven

Those Who Demand Attention

As Morgan, Sadie, and I sought a publisher for the book, a kind and valued Drexel colleague connected me with a few agents. I reached out, and sent along some of the early chapters. I appreciated the candor in their responses, especially since my contact was a) out of the blue and b) the result of old fashioned path greasing. They had some questions: Was this an academic or a personal exploration? Were we attempting memoir or writing a self-help book? Fair enough. But the main theme of their comments boiled down to this: don't challenge the audience. One told me that we shouldn't "damage the illusion that life is OK." Modulate your tone; don't vent. "Don't hammer them," one said. Based on the sample chapters, they concluded we had over-reached in our attempt to highlight the insensitivity still directed toward folks with intellectual disabilities. Folks won't just "snap out of it," one said. A keen observation about human nature, to be sure.

One comment in particular stood out for me—slapped me in the face actually—as I went through my notes to begin bringing our journey to a close. He spoke derisively of "those who demand attention by their difference."

Where to begin? Do we still say, "Oh no you didn't!"

Neil doesn't demand attention to drive awareness of his disability. He's not an activist, except when he's deployed as one without his knowledge by Special Olympics and related groups (though to be fair, we sign the photo release forms usually without thinking). The agent's tone-deaf comment speaks to the power of the narrative we've created and now inhabit about folks with intellectual disabilities. So let's also be held just the tiniest bit accountable here: *You've* made them into show ponies, reap and revel in the publicity and the self-congratulation, and now believe and tell the world that they want it that way. Bullshit. *You* demand attention for being temporarily kind to and engaged with them. For volunteering for one event, for making small monetary contributions to an organization or two, for allowing them to take a three-point shot—and then denying them the chance to walk with their high school's graduating class, as happened recently to a young man in Arkansas ("Update," 2016) . *You* dip your toes in our lives—pat a head, flash a smile, offer half-assed comments about how beautiful our sons and daughters are, and then you move on with your life, having knocked being kind to an intellectually disabled kid and his family off of your self-advancement list. *You* resume your fake anguish or congratulate yourself for stepping outside your emotional comfort zone. And then you go right back to using the word "retard." A 2017 Harris Poll found that 9 out of 10 of us have been present when the word was used. Half of us have been around when the word was directed at an individual with an intellectual disability (Heasley, 2017).

You—and Eunice Kennedy and the Shrivers—mount the movements, support the causes, but in so doing narrow the behaviors of our kids for public consumption. And let's not forget they altered a family member for the sake of political expediency. Their overcompensation, and the work of groups similar to Special Olympics, is all well intentioned, but it rarely proceeds from, encourages, or builds on genuine interaction with them. A significant percentage of teens and adults still believes that it's OK to "describe a thing or situation as retarded" (Heasley, 2017). *You* constrain their activities in inclusion classes and say little when politicians move to cut budgets, as is happening these days in Delaware. *You* indicate in forms both obvious and subtle that we should revel in—and be grateful for—the progress that society has made, for having more care options. At least they won't go right into an institution or group home; they can hang out in school until their 21! *You* expect us to be resilient and plucky, full-time full throated advocates for our kids.

You know what? Talk to the hand. You try living like someone has coated the backs of your eyes with mayonnaise.

I had a dream when I was seven years old: I was late for school; I was well aware that my second-grade teacher, a 40-year classroom veteran, did not tolerate tardiness, so I rushed down the stairs, out the door, and off to school, which fortunately was only about four blocks from our house.

I did so without my pants.

I'm certainly not charting any new Freudian or Jungian terrain here, but it shook me. The last image before I woke up was me standing in front of the class in my tighty-whiteys, soaking in shock and ridicule from my classmates. For about two years after the dream, I carried a softball sized Westclox alarm clock around with me—to breakfast, to the bathroom—to ensure that I wouldn't be late. Today, of course, I obsess about time with the aid of a Smartphone. I joke with my students and with Sheila that I'm 15 minutes early for everything, I tell them, and that it's all because of this dream I had nearly a half-century ago.

But these days, my obsession is more about trying to reclaim pockets of time from Neil's care, to capture every last second of time for myself and for us before he returns from school or camp. I leave at 8:45 a.m. on Tuesdays and Thursdays for a drive to Drexel that I can complete, even with some traffic congestion, in about 50 minutes, leaving me about an hour before I leave about a half-hour early for an 11 a.m. class that meets in a building directly adjacent to mine.

And what do I do with that time? Spin my wheels—revise my class notes rather than trust that I can speak intelligently about topics I've taught for nearly 25 years. Check my email. Grab coffee. Stare. I can't count the number of times that I have set the goal of engaging with Neil without counting the minutes. It's acceptable to make sure that he heads out for the bus on time, of course, but I'm talking about checking the clock in our office every ten minutes when we're spending weekend afternoons or days of school vacation together. I have, however, managed to dial back the fussing and anxiety about getting him into his chair promptly at 5 to feed him. And even that is so I have a decent chunk of time to spend with Sheila in the evenings. What's sad is that on those weekend days, it goes more smoothly when Sheila is upstairs or out with friends—his rate of pinching and hitting goes up dramatically when she's in the room, as if he knows it upsets her. I soldier on, telling her that the procedure has to be done—so brave! In actuality, my energy is spent reminding her how hard it is. I sometimes ramp up the fight for her benefit. Yet I miss her so, so much. The song "I Miss You" by Klymaxx plays in my head when we're apart, but it fights up there with resentful score-keeping.

Blame stress. Blame fatigue. Blame likely mental illness. Blame my parents for not teaching me how to deal with or reroute my anger. For not discussing that they both likely suffered from depression—my mom for sure suffered from postpartum depression after having giving birth to both me and my brother. I remember that she spent a lot of time in her room after he was born. The same woman hired to help her raise me while Dad was off working was hired to help raise my brother.

Talk about your bubble. The pop culture references, the ritual M*A*S*H and *West Wing* viewing—they're safe, convenient. At least I can be an expert in that, in them, even though Sheila sometimes remembers plotlines and actor's names more readily than I do. My arrogance sometimes extends to Neil's care, to the point that Sheila, in her "Outfit Fairy" guise, abandoned selecting Neil's clothes because of my editing. Most of it predates us; it's not a shared experience, except for the tolerance Sheila has for it. In all of this self-involvement, I put aside loving him. Or it's not a priority. I come from a long line of dithering pragmatists whose pragmatism isn't buttressed by a whole hell of a lot of common sense.

Then there's the vocabulary—"duke," "put them in the cooker booker," "banging and gassing"—it's all done to segregate, to make me the expert (in something) because she's so damned good at running everything else. It excludes her. A humble brag of sorts. Again, a lack of empathy. Yet it warms my heart when she uses them. Now it's to the point that I feel like she's started to treat me like an adolescent incompetent. It's totally my doing—the absent-minded professor as performance art. And then I figure out an aspect of my iPhone in just seconds. We had a conversation during our early dating phase, though after we knew we'd commit to each other. I told her that I'd eventually suck the life right out of her. And it's happening. I see the absolute and total love of my life going off and doing things—but I need a kick in the ass to remember, to consider what she's going through—her declining health. She has diabetes, she'll undergo surgery in a couple of weeks for a potentially cancerous thyroid. We've both eluded death. Sheila's first bout with cancer should have killed her. And if she hadn't nudged me to go up to check on Neil, I'd likely be dead of the infection that so severely damaged my hand. It happens in drips, peeling paint, rust. Her parents died within a year of each other. And all I can think of and ruminate on is how much I have to do in the evenings. Not that the staggering isn't a little bit real—but it's become the norm; I worry that she won't remember my only slightly less self-involved but slightly more joyous self. But there are still outbursts and deep dives into depression. It's been better since we've back from our 20th anniversary trip to the Caribbean that required formulation of a babysitting schedule that made a Rube Goldberg machine look like an inclined plane. Yet led by Sheila's determined and quite capable sister, and armed with a 16-page guide we produced (and that was the seed for this book), six or seven villagers gave Neil excellent care. We joked that we'd be totally satisfied so long as he stayed out of the hospital and came back to us in one piece. Not quite the truth, although I wondered if he was peering downstairs from behind his gate because he was sad we were leaving or if he was anticipating the arrival of visitors. An odd combination of sadness and relief came over me as we headed out the door. Yet we managed to keep talk of his care to a minimum on the trip; we sent some pictures and received some of Neil and Sheila's sisters playing Snoopy Soccer, which apparently involved throwing balls down our stairs at a dancing Snoopy I purchased at a Hallmark store for Sheila. Smiles came our way when we returned, but Neil got right back to the business at hand on the steps, and then looked for the villagers from the second his aunt closed the front door and headed for her car. Maybe he was getting us back for tearfully playing the "disabled son" card when we realized in the office of the resort in St. Maarten that we had arrived a week early. Fortunately, a kind staff member took pity on us and found us a room.

I rail inside when she gives me gifts that require assembly or a lot of time to use. I try to give her one-off gifts. Things that she'll enjoy, use right away. And I never get to use mine. Vessels of resentment. Empathy felt, but in a forced way, as if required by a teacher. We're separated by roles that are equally valid. But the immersion makes you think your role is more important. But it's not her fault! It's a product of her optimism, not just of her love for me. An expression of hope that we can still do all these things, go down all these paths, explore new and existing interests. Photography. My digital camera is now ancient. Learning to speak Spanish. These are aspirational gifts—a throwback to a simpler time, when we could focus on each other. Sheila acknowledges the loss, but does so with more ebullience and optimism than I do. It's also her defense, I would guess, against how much time it takes to care for him. Not being able to look at him for fear—of what? He might squawk, complain, grab, pinch. I start shaking some days the moment I get up or when I walk up the steps to change him on a weekend morning.

At times it feels like the desire to explore is dying in me—and I blame the two of them, when in fact it is totally on me. I am, after all, the grandchild of the mistress of routine. The last act of our Sunday visits with my grandmother was laying out her Monday morning breakfast setting—plate, bowl, silverware, small Kel-Bowl-Pak of Special K, coffee cup and saucer. This after watching baseball, football, golf, perhaps a game of catch in the parking lot behind her apartment building, and a Stouffer's dinner in front of the TV.

Anyway: this is why I'm sick and tired of people telling us Neil's is lucky to have us—lucky to have me. He's not. I'm lucky that he likely doesn't internalize or isn't apparently damaged by the bile I spew his way, the anger, the outbursts, which I now instantaneously repackage as playful raucousness. It's convenient for me. So long as there's no bruising, and because he can't tell a teacher or aide or bus driver what I've said or describe what I've thrown, I'm covered. His disabilities offer a measure of protection from prosecution. And in the bargain, I can play the dutiful father, enjoying Neil's company while fending off the nasty and quizzical looks, downplaying the severity of his challenges (calling it "mild cerebral palsy"), acting as if I don't give a shit about their discomfort, but every so often feeling pangs of embarrassment. But then feeling totally unconditional love when he snuggled next to me on the school bus back from a field trip to the Franklin Institute.

Let's go with this: Do not adopt, or at least think very carefully, about taking a flexible approach to adopting (*yay!*) if you have anger issues and a simmering depression and haven't made significant progress in dealing with them. But it's so damned exhausting—and that's with our growing roster of very helpful friends and associates. This is what they don't show on the news stories about the kids overcoming disabilities: how their parents have to juggle jobs, dogs (not literally, although it could be fun), their own health issues, extended families, and just trying to sneak out for a date once in awhile. Fetishization of the disabled abhors context. You get used to being in regroup mode; it's proverbially like being frogs in the pot. I wonder sometimes what it would feel like to not be in this mode. Where do these thoughts come from? Just so much to take care of—problem is, I've thought that for some time. It's my nature, to be overwhelmed, to make lists to fend it off, like my mother. I think is the look the same, the smile, the feelings. I doubt, but then when I have to leave her in the hospital, it's Sheila and Ron all over again. Perhaps I've never been as nice or as empathetic as I thought I was, or as I thought others thought I was. Writing my parts of this book is probably just an exercise in narcissism, of thin reflection, of exploitation. Yet I can see, taste, smell being selfless. I'm nice to my students, nicer than I am to Neil. I blame him for taking me away from my calling—how conceited is that? Just using the word devalues the struggle faced by folks who aren't working in their ideal jobs. There are glimmers of compassion. It may be true that I'm the most compassionate one in my original family, but that's like saying I'm the least violent criminal in a gang. I come off as the nice guy, but in my mind at times it's all been a grand imposition. How is it possible for a father, a parent, a dad, a human being to say that about his child? To so often treat him with such disrespect and disregard?

But, I say, it's assault, plain and simple. You can see the change in mood, in intent. But malicious? And where did he learn it from? I taught him to throw, sure, but I also taught him that it's OK to throw when you get angry—and shout. It's a good thing he can't speak, because I'm sure half of what he'd say when he was pissed would be profane. During one fit of anger, I hit myself with such force before Thanksgiving that I caused a long, Western Hemisphere-shaped bruise on my thing. I rationalized it—at least I didn't hit him. I didn't break anything or throw something. But that's not progress. All I could think about then was how the incident—which I don't even remember—would affect me, my thought process—about cleaning my damned conscience. Do I care that he might be bruised or suffer internal injuries when I wrestle him back between my legs to change his diaper? Of course I do—and not really. It's a set. The self-injury, the self-medication, the checking out, dropping your head in your hands and crying fiercely at the drop of a hat, or at a touching TV scene—all of this is beyond mere fatigue.

I got supremely pissed—but per form held it in under a blank stare—when Sheila suggested getting him down from his room a little earlier while he was on break last summer. I sort of filed it away, knowing that it wouldn't happen, and making a note to let it happen, and then wear her down mainly by having Neil be Neil. Eventually, I tell myself, the world will see my point of view—something to be proud of, right? I comply, sometimes in a surly fashion but to be fair I do a decent job of smiling. I've cut the frequency of my truly surly periods when the anger feels like it literally drips out of my eyes. Not a lot of slapping of late. You can hide behind the whole "we're just defending ourselves" riff—but it's still hitting your kid.

In a way, I guess, we move from bubble to bubble, ours and the ones created in ad hoc fashion by society. Some—A.I. DuPont Hospital—are warm, their occupants comforting. His medical file, kept at the local children's hospital, is so voluminous it would cause J.K. Rowling to blanche in envy. We panicked when his pediatrician—an original member of the team—let us know she was moving her practice. Our panic ended when she informed us she's staying in the area—and moving her office a little closer to us, thankfully. Again with the "what we have to do"—won't miss the trek to the office, though. That's why his recent flameouts at Barnes and Noble, where our story began, is so troubling. Will they take our privileges away? A recently hired private security guard roams about—he's been nice to us so far, but has sent a few glances of concern our way. What the hell would we do with these visits?

Outside of the yearly trips to Philadelphia for the Macy's Christmas light show and to Cape May, our travel is largely of a vicarious nature, thanks to Rick Steves and Rudy Maxa. I can't stand how quickly time seems to be passing and, at the same time, how interminable his care is and promises to be. Our lives are interchangeably fleeting and stuck. And I continue to make Sheila sad. After two or three of my most recent drumming sessions, I've sat in my leather chair, wringed my hands, and told her that she won't have to put up with me playing for much longer, such is the inflexibility in my fingers and wrists. It's not a big loss; we're not talking Buddy Rich—or even Richie Rich. But my dramatics make her *sad*.

I've been barely an observer in much of what my son has been through. It's actually checking out, after which I tell myself that it's because checking in is so damned hard. Another baby cries—live or on TV—and I nearly cry. He cries, and I have to nudge myself to soothe him. Then I cry the second *Daddy Don't You Walk So Fast* makes one of its rare appearances on radio. You would think after this much time, I'd be able to offer you at least a cursory description of my sadness. Let's see—A din. A hum. The volume is turned up when, for example, we receive a brochure from a charter school that wants to prepare Neil for college, or even when his teacher sends home pages of in-class work that he most likely had little to do with completing. But again, this is a difference between my lovely Sheila and I. She believes, or at least claims to believe, that he is capable of living a fuller life. I play along, mired in the day-to-day care that we both perform, but as house martyr, I believe I'm most responsible for.

It hits in waves: he'll never get married, never have kids. What's he going to do—shred paper for the rest of his life, under the somewhat watchful eye of a supervisor whose compassion begins when a news crew shows up? And what happens when his CF leaves him unable to work? We'll never have more kids. We'll have to take care of him in some fashion for the rest of his life, which we hope is as long as the CF and the improving array of medicines and treatments will allow. We fight. We are fought with. He lacks empathy and senses openings for aggressiveness, but brings us to tears with a smile, an air-kiss, or 30 seconds spent gently petting the dog, when he smiles contentedly while playing ball or climbing the stairs, when he flashes the Fosse moves and makes an excited O with his mouth.

My mind vibrates when I hit these stretches. Usually it starts in the morning when I'm changing him and he's kicked my chest or stretched out my groin for the fourth time. I blame Sheila; how come she's not up at 5 a.m. wrestling him? It's not fair—I'm out of here! And then, ten minutes later, when I've actually almost woken up, it goes away and I'm back to loving her endlessly and wishing we had more time for each other. I tell myself it's not major, and I do stupid childish things like penalizing myself by trashing a gift or something I've bought. But she knows this sometimes sucks. She knows how hard it can be. I just have to be hit over the head to reacquaint myself with her experience. He practically pulls the hair out of her head, and sometimes I think "See—see what I have to deal with?" I had a split-second of "thought so!" when she acknowledged when I was away for a conference that she wasn't able to change his diaper because of the hair pulling. My secondary reaction? Well, there goes another conference. I wouldn't dream of not letting her attend an annual knitting conference. I'll just sit and stew and barely communicate. And then text lovey-dovey. And then seethe. And then take it out on him. And then cry when I realize that I'm taking it out on him. The stress has opened a window for obligation to waft in. I'd like to get to the point where I'm doing the same kind, slightly bumbling act at home that I do when we're out with Neil. Sure we're supposed to help each other—or even just sit tight—when a foul mood hits. And being tired and sometimes buzzed exacerbates this difference. But I just have to find a way to drop the martyr routine. Just one day free of selfishness.

Several years ago, we visited my mom and dad at their home in western New York. We waited for my brother and his then soon to be wife to arrive, but they typically came late—and then kept to themselves in tight little knots of colloquy for the rest of the afternoon. They came nowhere near Neil, who was easily accessible on the staircase, until our last few minutes at the house when my brother made a cursory pass by his window in our rental car to deliver an indifferent wave. My now sister-in-law stood with my parents what I'm sure she considered a safe distance away.

About a week later, during a call with my folks, my dad, who could have taught master classes in name-dropping and parasocial interaction, informed us that my brother and his fiancé didn't want Neil at their upcoming wedding because of "those noises" he makes. "You've got to be fucking kidding me," was my reply. From the couch, Sheila urged me to be kinder. We went to wedding anyway, rationalizing our decision by invoking the "major mile-stone in his life" trope. During his first wedding reception in the late 1980s, attendees fended off the bride's mother, a religious zealot who agreed to accept guest testimony and facilitate conversions. With Neil home in the care of a close friend and a babysitter who split the 10 hours we were gone, we sat in a darkened section of a posh New Jersey banquet hall and listened as the bride's close friends unleashed a 25-minute inside joke medley set to the songs from *The Sound of Music*. None of the jokes referenced my brother. Still pissed off about her comment and missing Neil, I fired off an angry email to him. I rose to Neil's defense; I announced I'd never forgive them for what she had said at my folks' house that day and for his not pushing back against his wife's intolerance. Aside from a goodbye hug as we headed home after their reception, perfunctory Facebook birthday greetings (from me to him, not the other way around), and a few phone calls exchanged the week my dad died in 2012, including one in which I instructed him to "not be a dick" when they finally made it to western New York a week after the funeral because I feared he'd take advantage of mom's grief to acquire funds and items to which he's always felt entitled, we haven't communicated since.

But what about my own reactions to his sounds? He can't talk, but boy can he communicate. The persistence, the raging, is sometimes so sudden, but always so jarring, so harsh. Sheila is much more tolerant of this that I am. On a recent weekend, we got some cleaning done, actually took down the items from atop our cabinets and cleaned them, weeded out some unwanted things, and cleaned the tops, generating a significant amount of grease and renewing our discussion of whether we should have white anything when we finally find the time and money to renovate the kitchen. There was Neil tossing a bunch of old CD liner notes around, coming up to pat Sheila on the behind, getting into the trash, and finally letting the water in the faucet run gently over his hand. That was after taking all the toilet paper off the roll in the bathroom and mixing the dirty laundry with Sheila's shoes. We had to put up the "PAT screen"—a curtain that hides the laundry area pressed into service as a block to prevent items from ending up behind the washing machine where, of course, they will never be heard from again. I think my frustration is genuine with this—I do oversell it at times, reminding Sheila that the flow of work will not be smooth with Neil cavorting around and trying to touch the television in the hope it will work like the iPad, or opening and closing the drawers in the large TV stand, or pulling all of the books off of his bookcase. The line between thinking of certain activities—his favorite CD, for example, as a palliative (done just to have him stay in one place for five minutes) and recognizing how much he loves those, and the rambunctious, activities—is danced all over. The latter is more rare. You just run out of juice—this happened at the doctor's office this week. Twice. We leave these spaces as though there had been a bar fight—chairs tipped over and strewn across the floor, the paper used to cover the exam table almost completely off the roll and torn into balls thrown in the trash. Drawers and cabinet drawers open and shut loudly. The tops of stools spun vigorously. I try to clean it up but they're very kind—don't worry about it, they say.

He punctuates my breakfast with his shouting. It actually took me a significant amount of time to put changing his diaper mid-morning on my weekend schedule. He pulls at the staves of the gate and kicks it. He stands behind it and shouts. He tosses his cardboard bricks down the stairs. Every so often, I have to half-tackle him to get him on the ground to change his diaper. He lurches and rolls away. He no longer allows me to lift his legs up to clean him and slide the new diaper. Instead, he jams his legs down. I have to hope "vent" comes on or that I find a topic of conversation that causes this to end. I fend off his kicks to the groin. I roll him forcefully once or twice. Elbow his knees down before I get kicked in the chest. But recently, for the first time in a while, perhaps ever, calm has returned. I joke about "fighting the good fight" and "it's great if you can walk away from it" but this time I returned to love much more quickly. But just as quickly, the fight resumed. More shouting, more rolling side to side, more attempts to kick me as I attempt to collect his dirty clothes and bag up the soiled diaper. I added a hug—and a gentle tug of the diaper to prevent leakage—and a kiss to the top of his head to our ritual. He added lunging and jamming his face into my stomach. And so it goes.

I get angry at Sheila—my empathy just completely goes missing. I want him in a facility—let them deal with that. And yet I'm pissed at Joe and Rose Kennedy. It's just so endless sometimes. *Groundhog Day*—maybe that's why folks get so into Special Olympics and their activism. There are pockets of beauty and amazing—him in his little exam robe, for example, or on the swing, or climbing into his seat in the car. But in the end, after all of my internal ranting, my practiced indifference, a society that more often than not treats him as a chance for community service, and a news media that wouldn't know our life—our real life—if it clicked 250 times on yet another Kardashian story, he's loved. By many. Immensely. Boundlessly. But does he love us? Of course he does, I like to think, with a coda that given his developmental delays—he can't talk to us—if he feels the same deep love for my wife and I that we feel for him. That sounds petty and self-absorbed, I know, but he's hard to read when it comes to affection. Or maybe I'm just telling myself that because I'm too lazy to understand how he expresses affection. He smiles and blurts out "pa pa" when I come home from Drexel, and throws many warm smiles Sheila's way. And he kisses us lightly when we lean in. But we still hold out hope that someday his expanding range of feelings will culminate in a heartfelt "I love you" directed at one of us. Why aren't his looks of love and adoration enough?

I worry constantly about crushing his hand. I've never been able to take and hold it like Bill Bixby and Brandon Cruz did on those poignant beach walks during *The Courtship of Eddie's Father*. I've had to spend so much time holding it—walking, dragging him to the stairs. I think sometimes that he only wants my hand when he wants to get somewhere. Now that means he can do most of the work himself. He walks haltingly; he holds his hands out in front of him, elbows slightly bent, as if he's waiting for someone to position a pair of poles before he embarks on an Olympic ski jump. He turns better than before, and doesn't have to use large objects—our two Subarus— to stop himself. Yet the hand is still a means to an end. Now and then I acerbically comment that "he wants to do seven things," but we've managed to expand the list, or at least teach him to tolerate unlisted activities on the way to doing the ones he likes.

These coalesce in his "marauder" stretches. We rip up newspaper, but only as a prelude to him wanting to open all the drawers on our TV stand— avoiding our legs as we try to block him—and pushing something into the end table so as to make the lamp wiggle and its twin chains clink. He then goes after Sheila's knitting, hoping to unspool and pull on it. Sometimes the inner waiter kicks in and I move it to higher ground in time; sometimes he knocks the ceramic bowl on the ground and has at it. Then it's off to throw- ing dirty and clean laundry.

I stumble around, trying not to overreact. Now and then I'll still mutter "fucks," and recently whispered "I just want to shoot you" to myself. I wasn't facing him and had tucked my head into my chest. But he heard me. His energy dissipated. The look on his He processes our emotions. Sheila is constantly telling me not to give him the "big reaction" when he's yanking on my shirt collar or pinching my arm. Again, I've gotten better—and even managed to not do it to punish her, to ram home again the point that this is hard. Yet I worry I'm closing in on the point where I won't be able to feel joy about him, about us. I absolutely still do; it sometimes comes in the form of brief flashbacks to a happy moment from our shared past, or, because it's my turbulent mind we're referencing, to a favorite 1970s TV show where family crises could be resolved in thirty minutes with pot roast or quasi-divine intervention by Alice or Mrs. Livingston.

The catalyst for this movement came when Neil was about 3. We traveled to Sheila's sister's house for Easter festivities. We were at the stage when I was carrying Neil around a lot of the time, before he started to use a wheel- chair. Sheila and I alternated holding him on our laps during the meal—a go- to tactic at the time. We had left the house when one of us realized that we had forgotten something—his diaper bag maybe? I ran back inside to grab it. I shouted a goodbye and headed back to the car when my brother-in-law's mom say "he never gets a break." She hadn't seen me come back inside.

That moment—that five seconds—has for me become a pernicious mind-worm; it activated my anger, discussed now ad nauseum in these pages, and spurred the intermittent resentment I direct in my mind, and through my surliness when I'm in total asshole mode, at my amazing wife. It is of some solace that I can still be readjusted to realize that it might also be the moment that ends us if, even though this is the first time Sheila will have known about it. Her love honors me—but it's so damned much work for her. Right after the first of the year, she was enduring the latest of my joking suggestions/ aspirations that we move to a smaller house, maybe a condo. Neil would have his room, we'd have ours. I'd sell the drums and buy a smaller electronic kit. She could have a more manageable garden on a terrace. We'd have a view.

Sheila, she of the translucent blue eyes, the dazzling intellect, and persistent enthusiasm, turned to me and smiled, although she was miffed that I was playing the card again. "I've left too many gardens behind," she said.

As is painfully typical for me, my love and admiration for Sheila was tempered by perturbed disbelief that she didn't see the genius in my plan. Profundity hits me in time-release fashion. But gradually, I have come to love our little acre. We sit and hold hands on the deck, gaze at our cherry and red maple trees, think about when we planted them, remember how small they were when we did. We look at Neil's swing set and note that we'll soon need to buy him a seat the next size up. We share our fear about a recent test which revealed that CF has begun to ravage his lungs in earnest. A bronchoscopy has been postponed, since it would have meant another week at A.I. Dupont Hospital recovering first from the procedure and then the damaging effects of anesthesia. It took so long for him last year to bounce back from some simple dental surgery last summer. He looked so wan, ashen even, and defeated laying there in the bed. He wasn't back to his marauding/escalator riding ways until the first of this year. We complain about inflexible and clueless bosses, unrelenting bureaucracy, quirky, and ineffective co-workers, appointments to be made and those recently forgotten. Family stories are retold; the doings of siblings are dissected. Sheila's intricate plans to commandeer our eventual nieces and nephews for extended periods of time are discussed. I putter, trimming branches and pulling a few weeds. She urges me once again to relax.

Boy is there a long way to go. I'm perturbed, or offer only perfunctory comfort, when Neil gets upset as I leave the room and leave him in the care of one of our village denizens. He wants to be with me—darn the luck. And it appeared for a while this spring that our time at the bookstore had officially come to an end. Neil wasn't able to last more than a few minutes before thrashing and yelling when a once empty escalator would fill with people. He ended up seated at the base of the elevator, directly in front of folks getting on and off. At first, I did pretty well; I gently explained that we needed to share the escalator with others. We resumed the ritual. I subtly moved in front of him when he was at the bottom of the escalator cupping the hand rail. We took a few journeys, punctuated as always by his laughter at pings, pops, and squeaks, his curious looks at others, and my exaggerated steps on and off. But his anger at the erratic passenger flow only worsened. I picked him up twice—the first time to move him back to the handrail and the second, after signaling like an umpire calling a runner out to Sheila to indicate we had to leave, to put him in his wheelchair stroller. She chided me for lifting him up, but our goal had been achieved. I had to do it, I said. Later, at the Costco, Sheila noted that I had damaged Neil's dignity by so abruptly dragging him away from the escalator. The lifts revealed his tummy and his g-tube port. His screaming got louder. He lurched in his stroller, kicked at shelves, blocked the large glass door with his foot as we tried to leave. Sheila was right.

On the way home, we shifted into juggling, planning, Erich Brenn plate-spinning mode. There's always the home store about five miles from here, we said. It has refrigerators and ceiling fans, we said. Success! During a recent visit, Neil reveled in opening and closing the doors of units of all brands and watching as I spun the fans—or at least those that weren't too close to each other. I am beyond thrilled to report that thanks to some minor adjustments in the pre-escalator ritual—letting him watch for five or so minutes before embarking and giving the "everybody can use the escalator" speech—his behavior at the bookstore has improved dramatically during our last two recent visits. The authorities will not have to be called. And I'm less jealous of Sheila for horning in on our activity, so much so that I fully endorsed her suggestion to visit another local mall which has three stores with escalators, a fact I completely suppressed in my obsession with obsession. Sadly, the mall has seen better financial days, and may close.

But there's also been a noticeable uptick in his violent behaviors—louder shouting, more energetic—and scarier—thrashing when we don't allow him to do something, or when we want him to stop doing something. Like picking at our shins when we're standing nearby and he wants us to go up and down the stairs—or for no reason at all, as when Sheila sits on the couch and rips the newspaper into strips. We feel like puppets in a show. Reluctance to sit with him as he's being fed has for me at times turned to full-on dread. More angry tossing by me of his toys. How many times will he pinch or lurch forward so he traps my hands between his stomach and the Rifton tray? How many times will he reach behind him and over the back of the Rifton to yank on the tube carrying his food from the bag to his g-tube port?

I have apologized to my son for treating him at times like a cranky nurse treats even the nicest patients. For not engaging with him enough. For not kissing him enough. For feeling obligated sometimes to kiss him after lavishing affection on the dog. For manufacturing franticness only to underscore for Sheila how hard managing his care is. For my at times total lack of empathy. For watching the clock during our excursions like a bored employee—and for not truly appreciating those journeys, like a recent one to find new stairs to climb at his doctor's new office followed by lunch and well concealed fridge door-opening at a big box store, that seem to fly by. For darting around our living room during your treatments like an aggrieved janitor—Schneider from *One Day at a Time* if you like. For the moments lost to my anger and selfishness. For not appreciating how unappreciated my lovely Sheila feels at times, especially as she endures another day, another hour, another minute at her crappy job. For not being a sufficiently ardent cheerleader for her. For not being her champion. Finally, for not being all that much more compassionate than the folks whose behavior we've examined and at times criticized in this book. Hypocrisy, thy role is daddy.

But in those moments on the deck, we truly are holding up the sky together. My last goal in life is to get my head permanently out of my ass so that I can experience more of them.

References

About the history of Children's Hospital. (2017). Children's Hospital of Philadelphia. Retrieved from http://www.chop.edu.

Adams, R. (2001). *Sideshow U.S.A.: Freaks and the American cultural imagination.* Chicago: University of Chicago Press.

Allard, J. (2017, January 12). Why an inclusive classroom isn't the best fit for my autistic daughter. *Washington Post.* Retrieved from http://www.washingtonpost.com.

Bartholomew, D. (2015, July 18). Special Olympics swimmer from Northridge ready to win more gold medals. *Los Angeles Daily News.* Retrieved from http://www.dailynews.com.

Bell, S. (2015, July 26). Hometown heroes: Athletes take fitness skills home. *ESPN.com.* Retrieved from http://www.espn.com.

Bellamy, C. (2016, July 1). Pender mother sues over disabled son's school placement. *Wilmington Star-News.* Retrieved from http://www.starnewsonline.com.

Berger, P. (2017, April 13). Conflict in the classroom. *Rutland Herald.* Retrieved from http://www.rutlandherald.com.

Berkowitz, D. (1997). Non-routing news and newswork: Exploring a what-a-story. In D. Berkowitz (Ed.), *Social meanings of news* (pp. 362-375). Thousand Oaks, CA: Sage.

Biklen, D. (1987). Framed: Print journalism's treatment of disability issues. In A. Gartner & T. Joe (Eds.), *Images of the disabled, disabling images* (pp. 79-95). New York: Praeger.

Blair, D. (2014, August 3). Special Olympics athlete competing to be on the cover of *Runner's World.* WISH-TV. Retrieved from http://www.wishtv.com.

Bogdan, R. (1988). *Freak show: Presenting human oddities for amusement and profit.* Chicago: University of Chicago Press.

Boorstin, D. (1982). The image: A guide to pseudo-events in America. New York: Athaneum.

Braunsteiner, M-L. & Mariano-Lapidus, S. (2014). A perspective of inclusion: Challenges for the future. *Global Education Review, 1,* 32-43.

Brockley, J. (2004). Rearing the child who never grew: Ideologies of parenting and intellectual disability. In S. Noll & J. Trent (Eds.), *Mental Retardation in America* (pp. 130-164). New York: New York University Press.

Brown, S. (2016, February 9). Watch FRA manager with Down syndrome hit 3-pointer. *The Tennessean.* Retrieved from http://www.tennessean.com.

Brown, F., Evans, I., Weed, K., & Owens, V. (1987). Delineating functional competencies: A component model. *Journal of the Association for Persons with Severe Handicaps, 12,* 117-124.

Bruno, A. (2015, October 10). Special Olympics win was a magical experience. *Buffalo News,* A-10.

Bunch, G. & Valeo, A. (2004). Student attitudes toward peers with disabilities in inclusion and special education schools. *Disability and Society, 19,* 61-75.

Carey, J. (1992). *Communication as culture.* New York: Routledge.

Carey, L. (2015, October 19). Rosemary, the 'missing Kennedy,' remembered by Elizabeth Koehler-Pentacoff. *San Jose Mercury News.* Retrieved from http://www.mercurynews.com.

Castles, K. (2004). 'Nice, average Americans': Postwar parents' groups and the defense of the normal family. In S. Noll & J. Trent (Eds.), *Mental Retardation in America* (pp. 351-370). New York: New York University Press.

Cherkis, J. (2016, November 29). Jeff Sessions slammed a law protecting schoolchildren with disabilities. *Huffington Post.* Retrieved from http://www.huffingtonpost.com.

Chappell, B. (2015, March 13). Athletes help cheerleader with Down syndrome defy bullies. *National Public Radio.* Retrieved from http://www.npr.org.

Christians, C. & Carey, J. (1991). The logic and aims of qualitative research. In G. Stempel & B. Westley (Eds.), *Research methods in mass communication* (pp. 354-374). Englewood Cliffs, NJ: Prentice-Hall.

Cline, S. (2017, March 6). Chinese educators tour inclusion classrooms at Leddy School in Taunton. *Taunton Daily Gazette.* Retrieved from http://www.tauntongazette.com.

Cloud, D. (1996). Operation Desert Cloud. In S. Foss (Ed.), *Rhetorical criticism: Exploration and practice* (pp. 304-319). Prospect Heights, IL: Waveland Press.

Criss, D. (2016, September 20). Water boy with Down syndrome scores special touchdown as terminally ill mom watches. CNN.com. Retrieved from http://www.cnn.com.

Debord, G. (1995). *The society of the spectacle.* New York: Zone Books.

Delcamp, C. (2015, December 8). *7 News at 11 p.m.* [Television broadcast]. Boston: WHDH-TV.

D'Haem, J. (2016). *Inclusion: The dream and the reality inside special education.* Lanham, MD: Rowman and Littlefield.

Dicker, R. (2016, January 28). Unbeaten wrestler lets opponent with Down syndrome win match. *Huffington Post.* Retrieved from http://www.huffingtonpost.com.

Dobbin, M. (2015, November 2). Book review: 'Rosemary: The hidden Kennedy daughter.' *Washington Times.* Retrieved from http://www.washingtontimes.com.

Donahue, J. (Host). (2015, October 14). Rosemary: The hidden Kennedy daughter. *WAMC.com.* Albany, NY: Northeast Public Radio. Retrieved from http://www.wamc.org.

Doring, J. (2015, April 29). Athlete blog: Jonathan Doring to call shots at World Games. *ESPN.com.* Retrieved from http://www.espn.com.

Downes, L. (2015a, July 27). Special Olympics takes on the world. *New York Times.* Retrieved from http://www.nytimes.com.

Downes, L. (2015b, July 31). Special Olympics and the burden of happiness. *New York Times.* Retrieved from http://www.nytimes.com.

Downing, J. & Peckham-Hardin, K. (2007). Inclusive education: What makes it a good education for students with moderate to severe disabilities. *Research & Practice for Persons with Severe Disabilities, 32,* 16-30.

Dudley-Marling, C. & Burns, M. (2013). Two perspectives on inclusion in the United States. *Global Education Review, 1,* 14-32.

Dunlap, T. (2016, February 24). Father's emotional video about son goes viral. *People.* Retrieved from http://www.people.com.

Eagleton, T. (1991). *Ideology: An introduction.* London: Verso.

Ehrenreich, B. (2009). *Bright-sided: How the relentless promotion of positive thinking has undermined America.* New York: Metropolitan Books.

Eleven-year-old Celtic fan wins Scotland's goal of the month. (2015, February 20). *The Guardian.* Retrieved from http://www.theguardian.com.

Elliott, D. (1994). Disability and the media: The ethics of the matter. In J. Nelson (Ed.), The disabled, the media, and the information age (pp. 73-79). Westport, CT: Greenwood Press.

Fabrizio, D. (Host). (2016, April 25). The hidden Kennedy daughter. *Radio West* [Radio Broadcast]. Salt Lake City, Utah: KUER. Retrieved from http://www.kuer.org.

Ferguson, P. (2004). The legacy of the almshouse. In S. Noll & J. Trent (Eds.), *Mental retardation in America* (pp. 40-64). New York: New York University Press.

Fisher, C. (2015, July 16). Countdown to the Special Olympics World Games with Robin Roberts airs Thursday, July 23 at 9 p.m. on ESPN and Saturday, July 25 on ESPN & ABC. *ABC News*. Retrieved from http://www.abcnews.go.com.

Fisher, W. (1987). Human communication as narration: Toward a philosophy of reason, value, and action. Columbia, SC: University of South Carolina Press.

Fiske, J. (1987). *Television culture*. London: Routledge.

Foss, S. (2009). *Rhetorical criticism: Exploration and practice*. Long Grove, IL: Waveland Press.

Freeman, B. & Grindal, T. (2016, December 13). Inclusion matters for all students. *Huffington Post*. Retrieved from http://www.huffingtonpost.com.

Gans, H. (1979). *Deciding what's news: A study of* CBS Evening News, NBC Nightly News, Newsweek, *and* Time. New York: Vintage.

Gibson, B. & Schwartz, T. (1995). *Rose Kennedy and her family: The best and worst of their lives and times*. Secaucus, NJ: Carol Publishing Group.

Gilman, S. (1982). *Seeing the insane*. New York: J. Wiley, Brunner/Mazel Publishers.

Gleeson, S. (2015, July 29). Special Olympics has message bigger than sports. *USA Today*. Retrieved from http://www/usatoday.com.

Goffman, E. (1963). *Stigma: Notes on the management of spoiled identity*. New York: Simon and Schuster.

Goldberg, E. (2014, November 12). JFK's sister's lobotomy was 'tragic choice,' new book about disabilities reveals. *Huffington Post*. Retrieved from http://www.huffingtonpost.com.

Gordon, M. (2015, October 11). Family secret. *New York Times Book Review*, 12.

Gould, S. (1996). *The mismeasure of man*. New York: W.W. Norton.

Grida, J. (2017, January 5). How state measures teacher's performance unfair. *News-Press* (Fort Myers, FL). Retrieved from http://www.news-press.com.

Hall, S. (1975). *Introduction*. In A.C.H. Smith (Ed.), *Paper voices: The popular press and social change* (pp. 11-24). London: Chatto and Windus.

Haller, B. (2010). *Representing disability in an ableist world: Essays on mass media*. Louisville, KY: Advocado Press.

Haller, B. & Zhang, L. (2017). Stigma or empowerment? What do disabled people say about their representation to news and entertainment media? *Review of Disabilities Studies, 9*. Retrieved from http://rds.hawaii.edu.

Hallin, D. (1986). *The uncensored war*. New York: Oxford University Press.

Heasley, S. (2015, October 27). Target ad includes model with disability. *Disability Scoop*. Retrieved from http://www.disabilityscoop.com.

Heasley, S. (2017, March 2). Poll finds widespread use of 'retard.' *Disability Scoop*. Retrieved from http://www.disabilityscoop.com.

Higgins, J. (2015, October 2). New books describe Rosemary Kennedy's path to, life in Wisconsin. *Milwaukee Journal Sentinel*. Retrieved from http://www.jsonline.com.

Higgins, P. (1992). Making disability: Exploring the social transformation of human variation. Springfield, IL: Charles C. Thomas Publisher.

History of NADS. (2017). *National Down Syndrome Association*. Retrieved from http://www.nads.org.

Holley, P. (2016, February 26). Why this father says 'Down syndrome is the best thing that ever happened to me.' *Washington Post*. Retrieved from http://www.washingtonpost.com.

Holohan, D. (2014, November 26). 'Fully Alive' is Timothy Shriver's story of the Kennedy family's relationship to the Special Olympics. *Christian Science Monitor*. Retrieved from http://www.csmonitor.com.

Holohan, M. (2016, February 16). Team manager with Down syndrome sinks game-ending 3-pointer against brother's team. *Today*. Retrieved from http://www.today.com.

Jones, K. (2004). Education for children with mental retardation: Parent activism, public policy, and family ideology in the 1950s. In S. Noll & J. Trent (Eds.), *Mental retardation in America* (pp. 322-350). New York: New York University Press.

Jorgensen, C. (2005). The least dangerous assumption: A challenge to create a new paradigm. *Disability Solutions, 6*, 1-15.

Kamenetzky, A. (2015, July 23). Divisioning creates fairness in Special Olympics. *ESPN.com*. Retrieved from http://www.espn.com.

Kamenetzky, B. (2015, July 25). L.A. nimble, ready to host Special Olympics World Games. *ESPN.com*. Retrieved from http://www.espn.com.

Kennedy. T. (2013, November 21). Remember my Uncle Jack's legacy of compassion. *Milwaukee Journal Sentinel*. Retrieved from http://www.jsonline.com.

Kimbrough, R. & Mellen, K. (2012). Research summary: Perceptions of inclusion of students with disabilities in the middle school. Retrieved from http://www.amle.org.

King, S. (2006). *Pink ribbons, Inc.* Minneapolis: University of Minnesota Press.

Koffler, J. (2015, July 24). Five inspiring athletes who will get you excited for the Special Olympics. *Time*. Retrieved from http://www.time.com.

Krossel, M. (1988). Handicapped heroes and the knee-jerk press. *Columbia Journalism Review*, 46-47.

Kumar, A. (2013, August). Normalization: Guiding principle of equal opportunities in education for children with disabilities in India. *European Academic Research, 1*, 667-676.

Kunthara, S. (2015, July 25). Michelle Obama, celebrities attend Special Olympics opening ceremony. *KNBC-TV*. Retrieved from http://www.nbclosangeles.com.

Lacroix, C. & Westerfelhaus, R. (2005). From the closet to the loft: Liminal license and sociosexual separation in *Queer Eye for the Straight Guy. Qualitative Research Reports in Communication, 6*, 11-19.

Larson, K. (2015). *Rosemary: The hidden Kennedy daughter.* Boston: Houghton Mifflin.

Leahy, M. (2017, April 30). Best Buddies prom offers so much to so many. *Fairfield-Suisun City Daily Republic*. Retrieved from http://www.dailyrepublic.com.

Lev, M. (2015, July 21). ESPN has special plans for the Special Olympics World Games. *Orange County Register*. Retrieved from http://www.ocregister.com.

Liebetrau, E. (2015, October 12). Larson pulls Rosemary Kennedy from the shadows. *Boston Globe*. Retrieved from http://www.bostonglobe.com.

Lloyd, J. & Guinyard, T. (2015, August 3). Missing athlete found hundreds of miles from Special Olympics. *KNBC-TV*. Retrieved from http://www.nbclosangeles.com.

Longmore, P. (1997). Conspicuous contribution and American cultural dilemmas: Telethon rituals of cleansing and renewal. In D. Mitchell & S. Snyder (Eds.), *The body and physical difference* (pp. 134-160). Ann Arbor, MI: University of Michigan Press.

Longmore, P. (2003). *Why I burned my book and other essays on disability.* Philadelphia: Temple University Press.

Longmore, P. (2005). The cultural framing of disability: Telethons as a case study. *PMLA, 120*, 502-508.

Longmore, P. & Umansky, L. (2001). Introduction. In Longmore, P. & Umansky, L. (Eds.), *The new disability history: American perspectives.* New York: New York University Press.

Lule, J. (2001). *Daily news, eternal stories.* New York: Guilford.

Mandal, A. (2014). Down syndrome history. *News-Medical Life Sciences*. Retrieved from http://www.news-medical.net.

Marion H. Stiffler, 73; taught retarded pupils. (1981, August 17). *Rochester Democrat and Chronicle*, 9.

Marotta, T. (2010, August 25). What the 'other sister' did for the Kennedys. *Huffington Post*. Retrieved from http://www.huffingtonpost.com.

May. J. [Host]. (2008). *Top Gear* [television broadcast]. London: British Broadcasting Corporation.

McAfee, T. (2015, October 7). Patrick Kennedy now suspects mental illness was behind two 'Kennedy Curse' family tragedies. *People*. Retrieved from http://www.people.com.

McAfee, T. & McNeil, L. (2015, October 22). Inside Ted Kennedy's special bond with his sister Rosemary: 'He related to her on an emotional level.' *People*. Retrieved from http://www.people.com.

McDermott, J. (2016, July 13). RI friends with Down syndrome premiere their epic zombie movie. *Providence Journal*. Retrieved from http://www.providencejournal.com.

McGinnis, A. (2014, August 1). Obama commemorates Special Olympics anniversary with star-studded White House event. *Reuters*. Retrieved from http://www.reuters.com.

McLeskey, J., Landers, E., Williamson, P., & Hoppey, D. (2012). Are we moving toward educating students with disabilities in less restrictive settings? *The Journal of Special Education, 46*, 131-140.

McNeil, L. (2015a, September 2). The untold story of JFK's sister, Rosemary Kennedy, and the disastrous lobotomy ordered by her father. *People.* Retrieved from http://www.people.com.

McNeil, L. (2015b, September 3). Fascinating first glimpse of never-before seen pictures of Rosemary Kennedy. *People.* Retrieved from http://www.people.com.

McNeil, L. (2015c, September 5). 'He was very natural with her': Inside J.F.K. Jr.'s special bond with his Aunt Rosemary, the 'hidden' Kennedy. *People.* Retrieved from http://www.people.com.

Mirecki, B. (2015, July 16). Hometown heroes: Bill Engvall reunites with Special Olympics. *ESPN.com.* Retrieved from http://www.espn.com.

Mitchell, L. (1989). Beyond the Supercrip syndrome. *Quill,* 18-19.

Mizoguchi, K. & McNeil, L. (2016, March 22). Author who knew Rosemary Kennedy says Emma Stone is 'ideal choice' to play her. *People.* Retrieved from http://www.people.com.

Montero, D. (2015a, July 18). Everything you need to know about the 2015 Special Olympics World Games. *Los Angeles Daily News.* Retrieved from http://www.dailynews.com.

Montero, D. (2015b, July 20). Special Olympics World Games seen as boost to Los Angeles-area economy. *Los Angeles Daily News.* Retrieved from http://www.dailynews.com.

Montero, D. (2015c, August 2). Special Olympics World Games closing ceremony salutes athletes. *Los Angeles Daily News.* Retrieved from http://www.dailynews.com.

Morris, S. (2015, October 2). The saddest story ever told. *Wall Street Journal.* Retrieved from http://www.wsj.com.

Nanez, D. (2016, February 9). Why executives came from New York to watch an amazing Arizona high school basketball game. *Arizona Republic.* Retrieved from http://www.azcentral.com.

Nelson, J. (1994). Broken images: Portrayals of those with disabilities in American media. In J. Nelson (Ed.), *The disabled, the media, and the information age* (pp. 1-24). Westport, CT: Greenwood Press.

Nelson, J. (2015, July 18). Colton family embodies "everything the Special Olympics is all about." *San Bernadino Sun.* Retrieved from http://www.dailynews.com.

Nirje, B. (1985). The basis and logic of the normalization principle. *Australia and New Zealand Journal of Developmental Disabilities, 11*, 65-68.

Nowakowski, A. (Host). (2016, May 11). 'The Missing Kennedy': A call for love, empathy, and understanding. *WUWM.com.* Milwaukee: Milwaukee Public Radio. Retrieved from http://www.wuwm.com.

O'Brien, G. (2004). Rosemary Kennedy: The importance of a historical footnote. *Journal of Family Studies, 29*, 225-236.

O'Neil, D. (2015a, June 1). Special Olympics makes health a global priority. *ESPN.com.* Retrieved from http://www.espn.com.

O'Neil, D. (2015b, August 4). Special Olympics movement continues after World Games. *ESPN.com.* Retrieved from http://www.espn.com.

Peter, J. (2015, July 26). Dustin Plunkett's journey leads to dream job at Special Olympics. *USA Today.* Retrieved from http://www.usatoday.com.

Plaschke, B. (2015, July 25). Special Olympics opening ceremony is out of this world. *Los Angeles Times.* Retrieved from http://www.latimes.com.

Players leave court mid-game to confront bully of cheerleader with Down syndrome. (2015, March 13). *Foxnews.com.* Retrieved from http://www.foxnews.com.

Powell, D. (2015, July 18). Larson sheds light on Rosemary, the hidden Kennedy daughter. *Charlotte Observer.* Retrieved from http://charlotteobserver.com.

Rich, K. (2016, March 21). Emma Stone may forever change the way we see the Kennedy family. Retrieved from http://www.vanityfair.com.

Richardson, K. (2015, July 20). Torch to come running through South Bay. *Torrance Daily Breeze,* A1.

Rocha, V. & Hamilton, M. (2015, August 3). Police locate second missing Special Olympics athlete, a teen from Ivory Coast. *Los Angeles Times*. Retrieved from http://www.latimes.com.

Rogers, J. (2015, July 30). Striking photos of the life-changing Special Olympics clinic. *Huffington Post*. Retrieved from http://www.huffingtonpost.com.

Rosemary Kennedy, 86; sister of JFK. (2005, January 9). *Los Angeles Times*. Retrieved from http://www.latimes.com.

Rosemary Kennedy dies at 86. (2005, January 7). *USA Today*. Retrieved from http://www.usatoday.com.

Rosemary Kennedy's dad ordered her lobotomy to prevent pregnancy, new books claim. *Inside Edition* [Web Broadcast]. Retrieved from http://www.insideedition.com.

Santoli, S., Sachs, J., Romey, E., & McClurg, S. (2008). A successful formula for middle school inclusion: Collaboration, time, and administrative support. *Research in Middle Level Education Online, 32*, 1-13.

Schlichenmeyer, T. (2015, November 11). Books: 'Rosemary: Hidden Kennedy daughter' a riveting read. *Times Record*. Retrieved from http://www.swtimes.com.

Schudson, M. (2003). *The sociology of news*. New York: W.W. Norton.

Shepherd, K. (2015, July 30). Volunteer clinic provides care, supplies to Special Olympics athletes. *Los Angeles Times*. Retrieved from http://www.latimes.com.

Shocking details! Inside Rosemary Kennedy's disastrous lobotomy ordered by her father – abandoned for 20 years! (2015, September 2). *Radar Online*. Retrieved from http://www.radaronline.com.

Shriver, E. (1962, September 22). Hope for retarded children. *Saturday Evening Post,*71-75.

Shriver, T. (2014). *Fully alive: Discovering what matters most*. New York: Sarah Crichton Books.

Silberman, A. (2016, May 19). UVM student wins social inclusion grant. *Burlington Free Press*. Retrieved from http://www.burlingtonfreepress.com.

Simon, S. (Host). (2015, October 3). A hidden – but quietly influential – life in 'Rosemary.' *Weekend Edition Saturday* [Radio broadcast]. Washington, D.C.: National Public Radio.

Siperstein, G., Parker, C., Bardon, J. & Widaman, K. (2007). A national study of youth attitudes toward the inclusion of students with intellectual disabilities. *Exceptional Children, 73*, 435-455.

Sklar, D. (2017, January 9). Poway educator among finalists for national teacher of the year. *Times of San Diego*. Retrieved from http://www.timesofsandiego.com.

Smith, P. (2010). Whatever happened to inclusion? The place of students with intellectual disabilities in general education classrooms. In P. Smith (Ed.), *Whatever happened to inclusion? The place of students with intellectual disabilities in education* (pp. 1-20). New York: Peter Lang.

Some Special Olympics competitors forced to sleep on Los Angeles gym floor. (2015, July 23). *FOX News*. Retrieved from http://www.foxnews.com.

Sontag, S. (1977). *Illness as metaphor*. New York: Farrar, Strauss, & Giroux.

Special Olympics International website. Retrieved from http://www.specialolympics.org.

Storey, K. (2004). The case against the Special Olympics. *Journal of Disability Policy Studies, 15*, 35-42.

Storey, K. (2008). The more things change, the more they are the same: Continuing concerns with the Special Olympics. *Research and Practice for Persons with Severe Disabilities, 33*, 134-142.

Stuart, R. (2015, December 29). How a model with Down syndrome made it to the catwalk. *CNN.com*. Retrieved from http://www.cnn.com.

Stump, S. (2014, December 23). Champion gymnast with Down syndrome overcomes obstacles, inspires others. *The Today Show* [television broadcast]. New York: National Broadcasting Company. Retrieved from http://www.today.com.

The Meadowood program. (2014). Newark, DE: Red Clay Consolidated School District.

Thomas, G. (2014, July 24). Mill Valley woman with Down syndrome a winner at national Special Olympics, a role model back home. *KNTV-TV*. Retrieved from http://www.nbcbayarea.com.

Thomson, R. (2001). Seeing the disabled: Visual rhetorics of disability in popular photography. In P. Longmore & L. Umansky (Eds.), *The New Disability History* (pp. 335-374). New York: New York University Press.

Thompson, J. (1990). *Ideology and modern culture: Critical social theory in the era of mass communication.* Stanford, CA: Stanford University Press.

Tomlin, J. (2015, July 25). Special Olympian will walk with teammates. *High Point Enterprise.* Retrieved from http://www.lexis-nexis.com.

Trent, J. (1994). *Inventing the feeble mind: A history of mental retardation in the United States.* Berkeley, CA: University of California Press.

Trevino, C. (2015, July 18). Bocce champ Tiaunta Gray ready for Special Olympics World Games debut. *Los Angeles Daily News.* Retrieved from http://www.dailynews.com.

Wasu, S. (2016, April 26). Gilbert parents fight for child with Down syndrome to stay at home school. ABC-TV15 [television broadcast]. Phoenix, AZ. Retrieved from http://www.abc15.com.

Weil, M. (2005, January 8). Rosemary Kennedy, 86; President's disabled sister. *Washington Post*, B6.

Welch, K. (2015, September 9). With gratitude to Rosemary Kennedy from the mom of a child with special needs. *Huffington Post.* Retrieved from http://www.huffingtonpost.com.

Williams, M. (2017, January 11). Ending an 'old school' way of teaching special ed. *Waynesboro News-Leader*. Retrieved from http://www.newsleader.com.

Williams, M. (2017, February 4). Seeking inclusion classrooms for all. *Richmond Times-Dispatch*. Retrieved from http://www.richmond.com.

Wilson, M. (2015a, July 22). Geneva Special Olympian reaches international level in rhythmic gymnastics. *Chicago Daily Herald.* Retrieved from http://www.lexis-nexis.com.

Wolfensberger, W. (2011). Social role valorization: A proposed new term for the principle of normalization. *Intellectual and developmental disabilities, 49,* 435-440.

Wood, M. (1975). *America in the movies.* New York: Basic Books.

Woodruff, J. (Host) (2016, March 1). L.A. schools grow more inclusive, but at what cost? *PBS News Hour* [television broadcast]. New York: Public Broadcasting System. Retrieved from http://www.pbs.org.

Zhang, L. (2015, August 3). Second Special Olympics athlete found after disappearing from Los Angeles airport. *U.S. News and World Report.* Retrieved from http://www.usnews.com.

Zirin, D. (2014). *Brazil's dance with the devil: The World Cup, the Olympics, and the fight for democracy.* Chicago: Haymarket Books.

Zola, I. (1991). Communication barriers between "the able-bodied" and "the handicapped." In R. Marinelli & A. Dell Orto (Eds.), *The psychological and social impact of disability* (pp. 139-147). New York: Springer.

CPSIA information can be obtained
at www.ICGtesting.com
Printed in the USA
LVHW011546180820
663527LV00004B/446